Sept 23ᵗʰ 2016

UNDER CURRENT CONDITIONS

To Andy
Best Wishes

Dennett Press

UNDER CURRENT CONDITIONS

KYLE DARCY

DENNETT PRESS

CANTON, MASSACHUSETTS

2011

For Richard, Lisa, Shelley
and Tory

Prologue

The rabbit froze motionless beside a pile of granite boulders on the other side of the street. His animal instinct took over when I appeared on the scene with my wire-haired fox terrier. This fight or flight reflex was so unnecessary, since Perkins was on a leash. Even if he had not been restrained, his twelve-year-old frame could never have caught the rabbit before it disappeared into the thick brush cover, no more than three quick hops away.

Perkins stopped in his tracks, tail rigid and nose raised in the air sniffing excitedly. Perhaps in his prime he would have had a chance at catching this prey, but those days were gone. The rabbit had no need to fear him. Perkins posed no threat whatsoever.

What happened next made me realize that for humans, life is no different than it is for the rest of the animal kingdom. We too possess instinct; however, it has been several thousand years since we lived in caves and relied on it to assess danger. Although not honed to the degree of our primitive ancestors, we still have this sense. Our dealings with others are predicated upon whether or not we perceive them to be a threat. The handshake, a custom originally developed to show that no weapon was being carried, has been relegated to a ritual performed as a subconscious compliance with social etiquette. In our modern world, we rely on instinct to judge the people we encounter throughout our day.

Just like this rabbit, sometimes we too can get it wrong and with disastrous consequences. I was no threat to this creature, nor did he have any reason to fear Perkins. This basic animal instinct which had served him so well in the past and caused him to remain completely still would, in fact, contribute to his demise. One moment he was sitting by the rocks – the next, he was being carried off by an eagle. What a life lesson to witness.

The author wishes to thank Martin Quinn for this introduction.

Introduction

Everything you are about to read actually happened to me. Of course, there has been the obligatory changing of characters' names, but not places. The names of four people and one dog, however, remain unchanged.

Perhaps you are reading this in a public place: a book store or library; an airport or train station on your way to work; or maybe relaxing on the beach. Take a moment and look around. What do you see? Ordinary people. I might even be one of them. During the past week, these people woke each morning, ate breakfast and went to work, or possibly stayed home to take care of their children. They did the same thing the week before, and probably the week before that. Why? Because this is what ordinary people do. Days add up to weeks and weeks roll into months. We all get caught up living life the only way we know how; one day at a time.

But what if something unusual were to happen during the course of your day. Something trivial. A button gets jammed on your cellular phone, for example. That isn't going to change your life. Or is it? What if something equally insignificant happens, and perhaps something else again. Each incident by itself gives no indication that it is contributing to your normal life beginning to spiral out of control. Nevertheless, each one is gently pushing you in that direction. Like a freight train slowly leaving a stockyard, it would be easy to stand on the roof of a boxcar. Even if the train were to travel a little faster, then a little bit faster again, before you know it you are being carried along at quite a pace. Suddenly you realize you need to hold on, but there is nothing to hold on to and there are bends and bumps ahead. Look out!

I too was living a normal life, like everyone you see around you: doctors, carpenters, school teachers, lawyers, salesmen, housewives, the list is endless. I happen to be an engineer. How did this come to be? My father was a marine engineer and I became immersed in his profession. Many children do not get an opportunity to fully appreciate their parents' work. For me, it was different. I can still recall as a three year old, holding my father's hand as I struggled to climb the steep gangplank of a large ocean-going liner. As a four or five year old, I walked around below these monstrous vessels while they were being repaired in the dry-docks of Harland and Wolff in Belfast, Northern Ireland. The same shipyard where the Titanic was built in 1912. Having been exposed to this and the other rich engineering history this region has to offer, it was no wonder that I graduated from the University of Ulster, with an engineering degree, in the mid 1980s. By then, Northern Ireland was making another kind of history. The sectarian conflict which divided its Catholic, Nationalist community from its Protestant, Loyalist neighbors, made it a less than desirable place to raise a family. By 1999, when this story takes place, I had been living in Boston, Massachusetts for ten years with my wife and thirteen year old son.

Every creative writing class will stress the need to capture the reader's attention early in the plot. Perhaps if I wanted to embellish the story, I could have done so in order to satisfy this need, but then it would not be true. No martini cocktails, "shaken not stirred." No glamorous models or fabulous resort settings. Just an account of the daily life of an engineer with probably too much detail and focus on seemingly insignificant aspects. But you have the benefit of my warning before turning the next page. This ordinary life was actually heading seriously out of control. Will you be able to detect future consequences of events or conversations as the story develops? I cannot take credit for developing the plot. I just lived it.

Still want to read on? Then check all the buttons on your cellular phone are working correctly before you continue. You have been warned!

Martin Quinn

11:35AM - Friday March 5, 1999

The unmarked cruisers, windows tinted and lights pulsating rapidly, were double parked outside the Boston Harbor Hotel. Several imposing figures escorted a somewhat disheveled man towards the waiting vehicles. Despite the brisk March temperatures, their charge wore no winter coat. On the other side of Atlantic Avenue, a reversing concrete truck caused a speeding bicycle courier to weave in and out of traffic with all the finesse of an Olympic skier. The cyclist approached this occupational hazard as if it were a new level in a video game. A pursuing trolley tour-bus was unable to replicate these maneuvers. Its driver stopped and acknowledged the reversing truck with a jovial ringing of a ship's bell. The tour's youngest passenger welcomed this interruption since he was intrigued by the drama unfolding outside the hotel.

"Dad, are those guys FBI?"

"Maybe, or they could be Boston Police detectives."

Martin Quinn climbed into the rear of the cruiser parked closest to the curb. Both vehicles gave a short burst of their sirens as they cut across the traffic and sped off. Quinn was thrown to his right as the car turned sharply to travel underneath the elevated I93 Expressway.

"My life will never be the same," he thought, trying desperately to identify where it all went wrong.

Four weeks earlier ...

6:45AM - Wednesday February 3, 1999

Martin Quinn was never quite content with the location of their office. It was, however, ideal for his business partner, Eddie Gallagher. Having Cove Construction situated within the administration building of a marina just south of Boston, served two purposes for Eddie. First, it was where he moored his boat. Second, it was less than a ten-minute commute from his house in Quincy, a benefit of which Gallagher rarely availed, since he was still employed, full-time, with another construction contractor, Milano Excavating. Martin had also been employed by Milano. It was agreed when they started Cove Construction that he would be first to leave, when the new company's workload could support his salary. In time they hoped Cove would carry both of them, however so far, only Martin made the daily commute from his home in Stoughton to the Marina Bay section of Quincy.

The last two miles to Cove's office were worth the battle through highway back-ups and traffic jams which plagued Boston commuters. Quincy Shore Drive was unique and inspirational on every occasion. From Martin's perspective, he just could not get any closer to his Irish homeland without getting his feet (or tires) wet. During storms, the ocean tumbled over the sea wall and lashed out at traffic, as well as unfortunate pedestrians within its reach. On this bleak New England winter morning, snow and ice encrusted waves broke incessantly across the shoreline. It was not only during winter months when Martin enjoyed the scenic commute along the Atlantic Ocean. The route on summer days was decorated by scantily clad girls lapping up the sun's rays while jogging or relaxing along the seawall. As in other scenic regions throughout the state, commercial vehicles were banned by the Commonwealth of Massachusetts. On this road, however, the authorities had gone one step further by installing traffic lights every six hundred yards which were phased to slow the traffic. It was just impossible for Martin to miss any of the beautiful sights!

Quinn knew he would have no time for sight-seeing that day, or for the foreseeable future. His ride to work had been punctuated by telephone calls from field superintendents on different Cove jobsites. He parked his black Jeep outside the office. There was never a problem finding parking space in February, unlike the summer months, when the marina was much busier. As he walked towards the office building, his cell phone rang again. It was his wife, Margaret.

"Don't forget to pick up Brendan at the rink tonight."

"I hadn't forgotten, Love."

"Also, the mortgage company left voicemail. Did you send them a check?"

"I put it in the mail yesterday. There's no need to worry. I'll give you a call later. Love you."

Cove Construction was located on the second floor of the administration building, directly above "The Chantey Pub." Clients visiting the office would often joke that the close proximity to the bar was the real reason two Irish men had chosen this location. Any protests to the contrary were futile.

Sandra, the office manager, greeted him with the usual, "Good morning," and a fist full of phone messages. She had only been working with the company for four months. A Professional Engineer, her previous employers had been design consultants. Quinn and Gallagher both agreed that hiring a registered engineer elevated their young company's profile within the local industry.

"Eddie called looking for you. He said he couldn't get you on your cell."

"I'm not surprised. The phone never stopped ringing since I got into my truck this morning. I'll call him now," Quinn replied, picking up the phone on his desk.

"What are you doing tonight? Can you come over to the house?" Gallagher inquired.

"What's up?"

"I can't go into things at the moment, but Fred Ross called me. He's got a very interesting job that he wants us to help him with. I told him we might be able to meet tonight, but I wanted you to be there as well."

Fred Ross was a name Martin Quinn just did not want to hear. It brought back unpleasant memories of an insidious individual. Eddie explained that Ross was free-lancing as a developer / construction manager. Martin had no interest in hearing about him or any of his endeavors. Five years earlier, he and Fred Ross had worked for the same general contractor, Boston Building Associates. Quinn was well aware of Fred's character, or rather, lack thereof. Ross worked in BBA's estimating department, while Quinn was employed as a project manager. Working with Fred for over three years had taught Martin that any movement of Ross' lips was an indication he was not telling the truth.

Eddie Gallagher's experiences with Fred were different. He encountered him from the perspective of a subcontractor. When BBA was invited to bid on a project, its estimating department would solicit quotes for the various elements. Since Ross was privy to these proposals, Gallagher viewed him as a source of valuable intelligence as to how Milano's bids on sitework matched up against others. In return, Fred received favors, such as landscaping improvements at his house.

Once BBA was awarded a project, the job files were transferred to an assigned project manager. On estimates involving Ross, there were always several sub-bidders who were well informed as to how their proposal compared with the competition. It disgusted Quinn to know someone in BBA's office was impairing the project managers from securing beneficial deals for the company. He could usually work out the type of home improvements Ross was planning from the nature of his inquiries about subcontract negotiations. Despite all this, Eddie was very philosophical about his relationship with Fred. "Everyone has an asshole," he once explained. "We're not very proud of it, but it serves a very important function. Fred's just another asshole!"

9:30PM - Wednesday February 3, 1999

It was not practical for Martin to meet with his business partner any earlier on a school night. Gallagher was a single parent with two young children. Usually it was after 9:00 before Eddie had finished dinner, helped his children with their homework assignments and got them off to bed. Martin had no objection to scheduling these late night meetings at Gallagher's house. Margaret, however, was less tolerant of this arrangement. She disliked that Eddie's family circumstances meant it was Martin who always made this trip. She believed her husband sacrificed too much of their family time for Cove Construction.

When Martin arrived at Gallagher's house, he found Fred Ross and Eddie reviewing a set of blueprints which had been rolled out on the kitchen table.

"Mr. Quinn, an honor and a privilege as always."

"Whatever Fred," Martin muttered. Even saying the name seemed to leave a bad taste in his mouth.

The plans related to the construction of an aluminum raceway for carrying nearly two miles of fiber-optic cable along the side of the Jamestown Bridge in Jamestown, Rhode Island. ("Raceway" is an industry term for a conduit or tube system which carries and protects a utility, such as a fiber-optic cable.) Somehow, Ross had convinced the design engineer that he be allowed to bid on this project. According to Fred, Seahorse Communications had awarded his company, RossCon Enterprises, a contract to furnish and install the aluminum raceway. This construction company was the product of Fred's creative flare, presented with the aid of a good laser color printer, in a fashion that apparently impressed the folks at Seahorse. Regardless of Martin's prejudiced opinion of Fred, he had to acknowledge that there was probably no one better at securing the confidence and trust of potential clients, while having very little technical knowledge himself.

Ross explained that Congress' deregulation of the communication industry meant that television cable companies were allowed to offer their customers a telephone service, while telephone companies were permitted to provide cable television. In addition, both industries could compete for their share of the lucrative and rapidly expanding internet market. Technical advances in fiber-optic science were the main reason for the revision of legislation that governed these enterprises. However, cable companies that wanted to offer phone service were being held to a greater standard of reliability than when they only provided cable television. With provision of a telephone service came the responsibility of supporting the 911 emergency system. Loss of 911 coverage, for even a minimal period of time, had more serious consequences than a household losing its day-time soaps. Consequently, cable companies like Seahorse, which wanted to compete for a share of the telephone market, had to make substantial improvements to their infrastructure. This Jamestown Bridge crossing project was a major component of Seahorse's plans to compete with the country's leading telephone companies. The largest in the area, CellTell Atlantic, already had an old submersed copper core cable installed across Narragansett Bay. This cable was in poor condition and the subject of grave concern for its owners. Despite three years of negotiations with the Ocean State Bridge Authority, CellTell Atlantic had failed to get permission to attach its own fiber-optic cable raceway to the bridge. Seahorse managed to negotiate an easement, but its agreement with the bridge's owners also mandated that they permit their competitor,

CellTell Atlantic, to lease space within the new raceway.

Ross concluded that he had negotiated a base contract price of $400,000. The completion date was set for May 7, 1999; however, Seahorse was willing to pay a $20,000 bonus if the work was completed by April 15. Martin laughed at the thought of Fred committing to such terms, because this job was clearly way out of his league.

"Fred, this is one and a half miles of specially manufactured aluminum raceway. You can't just pick it up off the shelf at any hardware store. It's February 3, and you told Seahorse that you'd have it installed by May 7?" Martin questioned with disbelief.

Eddie tried to adopt a more positive response to the news.

"We need a couple of days to work on this. How about we meet here again on Saturday morning?"

* * * * * * * *

It was after midnight when Martin closed the garage door of his home.

"How'd the Bruins do?" he asked, climbing into bed beside Margaret.

"Not very well, they lost 2-0."

"It's always hard to come out of Chicago with any points," he conceded and reached over to kiss his wife good night.

8:30PM - Thursday February 4, 1999

Xavier Santos relaxed in his chair and sipped another mouthful of tequila. The comfortable study in his large Newton, Massachusetts residence was a testament to the legacy of his late father. Custom-made furniture in a classical style decorated this room and others throughout the home. Unfortunately, none of the pieces suited his wife's contemporary taste. Maria Santos took charge of interior design in the kitchen and other common family areas. Consequently, all the Santos heirlooms were banished to Xavier's private study as well as guest bedrooms on the second and third floors. Not even the most diplomatic *Antiques Road Show* expert could have faulted her for adopting such a policy. An appreciation of their sentimental value to her husband was the only thing that prevented them from being set out on the curb as trash.

Santos gazed fondly at the framed photograph sitting on the corner of his desk. His smiling father was standing with his arm around Colombian international soccer star Andres Escobar. Xavier recalled taking the photograph in 1994 when many of his father's home country's soccer stars visited his nightclub in Boston after they had defeated Northern Ireland in a friendly match at Foxboro Stadium. Ironically both men were shot dead on the same day, only one month after the photograph was taken. Eduardo Santos met his maker minutes after driving his Mercedes convertible out of their garage on the morning of July 2, while Escobar scheduled an emergency meeting with St. Peter after being murdered in Medellin, Colombia. The soccer star's fate was allegedly sealed when he scored an own-goal during his team's World Cup soccer game against the

United States. The result of this error was the elimination of Colombia from the competition, causing significant gambling losses for unforgiving drug lords back home.

9:55AM - Saturday February 6, 1999

Martin thought it best not to disclose to Margaret that he was meeting with both Eddie Gallagher and Fred Ross. He avoided any discussion about why he had to work on a Saturday, but assured her that he would be home by 1:00, since Brendan had a hockey game that afternoon.

Although this fiber-optic bridge project seemed like an interesting and profitable endeavor, the fact that Fred Ross was involved concerned him. Cove had been operating for two years and only recently had the business generated enough revenue to support Martin's full-time employment. His company specialized in site development, foundation construction and underground utility work. Seahorse's project involved the manufacture and installation of eight thousand linear feet of an aluminum conduit system, on a highway bridge structure, seventy miles away in Rhode Island. It was something with which Cove had absolutely no experience and was made even more difficult because of aggressive time constraints. Nevertheless, Martin knew that Fred had approached Cove because of Quinn's reputation for overcoming seemingly impossible tasks.

Eddie and Martin had discussed the project in detail over the previous two days, during which time Gallagher relayed to Ross that Cove would be willing to do the job for $340,000. In the event the work was completed by the April 15 bonus deadline, a further $10,000 would be paid. Thus, Fred would make $70,000 for doing nothing other than find the job. This calculation of RossCon Enterprises' profit was based on Seahorse paying $400,000, in addition to the bonus. Quinn suspected Fred had been economic with the truth regarding his company's compensation terms, but unfortunately there would be no way of verifying this information. Ross had indicated he was satisfied with this deal and confirmed their meeting for Saturday morning.

Neither of Eddie's children was home when Martin arrived. Both had been invited to a birthday party which included a bus trip to the New England Aquarium in Boston. By 10:30, Fred had not yet arrived.

"Typical," Quinn vented, "I thought we agreed to meet at 10:00. Call him and find out where he is."

Gallagher got Ross on the phone only to be told that he was "too sick" to leave his house.

"Listen Fred," Eddie explained, "we're already a week into February. If you want to complete this project within the next year, let alone by April 15, then you need to give us a set of plans so we can get started."

"How about we meet tomorrow afternoon?"

"I can't, but maybe Martin can. He'll be the one working on this. We have to get things moving and I've a full work load at Milano."

Quinn reluctantly agreed to go to Ross' house the following day to get the plans. Before ending the call, Fred also informed Eddie that he needed Martin to accompany him to a meeting which was scheduled for Thursday morning with Seahorse Communications.

"Classic Ross," Martin sighed with exasperation. "What an asshole! Why couldn't he call you earlier this morning and save me the hassle of driving over here?"

There were times when Quinn felt Eddie Gallagher had no appreciation of the inconvenience caused by nonsense like this. Fred Ross canceling their meeting without any notice had very little impact on Eddie's Saturday plans, but such was not the case for Martin. It had taken three hours of his day driving back and forth from Stoughton to Quincy only to get committed to another meeting on Sunday. This too would have no impact on Eddie's weekend. If Margaret only knew, she would have every right to be angry. Martin, however, was conscious of how difficult it was to keep Cove Construction operating and this fiber-optic raceway installation certainly had the potential to be quite lucrative.

On the drive back home, Martin thought about Margaret's dislike of both Fred Ross and Eddie Gallagher. Whereas he shared her evaluation of Fred, he did not feel the same way about his business partner. He was conscious they each had different strengths and was understanding of the restrictions that Gallagher's home life imposed. They were not clones – just business partners. Nevertheless, Margaret believed that even though Martin and Eddie were equal shareholders in Cove Construction, it was her husband who sacrificed the most, especially since he had given up the security of his previous position for the fledgling Cove. Her feelings were understandable because she was not privy to the contributions Eddie made. She only saw Martin's effort which was magnified by meetings on weekends and evenings at Gallagher's house. As far as she was concerned, her husband did more than his fair share. From her perspective, this Saturday morning was yet another occasion when Martin was not at home with his family, so that Eddie could be with his. Quinn blocked out such thoughts. He had a mortgage to pay and $22,000 a year for Brendan's school fees at Thayer Academy. Cove was their only source of income. The saying, "having all your eggs in one basket," was never more appropriate.

When it came to Fred Ross, Martin and Margaret were in complete agreement. Both distrusted the man.

4:00PM - Sunday February 7, 1999

Martin hoped the meeting would not interrupt his family's Sunday, too much. The Bruins' third period at the Boston Garden was just beginning as he turned off the car radio. Ross had a knack of annoying him without even trying. "I should be at home watching the hockey with Margaret and Brendan, but instead I have to meet with this clown!" he thought to himself.

Fred lived in Easton, just ten minutes from Martin, in a 3,500 square foot, brick-faced house, set on a one-acre landscaped lot. The marble floors of the foyer extended into a formal dining area. As he followed Fred into his home office, Martin glanced into the kitchen where gleaming granite counter tops accented top of the line cabinets and professional grade stainless steel appliances. Quinn was impressed.

He sat down in front of Fred's desk, foolishly thinking he was there to discuss Seahorse's fiber-optic project, get the set of plans, and then leave. Ross, however, had a different agenda. He wanted to discuss construction of a new school bus depot in Bedford, Massachusetts. After listening politely for several minutes, Martin explained that he did not have time to give another job the attention it warranted. Considering they both had to meet with Seahorse on Thursday morning, he asked Fred to give him the plans for the Jamestown, Rhode Island job, so he could start reviewing them.

"What do you think we should do to prepare for the meeting with Seahorse?" Fred asked.

"We need to make a sample support bracket to see how it fits against the bridge and exactly how it will support the raceway sections which will span between them."

"What will you make it from?"

"Aluminum, just like the design calls for. If I take the blue lines today, there's a good chance I'll have it ready for Thursday."

"I don't have the plans," Fred confessed. "We've got to pick them up from my friend, Ian Goodwright. He only lives two streets away."

Martin knew immediately that something was wrong. It confirmed all his suspicions and reservations about having anything to do with Ross. "Cove must be in competition with some other company for this work," he thought. "There can be no other reason why Fred has given away his only set of blueprints, unless he's considering using someone else."

"Come on, we'll use your car, I think you're blocking me," Ross suggested.

The Jeep started to the noise of the Boston Bruins firing the puck on New Jersey's goal. Fred reached over and turned down the radio.

"I can't believe you did that," Quinn scolded, turning the volume back up. "Ice hockey's my favorite sport and the Bruins are my third favorite team."

"Sorry – and who are the other ones?"

"My son plays hockey at Thayer and also for his town in a youth league. Those two teams are my favorites of course."

A few minutes later, Fred asked Martin to stop outside a beige colonial house. As the Bruins turned up the pressure on the New Jersey Devils, Martin observed a conversation between Ross and a tall, fair-haired gentleman. This brief encounter at the front door ended when a roll of plans was relinquished. On the drive back, Fred explained that he had contacted Ian Goodwright after his initial discussions with Seahorse, because he owned an aluminum fabrication shop.

Back at the Ross residence, Fred stalled before getting out of the vehicle and began to query Cove's price for completing the work. Martin and Eddie had privately estimated the job costs at $270,000. Quinn was not prepared to re-open negotiations with Ross. He understood that Cove Construction and RossCon Enterprises had a deal for $340,000 – end of discussion.

9:00AM - Monday February 8, 1999

Quinn had found it difficult to sleep during the night, continuing to question in his mind the wisdom of getting involved in any business venture that involved Fred Ross. By the time he drove into the parking lot of Anderson Aluminum, he had been on two of Cove's job-sites and also stopped at a commercial printing shop to make copies of Fred's blueprints. Over the years, Martin had done some business with this aluminum fabrication company, so he was well aware of their capabilities. Their enclosed workshop area encompassed nearly two acres. Anderson's client base was wide and varied, running the full gamut from defense contractors to biotech laboratories. Quinn knew this company was the key to successfully completing the project. Upon entering the reception area, he introduced himself through a small sliding window and asked to speak with Carl Richards. Carl had been his contact on prior occasions, but none of these previous jobs were ever larger than $1,000. Consequently, he was not surprised when the receptionist reported that Mr. Richards was too busy to meet with him. Martin estimated that the blueprints he had under his arm represented at least $100,000 worth of work for the fabricator. He also knew that time was of the essence.

"This is quite a substantial amount of work. If Carl isn't available, perhaps there's someone else I can speak to?" he smiled, plying her with his Irish charm.

The sliding window was closed again and the receptionist disappeared. She returned promptly with another gentleman, who opened the door accessing the small reception foyer.

"Hi. I'm Jeff Anderson, one of the owners here. How can I help you?"

Quinn unrolled the plans and gave a brief outlay of the project. Within thirty seconds, the two men were walking towards a small office in the middle of the factory.

"Martin, I'd like you to meet our shop foreman, Louis Fusco. Perhaps you'd repeat what you just explained to me about your project."

Both Jeff and Louis were very interested in the presentation. Quinn emphasized his primary concern was that the job be completed competently and on time. Fusco was confident he would have a sample bracket ready by Wednesday afternoon. Martin left a set of the newly printed plans and cautioned both men about the confidential nature of the job. He guaranteed that if Anderson quoted a reasonable price and proved it was capable of completing the work on time, Cove would not solicit other bids. In return it was agreed that Anderson would not discuss the project with anyone else. Furthermore, Anderson needed to alert him if it received other similar requests for pricing.

Martin could tell the two men were somewhat taken aback by his warnings. Nevertheless, he knew that any deals involving Fred Ross had to be undertaken with the utmost care. Quinn could not afford to risk his relationship with Anderson Aluminum by having Fred weasel his way into the picture, jeopardizing the potential for Cove to put together a winning game plan.

After his meeting, Martin called Eddie from the parking lot.

"We're going to have to keep an eye on Fred. Yesterday afternoon when I was over at his house, he was still trying to chisel away at the $340,000 cost for the project. I thought we were beyond that."

Eddie tried to minimize Martin's concerns by suggesting prejudiced opinions of Fred were clouding his judgment. Quinn countered by alerting Gallagher to the fact that Ross had another company looking at the blueprints.

"Fred tried to brush it off by explaining that he asked his neighbor to look at the job when Seahorse first contacted RossCon Enterprises. I don't believe him because it doesn't explain why this guy had the plans as recently as yesterday. I'd say he's had the plans since after we met Ross last Wednesday evening. There was probably a screw up and Fred never got them back in time for our meeting on Saturday. He didn't seem too sick to me when we met yesterday!"

"We can still make good money on this job, even if we go down to $300,000. Let's get together with Fred on Wednesday evening before you two meet with Seahorse Communications. We can go over the costs again and straighten things out."

3:45PM - Wednesday February 10, 1999

Considering the short notice, Quinn was very impressed with what Louis Fusco managed to fabricate. It was not exactly what the blueprints had indicated, but it was made of aluminum and the assembly was a full scale, two foot long model that clearly showed how a bracket would work when attached to the bridge. As the two men walked back through the shop floor, Quinn suddenly grabbed Fusco's arm. He had spotted a fiberglass bin full of electrical components stamped with the name "SIEMENS."

"Would you be able to stamp 'SEAHORSE' on each of the assembly covers?" Martin asked.

"Sure, when it comes to aluminum, there's nothing I can't do!"

"Why don't you give me a small piece of aluminum stock and just stamp it with any of the name dyes you have, so I can give the folks at Seahorse a taste of what we can do for them."

"Excellent idea!" Louis agreed.

6:15PM - Wednesday February 10, 1999

Tory and Shelley were the best of friends. They car-pooled practically every day between Jamestown, Rhode Island and Braintree, Massachusetts. They would normally have been crossing the Jamestown Bridge by 6:15PM, had it not been for the fact that the school's yearbook photographs were taken that day. Tory was indifferent to this annual ritual. He was tired and judging by the congested traffic, it would be some time before he would eat supper. A glitch with the photographer's flash equipment had caused things to run late and as luck would have it, he and Shelley were his last two subjects. Like most women, she took more interest in these matters conscious that unlike her driving license, this picture would be featured in Thayer Academy's school yearbook. She had even stopped the photographer to straighten Tory's collar.

Shelley's husband, David, did not answer his cell phone when she called to explain why she was running late. Even without delays, however, the daily commute was becoming too much. This factor had spurred her into applying for a new position closer to home. Recently it seemed as if she and David communicated more via voicemail than by any other method. Tory did not really like David. There was no particular reason other than instinct. Shelley, however, was unaware of his feelings towards her husband.

9:20PM - Wednesday February 10, 1999

Ross arrived at Gallagher's house before Quinn, and shared his reservations regarding Martin's commitment. He had no basis for concern, but took the opportunity to undermine Eddie's business partner.

"I don't think he's focused on the project."

"That's not true. He's spent the last two days rethinking the design and getting a sample fabricated for tomorrow morning's meeting. He explained to me that it's impossible to meet your May 7 deadline without redesigning how the raceway needs to be fabricated. These are all issues that need to be addressed with Seahorse Communications. Remember, I work full-time for Milano. I can't get involved in these details. Now stop worrying about Martin's commitment."

Their conversation was interrupted when Quinn walked into Gallagher's kitchen with the sample bracket assembly under his arm. Both Ross and Gallagher were impressed by Anderson's work, but it was the dye stamp that really sold the program.

"The guys at Seahorse will love this," Fred exclaimed. "When we tell them that their name can be stamped on eight thousand feet of cable raceway, they'll be hooked!"

Martin reckoned there was no better time to sort out any questions Fred had regarding Cove's $340,000 price tag.

"I can't agree to pay you guys three-forty just like that. I still have to check some things out."

"Listen Fred," Martin snapped back, "that's the number you and Eddie agreed when he called you after we all sat here last Wednesday night. It's the number I told you we needed when you and I met at your house on Sunday afternoon and that's what I understood Cove would get paid when I took the plans and got this sample for tomorrow's meeting."

"Guys," Ross responded in a conciliatory tone, "maybe three-forty is the number. I just need a little time to check it out."

"You take all the time that you need," Quinn replied, "but understand this. I'm not going to the meeting with this sample unless it's clear how much you intend to pay us. Right now I believe we can make your May 7 completion date, but if this nonsense continues to eat into the work schedule, I've no idea how long it will take."

"Martin's got a point," Eddie interrupted. "We need to agree on a price, sooner rather than later. How about three-ten?"

"Maybe," Fred conceded, "but I want to give it some thought."

"Fred, if Seahorse has already given you the job then you need to get started right now, otherwise we'll stand no chance of getting the $20,000 bonus. What if Cove does the job and our companies split the profit on the base contract sixty – forty, with Cove taking sixty percent and Ross-Con Enterprises taking forty. If we meet the April 15 completion date, then we split the bonus fifty-fifty. Can you live with that deal?" Martin proposed.

The subsequent silence was too long for Quinn's liking.

"My life's not this empty!" he exclaimed. "I don't need this bullshit. I'm not going to any meeting unless we agree on what Cove is going to be paid."

Fred stood up, walked across the kitchen and opened the door. He was out of sight from where Eddie was sitting but nodded in his direction as he glared at Martin, "You'll do what he tells you."

Gallagher knew this was far more than Quinn would tolerate. He winked at his business partner and interrupted Ross before anything else could be said.

"Listen, Martin, you can't let Fred go to the meeting by himself. I've no doubt we can come to an agreement on the payment terms within the next few days."

Ross grinned like a spoiled child who had just got the better of his sibling during a squabble in which their father had intervened.

"Okay," Martin relented, "what time do you want to meet?"

"Eight o'clock at my house."

"Are you sure you can get up that early?"

"Behave!" Eddie scolded. "Now both of you get out of here, so I can get to bed."

9:25AM - Thursday February 11, 1999

Martin followed Ross' Yukon SUV into the parking lot of Bottazzi Associates, the engineers who had developed the initial design and would help acquire necessary permits. He had chosen to drive himself because he knew there was no way he could endure a road trip to and from Smithfield, Rhode Island, with Fred Ross.

"I can't remember the last time I saw you wearing a suit," Ross smirked as Quinn recovered the sample bracket from the rear of his vehicle.

Martin ignored the fashion critique and headed off in the direction of the building. The two men did not speak during an elevator ride to the third floor where they stepped out in front of two plate glass doors, each etched with the name "Bottazzi Associates." Beyond these doors, Martin could see a cherry reception desk with a black granite counter. Comfortable leather seats bordered three sides of a coffee table which also had a black granite top. Several construction industry magazines were neatly fanned out like a deck of playing cards on a blackjack table. The walls were decorated with professionally framed aerial photographs of completed projects, designed by the firm. An attractive young receptionist greeted the men when they entered.

"We have a 9:30 appointment with Tony," Fred announced.

"The others are already in the conference room," she replied, rising from her desk to accompany them into the meeting. "Coffee?"

"No thank you," they replied in unison.

"Did we just agree on something?" Martin thought to himself in horror. He attributed this minor slip to being distracted by the shapely form of their beautiful guide.

Anthony Bottazzi was already in the conference room along with one of his engineers, Scott Manning; and a project manager from Seahorse Communications, John Grasso.

"Why don't you show the class what you brought for 'Show and Tell' today?" Bottazzi suggested, once the introductions were addressed.

Quinn explained how the sample had been put together and why some aspects of it differed from the original design. Neither Anthony Bottazzi nor Scott Manning seemed to be upset by any of the modifications.

John Grasso was thrilled with the presentation, especially when it was explained that "SEAHORSE" would be stamped on all the cover sections along the raceway. Quinn knew he needed to temper John's enthusiasm and cautioned the group that a lot more work was required.

"Do you think we can make the May 7 completion date?" Grasso asked.

"With a bit of luck and a lot of effort, I believe it's possible," Quinn replied, "however the first thing I'd like to do this morning is visit the jobsite."

Tony Bottazzi explained that he had another appointment, but the others decided to reconvene at the bridge.

Thirty minutes later, all four vehicles were parked behind a row of concrete highway jersey barriers that shielded a maintenance area beside the Jamestown Bridge. John helped with the sample bracket, while Martin carried some tools. He brought two small cheap C-clamps, a thirty-foot tape measure and Vernier calipers: a precision engineering instrument for measuring the thickness of various structural elements. Quinn also had his leather Day-Timer organizer which accompanied him during every second of his workday.

The raceway was designed to attach outside the base of each post of a railing that ran the length of the bridge. It was comprised of a U-shaped lower trough which would carry the fiber-optic cables, along with a U-shaped top cover that encased both vertical legs of the lower section.

John led the party to a railing post which was accessible from both the sidewalk and a grass bank which sloped up from the water's edge along the side of the abutment. Since Martin had no intention of drilling into the structure that day, he substituted C-clamps for bolts. It took about fifteen seconds to secure the bracket in place and another five seconds to scale the side of the bridge. For John Grasso, the sight of Martin jumping up and down on the bracket satisfied two questions in his mind. First, there was no doubt that Quinn's bracket system would be strong enough and second, he knew for sure who Seahorse would get to do this job.

"Awesome!" Grasso exclaimed.

"John, it will take the weight of both of us," Martin assured him, "and we don't even have the bracket properly bolted to the bridge."

"I'll take your word for it. You've already convinced me."

Quinn jumped down and proceeded to take more measurements so he could modify the design. It was his intention to make a prototype, comprised of three brackets, along with two intermediate raceway sections spanning between them.

"Where do we go from here?" Grasso asked.

"Well, I want to prepare some manufacturing shop drawings and send them over to Bottazzi's office for their review. We can't begin fabrication, or installation in the field, until we have done so on paper."

"I'd like to show the sample to some people back at my office. Does your schedule allow for that today?"

"Not really. I have to get back to Boston for a 1:30 meeting, but why don't you and Fred keep it?" Martin suggested.

Ross' eyes lit up with delight at the thought of getting his hands on the sample. There were no objections from him and John Grasso appreciated Quinn's gesture.

"You can give me or Eddie a call later," Martin suggested to Fred as they parted.

2:45PM - Thursday February 11, 1999

Maria Santos took the Black American Express card from the salon assistant, returned it to her purse and lifted a coffee cup off the counter, taking care not to damage her newly manicured nails. She could have performed this weekly ritual with her eyes closed. Walking towards the silver Mercedes sedan, her attention was drawn to a white envelope wedged beneath a wiper blade. Maria's knees buckled in response to its content, causing her elbows to strike the hood with a dull thud as coffee splashed across the metallic paint finish.

Even though the subject in the Polaroid instant photograph had duct tape covering his eyes, she recognized him immediately. A sign suspended around her husband's neck read "CALL MY CELL PHONE - DO NOT CONTACT ANYONE."

Maria fumbled to unlock the door, before slumping into the driver seat. Her hands shook uncontrollably as she tumbled the entire contents of her handbag onto the passenger seat in a hysterical effort to find her cell phone. Frantically she dialed Xavier's number.

8:30PM - Thursday February 11, 1999

By 8:30, there had been no communication from Ross, so Martin called Eddie.

"I've heard nothing either," Gallagher reported.

"Call that little shithead and find out how things went after I left them," Quinn demanded. "Ross and Grasso were supposed to meet with engineers from CellTell Atlantic. I'll call you back in an hour. I'm at home, and Margaret won't appreciate you calling here."

One hour later, Quinn was back on the phone with Gallagher.

"Did you talk to him?"

"I did. Apparently the engineers at CellTell Atlantic have concerns about the welds."

"That's horseshit! There's nothing wrong with the welds. That shithead is up to something."

"Look, I'm only telling you what Fred said. Don't get all over me."

"What about the price for doing this job? What did he have to say about that? And where's the sample now?"

"He needs a few days to finalize the price and the sample's at Bottazzi's office."

"Whatever," Martin sighed. "Let's talk about something else that's been bothering me. I think we're going to have to get Brian Iverson to chase Roche for our money on the Canton job."

Paul Roche owned Commercial Construction Enterprises which was the general contractor on the construction of a new funeral home in Canton, Massachusetts. Cove had a subcontract to complete the sitework and concrete foundations. Brian Iverson was an attorney who Cove engaged on occasion.

"I'll call Brian tomorrow and have him start leaning on Roche," Martin concluded.

9:00AM - Friday February 12, 1999

Quinn needed to know what Ross was up to, yet understood the futility of simply asking him. "What would be the point? Fred's just going to lie," he told himself, suspecting Ross was soliciting other proposals. This task had become a lot easier because he had Cove's sample bracket to show prospective manufacturers. Martin knew that he had made a good impression with both John Grasso and Tony Bottazzi, but he needed to make sure Fred Ross did not jeopardize this. He decided to rush the preparation of manufacturing shop drawings and then send copies to both Ross and Bottazzi Associates. This would keep open a line of communication with someone other than Fred.

Martin placed a phone call to Attorney Iverson and, after explaining Cove's payment problems with the funeral home job, asked for advice regarding Fred Ross and the sample bracket which had not been returned. Iverson suggested talking to an attorney who specialized in the protection of intellectual property and provided contact information for two firms. He also instructed Quinn to make a copy of all his work on this project and mail it, in a sealed envelope, to Cove's office address. When Martin received his own package in the mail, he was not to open it, but rather store it in a safe place.

"If this goes to court," Iverson explained, "the judge will be given the task of opening this evidence, bearing the original postmark."

By 2:00 that afternoon, Martin had an independent draftsman committed to working over the weekend to complete the shop drawings. He had already mailed the self-addressed package and was in the process of explaining to patent attorney, Arthur Watson, the details of his dealings with Fred Ross. Watson requested that Quinn send him copies of any material related to the design, and scheduled a meeting for the following Wednesday.

8:50AM - Saturday February 13, 1999

Cove had a subcontract to build the foundations for a new pharmacy in the Boston suburb of Hyde Park. Robert Hayes, the project superintendent for the general contractor, had asked Martin to work the job on Saturday since there was snow forecast for later in the week.

"Do you want to go to the Bruins' game on Tuesday night? The ready-mix concrete sales rep gave me two tickets." Hayes asked, during morning coffee break.

"Why not, I'll pay for dinner in the North End before the game."

The rest of the Quinns' weekend revolved around Brendan's hockey games. Martin also avoided any discussion with Margaret regarding either Fred Ross or the Jamestown project. He wanted to give the attorneys and perhaps time itself, a chance to allow him to get the upper hand, before sharing any details with his wife.

7:45PM - Saturday February 13, 1999

Somehow Maria Santos managed to compose herself and comply with the kidnapper's instructions. The only silver lining to this whole episode was that she would never again have to look at the ugly footstool which had once languished forlornly in her husband's study. She smashed the ten pound sledge hammer down upon the custom piece of furniture, without any consideration to the care and devotion which had been put into its construction. It took three blows before the footstool revealed where it had been hiding one million dollars, in a cedar lined false bottom.

The last time this tool was used to uncover a similar bounty, it was in the hands of her husband. Maria had no knowledge of this incident. On that occasion, it only took one, well placed blow to its victim's left knee cap to reveal the whereabouts of drugs that had been stolen from Xavier's office at the nightclub.

Maria counted out the money into ten neat bundles. The kidnapper was demanding five hundred thousand dollars, which was only half of what the footstool had coughed up.

9:00AM - Monday February 15, 1999

Quinn marked up corrections on five 81/2 X 11 shop drawings received via fax from his draftsman and immediately sent them back. He was anxious to get them corrected and sent out that evening, by overnight delivery, to both Fred Ross' house and Bottazzi Associates. There was a local Federal Express depot which stayed open until 8:30. Even if it meant working late, he felt comfortable he could get the packages sent out that day.

By 8:00pm, Martin was locking his office door with two Federal Express packages tucked under his arm. He sent six sets of shop drawings to Bottazzi Associates, with a letter of transmittal, requesting the return of four sets with review comments. The transmittal also indicated that two sets of drawings had been sent to Fred Ross, in order to keep him informed of what was going on.

7:30PM - Tuesday February 16, 1999

Martin and Rob Hayes had eaten a good dinner and consumed several beers by the time they were sitting down to watch the Boston Bruins face off against the Tampa Bay Lightning. Throughout the evening, Quinn relayed details of his dealings to date with Fred Ross. Hayes was intrigued by the saga and insisted that he be kept informed as events unfolded.

Boston won the game 3-2 and Ken Belanger of the Bruins won both his fights, so all the home-team's fans left the game, satisfied with the evening's entertainment.

10:00AM - Wednesday February 17, 1999

Arthur Watson was a senior partner in the law firm of Van Acken, Tate and Armstrong whose offices were located in the financial district of Boston. As Martin waited in the elegantly furnished reception area, he took this opportunity to view some of the historic models and framed specification drawings decorating the space. One was a machine used in the manufacturing of leather boots, an invention stemming from the beginning of the twentieth century. Contrary to current filing procedures, the United States Patent Office, at one time, insisted all applications be accompanied with an actual working model of the invention. This practice had long since been abandoned primarily due to problems associated with storage and cataloging of such a vast inventory.

"Mr. Quinn?"

The voice interrupted inspection of a nineteenth century natural gas lamp. He turned to find a slightly rotund gentleman welcoming him with an outstretched hand.

"Arthur," Martin presumed.

He followed Attorney Watson into a conference room. Twelve ornate leather upholstered chairs with matching frames surrounded an impressive highly polished boardroom table. The walls had an oak wainscot which was topped off with a chair rail. The finish above was tan in color and appeared to have a suede texture. The perimeter of the solid gypsum ceiling featured an ornate crown molding. This detail was replicated on the border of a central recessed panel above the table. Concealed lighting washed this area and augmented decorative light fixtures located throughout the remainder of the ceiling.

Quinn had not spent more than sixty seconds in Arthur Watson's presence, but already he had a feeling of relief that any problems with Fred Ross would be resolved. Suddenly Martin realized why he felt so at ease. Arthur's character and appearance were very similar to those of his own father. He had been reassured during their initial phone conversation. The calm tone of Arthur's voice had completely set Martin's mind at rest. Then, and again at this meeting, Watson exhibited a confident manner reminiscent of Quinn Senior. He was also of similar height and general build. They even shared the same conservative dress sense. Arthur did, however, have slightly less hair and was perhaps ten years younger, most likely in his mid fifties. Even though Martin realized he had no evidence to support the way he felt, Arthur's resemblance to his father inspired faith in the attorney's legal expertise. He also recalled that Watson came recommended by Brian Iverson. This alone should have been an adequate endorsement. He accepted an offer of coffee and sat forward to reach for the freshly poured cup.

Watson confirmed he had reviewed the material which Quinn had sent previously and invited his client to elaborate on aspects of his dealings with Fred Ross. Arthur listened while jotting notes on a yellow legal pad.

When Martin finished, the attorney sat straighter in his chair and suggested that his office begin a search of the U.S. patent archives, to see if there was anything similar on file. He explained that Fred stealing Martin's idea was moot, if it had already been patented by a third party. Arthur recommended that an application be filed on Cove's behalf, if the search yielded no results of a similar patented system. Furthermore, Watson doubted that Seahorse Communications would tolerate Fred Ross' underhand behavior. He felt Quinn had taken enough precautions to support his position, in the event that legal action would be necessary.

* * * * * * *

While Martin was meeting with the patent attorney, Eddie Gallagher received a phone call from Fred Ross.

"Seahorse wants Martin to come to a meeting tomorrow."

"So why don't you tell him yourself? I told you before that he's the one running the job. I can't give it the attention it needs while I'm here at Milano's office."

"I tried calling him at the office. He wasn't there and I got no answer on his cell phone."

Ross explained that Seahorse had requested he carry out some value engineering to investigate the possibility of saving money with other designs. Consequently, he had another system for them to look at, but John Grasso had insisted Martin be present at the meeting.

"When and where's this meeting?"

"There's an Applebee's restaurant in Attleboro, just off Exit 4 on I295. We're going to meet at 4:00 tomorrow afternoon."

"I'll catch up with Martin and make sure he makes the meeting. But Fred, we've got to come to terms regarding payment for this job."

"I know, but Seahorse has complicated things by requesting I look at another design. We can't agree on a price until I've got a clear understanding of what they want me to do. I'm sure we'll have all this sorted out by the beginning of next week."

* * * * * * *

"Damn this Nextel phone," Martin muttered, as he made a futile attempt to call Sandra back at the office. It was only two months old and already giving him problems. He had made a decision to change the company's cell phone service to Nextel, because in addition to its regular cell phone mode, this system allowed him to get in touch with any of his employees by just pushing a button and talking on a private walkie/talkie channel. There was no need to dial a number and the airtime did not result in any additional charges. His crews liked the Nextel system too. It was easy to communicate on a jobsite when several operators were working in different pieces of excavating equipment.

Unfortunately for Martin, the number pad on his Nextel phone occasionally malfunctioned and prevented him from dialing the digits 4, 5, or 6. By choosing the two-way service, however, he was able to get in touch with Sandra, and ask her to call him using the cell phone mode. When Martin made the decision to get his company's key people onto the Nextel phone system, he kept his own regular Verizon cell phone. But in his rush to get out of the office that morning, he had accidentally left it under a pile of papers on his desk. When Sandra returned his call, the first thing he asked her to do was contact the Nextel dealership and report the problem with his phone.

Southbound traffic on I93 was backed up badly. Boston was in the middle of one of the world's biggest infrastructure construction projects, locally dubbed the "Big Dig." Urban planners and politicians had managed to implement a plan involving construction of forty miles of four-lane highway beneath the city of Boston and its harbor, so an existing elevated three-lane highway structure could be removed. The job had taken on a momentum and life of its own. Quinn recalled how a project of this nature would have been described back in his native Belfast. They would say it was like "Riding a Tiger," because once you've started, you can't stop or you'll be eaten!

The outcome of all this construction was that for twenty-four hours a day, seven days a week, Boston was basically one big jobsite. Unlike any other, however, it had to accommodate one million permanent residents, along with an additional two million people who commuted in and out of the city each day. Martin appreciated that in ten years time, Boston would benefit from these efforts, but right now, "what a mess, and what a cost!"

Twenty minutes after leaving the parking garage, he had traveled less than half a mile and had only managed to get onto the southbound lanes of the elevated Interstate 93, or "Expressway," as it had been proudly named by urban planners in the 1950's. Boston residents had since renamed it, "The Distressway." For the second time in as many days, Quinn spotted an eagle high in the sky. It glided effortlessly above the traffic without any apparent agenda. Suddenly Milano's main office number lit up his Nextel phone's screen. It was Eddie Gallagher.

"How did your meeting go?"

"Not bad, the attorney wants to do some research. Sandra said Fred Ross was trying to contact me. Do you know what he wanted?"

"There's another meeting and the guy at Seahorse Communications, John ..."

There was a pause while Eddie tried to recall John Grasso's full name. Martin prompted him and Gallagher continued.

"Yes, John Grasso wants you to attend. Ross says that Seahorse asked him to investigate the possibility of saving money by considering modifications to the design."

"That seems very strange if they want to make the May 7 completion date. When's the meeting?"

Eddie relayed the details before cutting short their call since he was working on a bid for Milano.

Quinn did not want to analyze the Seahorse Communications project too much. If there was a possibility Cove could get a productive job, despite Fred Ross' involvement, then it would be worth attending Thursday's meeting in Attleboro.

Later that afternoon, Martin contacted Federal Express regarding the shop drawing packages he had sent to Fred Ross and Bottazzi Associates. The customer service operator confirmed the signature, date and time for delivery of the Bottazzi package. She did not, however, have a confirmed delivery for the one sent to Ross.

"I don't understand," responded Quinn, "how can there not be a signature? Both packages were dropped off at your Randolph facility on Monday evening at the same time."

"The computer is showing that our driver did deliver the package to the Easton address yesterday morning, but no one was home to sign for it."

Martin was thoroughly frustrated and annoyed. The whole purpose of using the Federal Express service was to get written confirmation that Fred Ross received the shop drawings.

"We keep a form on file for many of our small business customers, authorizing us to leave deliveries when nobody is available to acknowledge receipt," she continued. "My computer shows that the package addressed to RossCon Enterprises was left between the storm door and front door at 10:36AM on Tuesday, February 16."

With the benefit of hindsight, it did not surprise Quinn that Ross had arranged for all Federal Express packages to be received without having to provide proof of delivery. It seemed an appropriate operating procedure for someone of Fred's character and it made Martin suspicious about what may be happening to Cove's shop drawings. Consequently he decided to call Anthony Bottazzi to make sure everything was okay. The drawings did not exactly reflect Bottazzi's design and Quinn felt it would be better to take the lead in explaining why he had made modifications. Developing a direct dialogue with Bottazzi would make it more difficult for Ross to undermine Cove's work.

"Hi Tony. I wanted to go over the shop drawings I sent you."

"I don't have them anymore. Fred Ross took them."

"Fred Ross took them!" Martin repeated in disbelief. "Why did he need to take all six sets? I sent him two full sets for his own use."

"Fred claimed he wasn't aware that you had sent out any shop drawings. He came here today at lunch-time and took everything you sent to our office. Apparently he doesn't want us to review them at the present time, because there's another design being considered."

Martin did not want to draw any more attention to this incident, so he ended the phone call trying not to sound too awkward. It was obvious Anthony Bottazzi was not aware of Fred Ross' character traits or he would never have surrendered all the copies.

Quinn knew Ross was definitely up to something, but decided not to share this development with his business partner. Eddie had a tendency to afford Fred the benefit of the doubt, often dismissing Martin's opinions as being too prejudiced. Quinn's patience, however, was being tested. Ross' behavior was beginning to jeopardize Cove's relationship with both Bottazzi Associates and Seahorse. It was also affecting Martin's relationship with Eddie. He constantly found himself adopting an opposing position in their discussions regarding Fred. Cove's commitments to its other clients were being diluted by the need to focus on this project. Furthermore, harmony in the Quinn household was being stressed by a project, the details of which he could not even bring himself to share with Margaret. Thursday's meeting in Attleboro was going to mean that he would be home late, yet again!

7:15AM - Thursday February 18, 1999

As usual, Shelley Tyre's car was the first vehicle to pull into the staff parking lot. Despite the early hour and busy schedule ahead, she was feeling energetic and eager to embark upon the day. When she accepted the position as Principal of Thayer Academy Middle School, Shelley promised herself not to allow this administrative role to completely separate her from what she truly loved: teaching. Four times a week she taught an eighth grade science class and that morning had decided to combine her love of teaching with another love: SCUBA diving. It took two trips between the car and her office to transfer all her equipment. Later she would use it to demonstrate practical applications of scientific principles and theory which her students had learned during the term.

Still shivering from the frigid morning air, Shelley hung her coat on the back of the office door. "Only a few more weeks and I'll be sitting on the dock in Tortola," she consoled herself.

4:00PM - Thursday February 18, 1999

As Quinn entered the restaurant, he could see John Grasso and Anthony Bottazzi across the dining room, where the hostess was seating them.

"How are you?" John asked, as Quinn approached.

"Good, John - yourself?"

"You remember Tony Bottazzi from the other week?"

"Of course I do," Martin replied, shaking the engineer's hand.

At that moment, Quinn spotted Ross' SUV reversing into the parking space beside John Grasso's truck. Fred then appeared to be waiting for two gentlemen who were getting out of a Cadillac sedan. Martin knew he only had thirty seconds before Ross would be inside the restaurant.

"What's the agenda for the meeting?" Quinn asked.

"We're all here at Fred's request," Bottazzi explained.

"Yeah," Grasso added. "He has a design idea from another engineer, but I told him I wanted both you and Tony to be part of any discussions."

"Not a problem." Martin assured him as he watched Fred slither around the tables towards their group.

Ross introduced the two men who accompanied him as Ian Goodwright and Alexander Stoltz. He explained that Goodwright owned Bay State Fabricators, a specialty metal fabrication business in Raynham, Massachusetts and Stoltz was an independent mechanical engineer.

Martin recognized Ian as the blonde gentleman from whom Fred had retrieved the original plans, on the Sunday afternoon when he went to

Ross' house. "This should be an interesting meeting," he thought, armed with the knowledge that neither John Grasso nor Tony Bottazzi had requested Fred Ross research alternative designs.

A waitress arrived at the table and introduced herself as Jill. She was petite, blonde and appeared to be in her mid twenties. As she opened her notepad to take their drink order, Quinn spotted a photograph slipped in behind a plastic pouch. It was of two young girls posing in swimsuits on a beach. The taller one appeared to be about four and was proudly holding the other child's hand.

"Are those your girls?"

"Yes," beamed Jill. "Alison is four and Heather is two. This was taken last summer."

"They certainly are two little angels," Martin remarked, as she held open the photograph for everyone to see.

"Thank you, they're good kids. Now, what can I get you gentlemen to drink?"

Anthony Bottazzi proposed Fred pay for the drinks and food, since he had scheduled the meeting. What could Ross say? Here he was in front of his new client, Seahorse Communications, as well as a new potential subcontractor. Fred made the best of the situation by agreeing to take care of the bill and then asked Alex Stoltz to expand upon his ideas for the project.

Alex explained that his design would be thirty percent lighter than what was currently being proposed. Ian Goodwright emphasized his company's ability to fabricate the components under an aggressive production schedule, since it already possessed many of the dyes and presses needed to manufacture Stoltz's design.

John Grasso appeared to be open minded and receptive to the proposal. He liked the production schedule benefits and even managed to

get Goodwright to assure him he could manufacture the raceway components by a date which would permit installation on the bridge prior
to the May 7 deadline. Tony Bottazzi was not so enthusiastic. He asked
Stoltz what accommodations had been made to ensure it would perform
satisfactorily at the bridge's expansion joints. Alex responded courteously
and acknowledged his design was far from complete and did not fully
address all the issues Tony was raising. He believed he would have to
visit the bridge and carry out his own field inspection before proceeding
any further. Nevertheless, Stoltz was confident he could finalize a design
which would satisfy subsequent scrutiny and review. It was then that John
realized Martin had not contributed to the discussions.

Quinn had strong reservations, but felt this was neither the time nor
an appropriate venue to air them. He had not invited these gentlemen into
the program. It was not his responsibility to explain that their proposal
was not practical. From what he could ascertain, Bay State Fabricators
specialized in furnishing aluminum trim and other light gauge metal and
plastic products to manufacturers of domestic appliances such as refrig-
erators or washing machines. These designs featured hidden clips which
held accent trim pieces in place, in an aesthetically pleasing manner.
Quinn's initial opinion was that their design was too flimsy. His experience of installing six hundred pound pieces of granite curb along the side
of highways provided insight as to the harsh environment that exists in
the proximity of heavy vehicular traffic. The resulting grit, sand, salt and
other debris can be punishing on anything other than the most robust of
structures. In addition, this application called for the fiber-optic raceway
to perform satisfactorily while exposed to whatever weather conditions
blew in from the Atlantic Ocean.

Martin felt sorry for Alexander Stoltz. His design had some merit
and it was obvious he was creative and knowledgeable regarding what

Goodwright's company normally produced. Quinn shuddered to think what sort of seductive representations Fred had made in order to get both Ian and Alex involved. Nevertheless, it was not his job to protect the world from Fred Ross. Besides, it was becoming more and more evident he needed to focus on protecting Cove Construction from this man.

"I think Alex is correct," Quinn replied. "It's unfair to be too critical at this point. He really needs to visit the bridge himself and finalize his design. At that time, we'll all be in a better position to give it the consideration it deserves."

The meeting concluded with Fred agreeing to bring both Ian and Alex to the bridge the following morning.

5:15PM - Thursday February 18, 1999

George Grey was ecstatic. It had been the most challenging test of his legal career to date; masterminding a flawless plan and executing it with cold calculated precision. Even though his drug dealing client was guilty of every crime with which he had ever been charged, it did not concern George that this man was, once again, back home with his family. It was, after all, what he had been paid to make sure would happen.

Fifteen years of working for the Suffolk County Sheriff's Department had numbed all his senses and emotions towards that section of society which choose criminal enterprise as a means to making a living. To Grey, their careers were no different from what many legitimate businessmen had to contend with, but considering the risks, it seemed only right that the most successful of them should be well compensated. Observing high-priced attorneys skillfully defend these criminal entrepreneurs had spurred him to labor through four years of law school at night. In 1993, these studies paid off when he passed the Massachusetts Bar Examination. Keeping his eye on the prize, George proceeded straight into private practice and joined the ranks of those defense attorneys who specialize in addressing the legal needs of the area's criminal community. Former colleagues in the sheriff's department helped him with both referrals and, on occasion, valuable intelligence regarding charges which had been filed against his clients.

He did not make a habit of accepting payment in cash but appreciated the need to make an exception on this occasion. Flicking his thumb through the last bundle of hundred dollar bills, Grey finished transferring the money from a black gym bag into the secure fire safe in his basement. Not even his wife knew the combination of its lock. She had no desire to know this information. Her husband continued to carry a concealed firearm since leaving the employment of the sheriff's department and Angela Grey insisted that it be kept locked in the safe immediately upon his return home each evening. Understanding only too well the allure the gun had for their two teenage sons, she had no interest in it or any other material pertaining to his work.

George smiled as he closed the safe door on three hundred thousand dollars cash, which would never be reported to the IRS.

6:15PM - Thursday February 18, 1999

O n the drive back home from Attleboro, Martin called Eddie.

"How did it go?" Gallagher asked.

"We have a problem. If John Grasso tells his boss that he's considering using Bay State's design, he'll probably get himself fired. However, if he's fortunate enough to get beyond that point and the bridge's owners see what Seahorse is proposing to use, then the project will be cancelled."

"What was wrong with it?"

"It's too flimsy and totally inadequate for this application. Fred's going to bring his two new guys to the bridge tomorrow morning, but neither John nor Tony is available to make that trip. If I call John Grasso tomorrow morning, I know for sure Fred won't be around and I can let him know privately how I feel."

"Well, you're in the best position to make this decision. I just hope it's the right one."

10:15AM - Friday February 19, 1999

Martin had to survey and price a small job at a retail plaza in Rockland, Massachusetts. He parked his Jeep in a remote corner of the parking lot and called 411 since he did not have a phone number for John Grasso. Quinn called three different Seahorse facilities before getting an operator who acknowledged John Grasso worked at that particular location.

"Good morning John. Martin Quinn here."

"Hi Martin. What can I do for you?"

"I wanted to talk privately regarding last night's meeting. I hope you don't think I'm out of line by calling you direct."

"Not at all, we're all on the same team. I don't want the project jeopardized by anything. So talk away."

"I'm concerned you'll lose your job and Seahorse will be chased off the bridge if you approach anyone in a position of authority and suggest installing that system."

Quinn explained in detail why he believed this new design would not perform satisfactorily. He was careful not to present an argument which would appear petty or driven by ego and supported his position by giving specific practical reasons based on sound engineering principles. By the time he had finished, Grasso was thoroughly convinced of the folly in giving the new design any further consideration.

"I'm glad I insisted that you attend yesterday's meeting. Ever since you brought that sample down to us the other week, I knew you were the right man for this job. Nevertheless Fred insisted that I meet with these other guys, so I did - but reluctantly."

"Fred told Eddie Gallagher, my business partner, that you asked him to research other design options and that was how I understood we all came to be meeting in Attleboro last night."

"It was Ross who requested that meeting. I've done nothing other than push him to get going with the system you demonstrated two weeks ago. That's why I gave him a full set of the bridge's as-built plans for you to study. How long will it take to get the raceway installed on the bridge?"

"John, the last time that I had anything to do with this project was two weeks ago when I left you guys with my sample. Fred has avoided Eddie Gallagher and me because he doesn't want to commit to a contract amount to pay Cove. He never gave me those as-built drawings of the bridge that you asked him to pass along."

There was a brief silence while Grasso comprehended the gravity of the situation.

"I'm sorry John," Martin continued, "but I haven't done anything, other than make the original sample bracket."

The two men spent the next twenty minutes, trading versions of all recent communications that Ross had with each of them. By the end of the discussion, it was clear what Fred had managed to achieve. Three weeks earlier, contrary to what he had represented to Quinn and Gallagher, Ross did not have a contract with Seahorse. All he had was an opportunity to submit a proposal and this had been offered somewhat reticently, since he had no prior experience of such work. But once Fred turned up with Martin and the sample bracket, he shocked both Tony Bottazzi and John Grasso. When Quinn left the meeting at the bridge, Ross found himself in possession of the original sample bracket. He was then able to embellish his story and represented to John Grasso that Cove Construction worked for him. John concluded by revealing that it was Martin's sample bracket and initial presentation which lead to Seahorse Communications signing a contract with RossCon Enterprises.

"How long will it take you to manufacture the components?" John asked again, but now with the panic and realization that precious time had been squandered by Fred's devious scheming.

"We haven't reached that stage yet. We can't begin fabrication based on that sample. We need Tony's office to complete its review of the shop drawings that Fred intercepted. We also have to make a prototype comprised of three brackets, with two full assemblies that will span between them, and then install this on the bridge so we can fine-tune any measurements before going into production."

Grasso was horrified, primarily because it was he who had recommended to his boss, Kevin Shaw, Director of Northeast Operations for Seahorse Communications, that they contract with RossCon Enterprises.

"This prototype, how long will it take you to get it fabricated and tested in place on the bridge?"

"Well, today is Friday," Martin thought aloud. "I believe I can have it installed on the bridge by noon-time next Thursday."

Quinn knew that he had made an aggressive commitment without any consultation with Anderson Aluminum. He was, however, confident about their capabilities. Besides, he enjoyed the challenge and wanted to reinforce John's trust in Cove Construction.

"Okay," Grasso replied. "But I don't want Fred to know we talked. I'm going to tell him that I've reconsidered things since last night and don't want him to give any further consideration to Bay State Fabricators. I'll direct him to proceed with your system and get a prototype fabricated. That way he'll instruct you later today to go ahead and put this together, but don't wait for his call. Get right on it!"

When Martin finished his phone call, he reached over to the passenger seat of the Jeep and picked up his Day-Timer. He thumbed it open at the entries for February 11, 1999. There, on the right hand side, were dimensions and small sketches which he had made during his visit to the bridge that day. He studied them for some time before satisfying himself that he had sufficient information for Louis Fusco to manufacture the prototype. Forty minutes later he was walking across Anderson's parking lot when he spotted an eagle, which for some reason, seemed familiar. "Is that bird following me?" Quinn wondered, as the predator circled above him.

When Louis appeared, he immediately gestured for Martin to step inside from the small hallway and join him in his office on the shop floor.

"Thank you for meeting with me at such short notice," Martin acknowledged, handing Louis two boxes of donuts. "One's for the office staff and the other's for your shop crew."

"You didn't have to do this," Louis replied, setting one box on the staff's kitchenette counter adjacent to the door to the shop floor.

As they walked through the aisles of storage racking, they had to side-step around forklifts, pallets of aluminum stock in various stages of fabrication, and work stations spitting sparks and shavings around the machinists' feet.

Louis' office was a ten foot by ten foot sound-insulated cabin with windows on all four sides. Although compact, it was neatly furnished with a plan table and work desk. It also housed a video monitor, streaming live pictures from different closed-circuit television cameras located throughout the facility. Anderson's premises were protected by twenty-four hour video surveillance, seven days a week. In the privacy of Fusco's office, Quinn explained in detail what he needed for his prototype. Although he was no longer in possession of the original sample, he soon realized there was no need to worry. Louis had, in fact, made two samples and produced the spare one for reference during their meeting. With the aid of Martin's field survey measurements from February 11, Fusco was left with a clear understanding of exactly what was required of him.

"I need to install this on the bridge next Thursday."

"No problem. By the way, I took a phone call yesterday afternoon from a company in Rhode Island. They wanted a price for supplying material with similar cross-sectional dimensions to what we're working with here. However, their quantity was ten times higher than what you said we needed. I told them that I'd work on developing a competitive price quote and would get back to them by Monday at the latest. I knew that would give me time to discuss it with you."

"It's obvious their quantities are far too high. Just go ahead and give them a proposal. I think I know who's behind this."

At that moment, Jeff Anderson entered the office. After quickly reviewing the details, he quoted a price of $2,500 for furnishing the prototype.

"I'll bring a check with me on Thursday morning," Quinn promised. "Oh, and Jeff, Louis tells me someone called looking for a price quote. Cove is definitely doing this job for Seahorse, but you may still get some inquiries from other sources. It's very important you don't discuss our two companies' business with any other party. Let me know if you receive other calls about this project."

Martin sensed Jeff was puzzled by these instructions, but Louis did not seem to mind. Nevertheless, Quinn was conscious of the need to guard against any approaches from Ross or companies acting on his behalf.

As he drove out of Anderson's parking lot, Martin felt somewhat relieved. For the first time it appeared he was getting the upper hand in his dealings with Fred. He decided to call Eddie Gallagher and update him regarding the morning's developments. Once again, his Nextel phone acted up and would not register a 4, 5, or 6. In frustration, he tossed it over his shoulder into the rear of the Jeep and then called Sandra, using his Verizon cell phone.

"Did you call the Nextel dealer about my phone?"

"I'm sorry - I forgot. I'll call them when we hang up."

* * * * * * *

While Martin was meeting with Louis Fusco, Fred Ross was returning home from a visit to the Jamestown Bridge when his cell phone rang.

"Hi, John. The guys at Bay State Fabricators are going to work on some design options over the weekend and get back to me either Monday or Tuesday at the latest," he responded positively to Grasso's inquiries.

"Well, that's why I called you, Fred. I need you to come to Tony Bottazzi's office this afternoon. I have some concerns that need to be addressed. I want to sit down with both you and Tony. Can you make a 3:30 meeting?"

"What do you want to go over?" Ross responded, hoping his work day was over.

"There's no point tying up cell phone time now. We can discuss that when we get together."

John Grasso could just have easily conveyed everything over the phone but he wanted Tony Bottazzi present for two reasons. First, Bottazzi had introduced RossCon Enterprises to Seahorse. John's anger had been tempered somewhat by an acknowledgement that this had led to finding Martin Quinn and Cove Construction. Second, Grasso wanted a witness to the instructions he was going to give Ross. After finishing this call, he contacted Tony Bottazzi and asked him to set aside thirty minutes for this meeting.

3:30PM - Friday February 19, 1999

John Grasso began by handing Fred Ross and Tony Bottazzi a letter addressed to both their companies, setting forth precisely how Seahorse wanted the project to proceed.

"What I'm about to go over, I've also covered in this letter. Since last night's meeting, I've given considerable thought to this project and have decided not to proceed any further with Bay State Fabricators' design. We don't have time to pursue options other than what you had Cove show me two weeks ago. So, from this point on, the only parties involved shall be Seahorse Communications, Bottazzi Associates, RossCon Enterprises, Cove Construction and finally Anderson Aluminum, who I understand is working for Cove. Also, since RossCon Enterprises is under direct contract with Seahorse Communications to complete this project, on or before May 7, I expect, by now, it has Cove properly signed under contract, and that Cove has its own written contract or purchase order with Anderson."

John paused to observe the acquiescent expression on Fred's face. "He's good," Grasso thought to himself. Ross gave absolutely no indication that he had any problem with the production of written contracts.

"I want you to meet here with Tony and me, every Friday afternoon until this project is successfully completed," he continued. "As the letter says in the last paragraph, you are not authorized to make any deviation from these guidelines without securing prior written authorization from me. Have I made myself clear?"

This was not the sort of meeting that Ross had been expecting. He was completely caught off guard by John Grasso's newfound authoritative tone.

"Very much so," Fred blurted out.

"Good," John replied abruptly, preventing any further discussion. The only thing Grasso wanted to hear from Ross was that he understood what was expected of him.

"I want you to have Martin Quinn make a full-sized prototype that we can install on the bridge. It should comprise of at least three brackets and have two intermediate sections, complete with covers, spanning between the brackets. I want it made from aluminum; however, I don't expect it to be anodized. How long will that take?"

"I'm sure I can have that for you by next Friday when we meet again."

"Good! Get Martin Quinn working on it immediately. Let me know if there are any problems. I don't want to hear of any deviations from this plan without me being involved. Don't be afraid to use that fancy phone you keep bringing out at our meetings."

Ross' cellular phone was extremely stylish and not much thicker than a few sticks of chewing gum. It seemed appropriate for him to have such a model. It was complimented by a soft leather-bound executive folder which contained a legal pad, slim pockets for securing documents, pen holders, and a calculator inside the front cover. Fred certainly had all the executive trappings which provided the illusion that he was just the man for the job.

The meeting broke up and Ross left with less of a spring in his step than when he first arrived. As he drove north on I95, he pondered how he could regain control of the project and wriggle out of the constraints in which John Grasso had placed him. His first call was to Ian Goodwright at Bay State Fabricators.

"Ian, Fred Ross here. I've got some bad news. Seahorse doesn't want to deviate from the sample that Cove had Anderson put together. Do you think you could manufacture their system if we're no longer able to pursue Alex's design?"

"I know I can, but it's going to cost more. Cove's sample is closer in specification to what Bottazzi called for. It's heavier and requires more aluminum."

"Take a good look at your budget numbers over the weekend and we'll talk on Monday. You've got to be more creative and find a way to cut costs. In the meantime, I'll put some thought into how I'm going to get your company back in the picture."

* * * * * * *

It was 5:00 by the time the garage door closed behind Quinn. This was the first evening, in quite a while, that he had managed to arrive home at a reasonable time. His hectic schedule over the previous weeks had been very demanding which had caused some friction with Margaret. Although this Seahorse project was looking more promising, he was still not comfortable explaining exactly what had happened to date.

The remainder of the weekend passed without a request from Fred Ross that Cove fabricate the prototype, as John Grasso had directed. On Sunday evening, Martin called Eddie to discuss Cove's work schedule for the upcoming week.

"Well, I'm sure John told him to call us," Martin surmised. "Fred will probably wait until the very last minute, after he's exhausted all other options."

"I don't know. You've had a better read of the situation."

Quinn sensed Gallagher was trying to distance himself from the proceedings and qualify his involvement, so that in the event things did not turn out well, he could exonerate himself of any blame.

The weather forecast on Sunday evening's 11:00 news, warned of a possible Nor'easter storm passing through the region later in the week. "I could do without this," Martin thought to himself. The possibility of having to work on the bridge while exposed to the North Atlantic Ocean in the middle of a raging snow storm was not at all appealing.

6:00AM - Monday February 22, 1999

Quinn's week began meeting with his crew at the funeral home jobsite in Canton. With a storm forecast for later in the week, he wanted to finish the last portion of the foundation. He had scheduled a concrete delivery for Tuesday, but decided to bring it forward to later that afternoon, so he could strip the formwork on Wednesday morning and back-fill the new foundation before the snow storm arrived. Martin decided to remain on this jobsite for the entire day and push the crew.

He called the ready-mix concrete supply company and rescheduled the order for 3:00 that afternoon. His request to bring forward this delivery was similar to many the concrete company would receive that day. Fortunately, Quinn's call was early enough to receive a positive response - others would not be so lucky.

Martin's problems would not end once the ready-mix trucks were emptied. The placement of concrete into the formwork often caused it to move. After it had been troweled off to the correct height, the alignment and plumbness of the formwork had to be adjusted. Any anchor bolts for future structural steel columns also had to be checked to ensure they had not been disturbed. Then, since it was winter, the formwork had to be wrapped in water-proof insulating blankets, the whole job area enclosed in tarpaulin tents and propane heaters placed throughout the enclosure, to ensure the fresh concrete did not freeze.

With all that had to be accomplished that day, it was 6:45 in the evening before Martin got into his truck to leave. As he drove off the jobsite, he realized he had given no thought to Fred Ross and Seahorse

Communications. A brief phone call to Eddie confirmed that Ross had not attempted to contact him either. Once again, Quinn's Nextel key pad acted up, so he used his Verizon cell phone to make this call. Martin considered calling John Grasso, but he had just spent thirteen hours crawling around a foundation pour and there was only so much even Quinn was prepared to do in one workday. Instead he finished the five-mile trip home listening to the radio and surfing between channels in an attempt to get an updated weather forecast. From all accounts, the Nor'easter was expected to hit the area sometime on Wednesday night. The WBZ 1030 radio presenter warned that the current conditions were nothing other than "the lull before the storm!"

Martin headed straight for a shower. The drive home from Canton was not long enough to warm him up after the long bitterly cold day he had spent with his crew. Margaret could tell that he was truly exhausted and made no reference to the fact it was nearly 7:00.

6:45AM - Tuesday February 23, 1999

Quinn's first stop was the Canton jobsite to check the propane heaters and makeshift tents which protected the foundation pour. He waited at the jobsite until 7:00 so he could talk with the general contractor's field superintendent. They agreed that on Wednesday morning, Cove would send a heavy crew to the site to remove the tents and formwork, as well as back-fill the foundations before the storm arrived.

Martin spent the remainder of the day at Cove's office in Quincy. He had many calls to make to his job superintendents. It was important that they made adequate provisions and modified their operations on each jobsite in order to prepare for the storm. Also, Cove had a contract to supply heavy equipment to a retail mall in Hanover, to remove snow from the parking lots. This meant two large front-end loaders, a backhoe and a small skid-steer loader had to be transported, prior to the storm reaching the area. He would also have to schedule his men to work shifts so the equipment would be properly manned at the mall. A significant Nor'easter could require as many as ninety-six hours of continuous equipment operation in order to keep the snow cleared.

It was 10:30 when he contacted John Grasso to let him know that Fred Ross had not yet requested that Cove fabricate the prototype.

"What the fuck!"

Martin had never heard John use profanity before.

"What's wrong with this guy? I sat him down last Friday and made it very clear as to what I wanted him to do. Now we've lost another week! How long is it going to take you to make the prototype after he asks you?"

"I thought we agreed I was to make the prototype regardless of whether Fred Ross contacted me or not. I'll have it at the bridge before noon-time on Thursday, just like I promised."

"Well that's a relief. But we'll have to postpone the bridge trip until after this storm passes."

"John," Quinn interrupted. "This job is seriously behind schedule. We can't set goals like this and then use the weather as a reason why we don't meet them. I'll be at the bridge before noon-time on Thursday, with the prototype – Nor'easter or not!"

"I like your attitude. I'm going to chase down Ross and ask him how you're progressing!"

* * * * * * *

Just before Quinn left his office for the day, he finally got Paul Roche of Commercial Construction Enterprises on the phone. When Martin inquired about the overdue payments, Roche responded with a litany of excuses.

"I don't care about any of that," Martin countered. "We just pushed the schedule to make sure the foundations were completed before the storm. Cove's been on your Canton job since mid-October and you haven't paid us one penny. If I don't get a substantial check real soon, then I'll be calling the owner and the bond company."

"I might be able to do something for you tomorrow," Roche relented sheepishly. "I'll call you in the morning."

4:30PM - Tuesday February 23, 1999

Attorney Grey rarely met with clients without an appointment, however, Xavier Santos was obviously in need of help. Besides, this man had been responsible for generating a considerable revenue stream for Grey.

"I know you don't usually do wills, but I trust you George, and after what happened, I now realize it's something I should'a done a long time ago."

His client was nothing like the confident criminal Grey knew from previous encounters. For the next hour, the two men worked on drafting a will for Santos. George finished by suggesting that Xavier take a sedative to help him sleep at night. The attorney was struck by the irony of a drug dealer who had a problem taking prescription medication.

"Listen X, give this guy a call," Grey instructed, handing him a card. "If you don't want to take any medication, you should at least talk to a professional."

Santos reluctantly took the psychologist's phone number. He was more appreciative that Grey had just helped him prepare a will than he was for the referral.

After Santos left, Grey considered his client's condition. He had known this man for five years and never seen him in such a state. Usually criminals of his stature were not vulnerable to this sort of soul searching until they found themselves inside a prison cell. So far, George had made sure this had not happened to Xavier, even though there were occasions when both of them thought that the District Attorney's Office was going to prevail. Santos always laughed when Grey explained why he worked so hard to keep him out of prison.

"X, they'll put you away for twenty years if you get convicted of dealing drugs in these quantities. That's twenty years with few reasons to send you a legal bill. You're far too valuable for me to allow that to happen. I don't mind them charging you, but I'm never going to allow them to get a conviction!"

Nevertheless, the experience which Xavier Santos had recently endured was far more traumatic than any stay in prison. The man had just survived a kidnapping which was only brought to a successful conclusion, days earlier, with the payment of a substantial ransom.

10:10AM - Wednesday February 24, 1999

Quinn was unable to concentrate on the paperwork which covered his desk. It troubled him that Ross had not yet requested Cove make the prototype. He considered the possibility that Fred had found another contractor to help him with Seahorse's project. The fact that Paul Roche had not called with positive news of payment for work on the funeral home job did not help matters either. His thoughts were interrupted by the office phone ringing. Sandra put the call through to his desk. "This had better be one of these two clowns," he muttered to himself.

"I have a check for you. Do you want to pick it up or will I put it in the mail?" Roche asked.

"I'll come and pick it up right now."

Commercial Construction Enterprises' offices were located in Scituate, Massachusetts, a small coastal town approximately twenty-five miles south of Boston. Martin had just started his engine when he got a phone call from Fred Ross.

"How's it going?" Fred inquired, as if the two men were close friends.

"Okay," Quinn replied in a disinterested tone. He had expected this phone call five days ago and had plenty of time to rehearse his lines for the "scene" and gave no indication he was aware of Fred's predicament.

"I need a prototype made up."

"What do you mean?"

Quinn did not want to make this an easy request for Ross, so he put him to the trouble of having to explain exactly what Seahorse wanted to see installed on the bridge. He felt that if Fred had any suspicions Martin and John Grasso were communicating directly, then this little charade would help dispel such thoughts.

"When do you need it?"

"Can you have it ready for Friday?"

"Fred, do you think I can just turn around and shit twenty-two feet of aluminum raceway out of my ass? That's just two days away!"

"Well, when can you have it ready?"

"Monday's the best I can do for you."

In his heart, even Fred knew he had done well to get this commitment. His own efforts with Ian Goodwright, at Bay State Fabricators, had yielded nothing. This left him with no option but to reach out to Quinn, just as John Grasso had instructed.

When the call ended, Martin immediately called John Grasso.

"Your ace just called me and wanted to know if I could have the prototype ready for Friday."

"What an idiot! What did you tell him?"

"I told him I would have it ready on Monday. That way, we can discuss what our best course of action should be with this clown, after you've had an opportunity to see the prototype tomorrow."

"Fair enough, but I can't see us getting to the bridge during the storm."

"John, you've been listening to Fred Ross for too long. I'll be on the bridge tomorrow at noon-time. If you're interested in seeing the prototype, just show up."

"Okay! Okay! I get the picture!"

* * * * * * *

As he left Paul Roche's office, Martin made yet another unsuccessful attempt to make an outgoing call with his Nextel phone. "$120,000 - well worth the trip," Quinn complimented himself as he tossed the phone onto the passenger seat. Although this was not everything that Commercial Construction Enterprises owed Cove Construction, it was a good beginning. Given his experience with Paul Roche, however, he would hold off celebrating until the check actually cleared.

Martin needed to be kept apprised of the impending storm and many of the radio news reports featured interviews with municipal highway department supervisors, state troopers and managers of hardware stores throughout the region. All described the impact the weather was expected to have on their jobs. Quinn was oblivious to all this hysteria. For him, life was beginning to turn his way and he very much doubted any amount of snow could knock it off course. He had a check for $120,000 from a client who had proven to be less than reliable, and for the first time in a month it seemed he was getting a grip on the Seahorse project.

Back at Cove's office, Quinn started to finalize his plans for the following day. The weather was certainly going to be a factor and he did not want it to prevent him from getting the prototype installed on the bridge. He decided he would use their company's Ford diesel formwork truck to make the trip. It had a twin rear axle, four-wheel drive transmission and a full cab which could accommodate six men. The eleven foot long aluminum sections of the prototype could be carried on the ladder rack which extended from the rear bumper to just beyond the front windshield. The truck was only one year old and nicely detailed with Cove's green logo on the factory's white-paint finish. There were tool boxes along each side of the eight foot rear truck bed which were water-proof and spacious enough to carry the three brackets. Martin would have two of his best laborers drive in this truck to Jamestown.

"Will we be working outside, Boss?" Jose Sousa asked, with a degree of disbelief, when he received word that he would be working regardless of the weather.

"Yes," Quinn replied, "but only for a short while, half an hour at most. I want you to pick up Manny Frias tomorrow morning and meet me at 7:00. There's a breakfast diner a quarter mile south of Stoughton center as you head towards Easton on Route 138. I'm not sure of the name, but you can't miss it. Just dress warmly."

Quinn spent the rest of the afternoon making calls to confirm the equipment was fueled and ready at the mall. Cove's lead superintendent, Chris Donovan, would be in charge of this operation. He would work the first shift with a crew when the snow started and then trade off with another crew led by his brother, Paul. Before leaving the office, Martin got word that the new foundations at the funeral home project in Canton had been backfilled. Cove was ready for the storm.

6:50AM - Thursday February 25, 1999

Zachary's Diner was only ten minutes from Quinn's home. The trip was long enough for him to hear news reports on the severity of the storm. It had started snowing at 3:00am, falling at a rate of one inch every hour. Most meteorologists did not expect it to stop until at least midnight. Quinn had decided to take his 1998 Ford Expedition for this trip. The storm made traveling to Jamestown too risky for his old Jeep Cherokee. The Expedition's weight, coupled with its superior four-wheel drive transmission and anti-lock brakes made it a much safer option. On his way to meet with Jose and Manny, he spoke with Chris Donovan who reported that his crew had been plowing snow at the Hanover Mall since 4:00am.

As Martin drove into the diner's parking lot, a strong Portuguese accent called out from his Nextel, "Morning Boss."

"Morning Jose, what's your e.t.a.?"

"Five minutes at most. I just got off Route 24. Six cars slid into each other at Exit 17 and caused a back-up."

Again, frustrated by his Nextel keypad, Quinn called Louis at Anderson Aluminum using his Verizon cell phone. He just wanted to make sure the raceway prototype was ready to be picked up as promised.

"It's all set; don't forget to bring the check."

"You're a good man, Louis! I'll see you at eight o'clock."

The diner was packed with snowplow drivers and sanding truck operators, many of whom had been on duty all night. Martin found a table and the three men ordered breakfast from a young waitress who appeared to be nothing other than calm and collected, despite the volume of customers that had invaded the restaurant. Quinn never had any problem with Jose or Manny's work ethic. For that reason, he chose them for the trip to Jamestown. He warned the two men not to disclose any aspect of their assignment to anyone, explaining that the project was very sensitive. As all three ate hearty breakfasts, Martin described their task for the day.

It should have taken no more than ten minutes to get to Anderson Aluminum; however, weather conditions were such that it took over half an hour, which included a brief stop at Dunkin Donuts. Martin exchanged two boxes of donuts for a welcoming handshake from Louis Fusco. They proceeded onto the shop floor, where two, eleven foot long sections of aluminum raceway were laid out end to end, with corresponding covers above each. Three brackets, designed to support these components, were positioned, one at each end and one between the two lengths of raceway.

"Excellent," Quinn acknowledged.

"I can't believe you're going down to Rhode Island in this weather!" Louis remarked.

"No choice, the schedule for this job doesn't have any accommodation for weather delays."

Martin unzipped the leather cover of his Day-Timer and retrieved an envelope labeled, "Anderson."

"Here's your check for twenty-five hundred."

"I have some paperwork for you," Louis replied, reaching down to recover a shipping manifest, partially trapped beneath one of the brackets. It identified Cove's C.O.D. order to be shipped via "Customer Pick-Up."

The morning traffic was severely impacted by the horrible road conditions. A convoy of snow plows and salt sanders slowed traffic to the degree that a pedestrian would have been able to overtake even the most powerful of European sedans. Quinn checked his rear view mirror and saw Jose and Manny following him with their precious cargo. "There's no way they're going to lose my trail at this speed!" he mused.

As they merged onto Interstate 95's southbound lanes, the traffic problems eased significantly, although he pitied the folks on the northbound side of the highway who were practically at a complete stop.

He had hardly traveled two miles when he received a call from John Grasso.

"Good morning, Martin. Surely you're not driving in this weather?"

"I'm already en route and one of my crews is following with your prototype secured to their ladder rack. We should be at the bridge by noon-time."

"You're unbelievable," Grasso replied. "Call me if you get into any bother, otherwise I'll see you then."

Martin soldiered on with the Portuguese contingent in his wake. Road conditions were perilous, however, by 11:50 they were approaching the Jamestown Bridge. He could see John Grasso's Seahorse pickup truck parked in the maintenance area on the northbound side. It had strobe hazard lights which pulsed rapidly, warning other drivers of its presence at the side of the highway. He dialed John's number on his Verizon cell phone.

"We're here!"

"Yes, I just spotted you guys through the snow."

"We'll see you in five minutes."

Since Rhode Island's Route 138 was a divided highway at this location, the little convoy had to pass over the bridge, take the first exit, get onto the northbound side of Route 138 and travel back over the bridge again. Cove's two vehicles parked just beyond the Seahorse pickup truck at 11:58AM. Grasso was already standing beside the Expedition by the time Quinn had turned off its engine and wrestled himself into a jacket recovered from the rear seat.

"You're two minutes early!" John announced with a smile as they shook hands.

"I wish we didn't have to work in this weather, but the schedule's just too tight."

All four men carried the prototype pieces to the same area of the bridge where Martin had met three weeks earlier with John Grasso, Fred Ross and Scott Manning from Bottazzi Associates. Once again, small C-clamps were used to hold each of the brackets in place. Jose and Manny set the eleven foot long raceway sections into position, spanning the two gaps between the brackets. They continued to assemble the covers and locking-brackets at each railing post. The simplicity and ease at which the components came together, belied the painstaking effort and time that Quinn had invested in their design.

It took Martin and his crew no more than three minutes to install twenty-two feet of prototype raceway on the bridge. Snow continued to fall but it was more of an annoyance than an impedance to their efforts. They had chosen to access a section of the bridge on the embankment which enabled them to make the installation at a comfortable waist height. Quinn knew that the rest of the job would not be this easy since all activity would be staged from the sidewalk. Completing the work would require his crew to reach through the vertical bars of the railings that prevented pedestrians from falling off the bridge.

John Grasso was ecstatic. "This is fantastic," he exclaimed while photographing the assembly.

To prove how resilient the system was, Martin climbed onto the mid span of one raceway section and instructed both Jose and Manny to do the same on the other.

"Wow!" Grasso exclaimed, taking aim.

"Damn it! My camera has frozen," he announced to the trio perched precariously on top of the raceway, with snow lashing their faces.

"Hold on, I've got another camera in my truck," he pleaded, scampering back through the snow drifts.

Quinn and his two employees held onto the bridge like three trapeze artists, posing proudly prior to their finale in the Big Top. Grasso returned and took another three photographs using a Polaroid instant camera. Martin could not believe how thrilled John was.

"If you've got enough pictures, we need to take this down before we're frozen to the bridge!"

"Sorry," Grasso replied. "Let's get everything and everybody back into the trucks."

When Quinn was satisfied that his men had all the raceway components securely tied to the ladder rack, he dispatched them on their way so they could get out of the storm.

"Drive safely," he instructed, "and when you get home, Jose, put all this inside your basement. Remember, neither of you is to discuss where you were working today. The next time I need these aluminum sections, I'll let you know."

"Okay Boss," they replied as Jose shifted the truck's transmission.

John Grasso suggested that he and Martin get some lunch or at least a cup of coffee, so they could discuss what needed to be done next.

"Just follow me," he shouted from his truck, "there's a small restaurant five minutes from here."

Quinn and Grasso both kicked snow off their boots before entering the restaurant. The only other patron, an elderly gentleman, was sitting at the counter cradling a cup of coffee. The business obviously catered to the summer trade. An overwhelming list of ice cream flavors was displayed on a large notice board behind the cash register. Fortunately, there was also a good lunch menu, since it was a freezing February afternoon and snowing a blizzard! A waitress followed the two men to a window booth, gave them menus, and took their drink order.

"Martin, I need to know what your agreement is with Fred Ross for this project."

"Normally I'd be uncomfortable discussing such arrangements, John, but we're in this together now and somehow we have to repair the damage Ross has caused."

"I dread to think what would have happened if you hadn't warned me. Seahorse Communications doesn't give up control of its projects to other parties. Ross' continued involvement with this job is solely at my discretion. I need to know exactly what he has asked of your company and what you've represented to him you can do."

Quinn shared with Grasso how Ross had approached Cove saying he had already been awarded the contract to furnish and install the raceway across the bridge. He chronicled how Cove's initial proposal of $340,000 to complete the work was refused, as well as a subsequent offer of $310,000 plus a $10,000 bonus for having the raceway in place on or before April 15. Cove finally suggested completing the work on a time and material basis, taking 60% of the profit while Fred would take 40%, for essentially doing nothing. Martin reported how this too was unacceptable to Fred.

"That greedy little fuck," John blurted out, covering his mouth when he realized the waitress was nearby with their food. "So he never came to terms with your company regarding an amount for completing this job? That first meeting and your sample was the very reason we awarded him the contract! I've been giving him information related to the existing bridge structure ever since we all met at Bottazzi's office and then rode out to the bridge. That's why I insisted you meet with Ross' other engineers regarding the design change he was proposing."

"Fred told me this change was your idea. He said you had told him to check out other systems which might reduce the project's cost."

"I never gave that lying sack of shit any such instructions," Grasso protested. "I had no problem with the budget. When I first met you, I thought you worked for him. With you on his team, I was more than comfortable about how the job would be done."

Both men realized that their soup and sandwiches were also becoming victims of Fred's nonsense, so they took a break to eat the chowder before it got cold.

"This is what's going to happen," John resumed. "Fred's supposed to meet with Tony Bottazzi and myself tomorrow afternoon. I'm going to insist that he bring an executed contract with your company to that meeting. So he's going to have to come to terms with you before he meets with me. I don't want you to agree to anything less than $400,000 for getting this job done by April 15. I want the project completed well before our May 7 deadline with CellTell Atlantic. Seahorse has agreed to pay him enough that he can well afford to pay you guys for taking care of all the work."

Martin looked shocked and was about to express his gratitude when John quickly continued.

"Don't even think of thanking me," Grasso warned. "Fred Ross is a greedy little fuck and really shouldn't be involved any longer. He does, however, have a signed contract even though he secured it by lying and misrepresenting himself. If he agrees to pay you what you deserve, then he'll finish out this project and get adequately compensated for doing nothing other than introducing you to our company."

"Well, I still want to say thank you, John. That said, we need to get busy or we're going to have no chance of making the April 15 deadline. So, if things don't get sorted out by tomorrow afternoon when you meet Fred, then you and I are going to have to talk again."

"I understand that, but I want to give Ross one last chance to stay involved, but only by compensating you properly for doing the work. It's going to be complicated to undo the contract he has with our company, and unfortunately it was me who recommended that my boss award him the job!"

The two men finished their meals and left the restaurant. It was still snowing hard and Grasso reiterated his appreciation that Quinn had come out in the bad weather to demonstrate the prototype. Both vehicles fish-tailed out of the parking lot with their tires leaving signatures in the fresh snow.

The drive back to Stoughton was a lot better than Quinn had anticipated. His only problem was that he felt his throat beginning to tighten. He had obviously spent too long hanging off the side of the bridge for the photo shoot. His plans for the rest of the day would be to get to a pharmacy, stock up on cold and flu medication, and get into a hot steamy shower. At least he knew the trip had been well worth the effort. John Grasso's response to the prototype installation and his assurance that Cove would be paid $400,000 for this job was actually beginning to make Martin feel elated. When he thought about Cove's other projects and how difficult it could be at times just to break even, this fiber-optic raceway program for Seahorse was certainly in a class of its own. He called Eddie and briefed him on how well the bridge installation had gone, as well as how much John Grasso wanted to pay them. When he was finished, Quinn got back to the sobering business of organizing Cove's other work. He called Chris Donovan who had spent over ten hours with a crew clearing snow at the Hanover Mall. From all accounts, the storm was projected to continue for at least another twelve to sixteen hours. No sooner had he finished this conversation, when he received a call from Robert Hayes concerning the Hyde Park pharmacy project.

"Martin, this weather is killing my job here."

"What weather? We didn't get any snow in Stoughton."

"Get the fuck outta here. Listen, they expect the snow to stop some time tomorrow. Can you give me a crew on Saturday morning, to clean up around the foundation, change out the gas cylinders, and repair any damage to the tarp enclosures?"

"Not a problem, Rob. I'll send two guys and meet you on site myself, first thing Saturday morning."

3:00PM - Thursday February 25, 1999

"Hi John. Is Tony expecting you?" Tanya asked when Grasso entered Bottazzi Associates.

"I don't think so, but something's come up. Has he got a minute? This shouldn't take any time at all."

"That's okay. I just panicked when you walked in because I have you in Tony's schedule for tomorrow afternoon at 3:00 with Fred Ross. I thought I'd messed up. Tony's here. He doesn't have anyone with him at the moment, so why don't you go on down to his office."

As John Grasso walked down the hallway, all he could think about was that Tony Bottazzi was responsible for introducing Fred Ross to Seahorse.

"John, how are you?" Tony greeted, blissfully unaware of the reason for the visit.

"Not good," he replied, tossing three Polaroid photographs onto the desk. "Your buddy, Fred, has been fucking with me for the past month, and I'm bullshit! Do you recognize anything or anyone in these?"

"What do you mean? I don't understand," Bottazzi protested, squinting at the images. "When were they taken? The weather must have been horrible. Is that the Jamestown Bridge?"

"Full marks, Tony," Grasso complimented him sarcastically. "That's Martin Quinn with his crew, three hours ago, on the side of the Jamestown Bridge. Ross has been feeding me a line of shit for weeks, ever since Martin Quinn was down here in this office. Where the hell did you find this guy? I feel like slapping him across the side of the head. Do you realize Martin Quinn has had nothing to do with this project since he brought down that sample? Ross has relayed no information to him and Quinn was the guy who manufactured the sample in the first place. Fred Ross has spent the whole time keeping all information to himself, while trying to get someone else to make it for less money. Tomorrow afternoon when he comes in here for the weekly progress meeting, it's going to be real fucking interesting, Tony! He has no idea I've already reviewed the prototype in place on the bridge. He was supposed to have it ready for me tomorrow, but he only asked Quinn to start making it yesterday! I guess he couldn't find anyone else."

"I don't know what to say," Bottazzi responded despondently.

"You don't have to say anything and especially not to Ross! I want to see how he responds to my questions when the three of us meet here tomorrow."

Tony Bottazzi could not believe what had been placed before him and understood that John Grasso had every reason to be annoyed. He had, in fact, very good reason. As Grasso lifted the photographs, he repeated his warning.

"Do yourself a favor, Tony, and don't mention any of this to Ross. I've got to get out of here. I'll see you tomorrow afternoon."

3:45PM - Thursday February 25, 1999

Fred Ross was sitting in his home office when he received John Grasso's call.

"Hi John," he responded. "I'm doing well. Staying out of this weather, though. How about you?"

"Can't say I was as fortunate as you, Fred, I had to work in it today. I wanted to remind you about our meeting tomorrow afternoon. We can't allow the weather to interrupt the work schedule – well certainly not our meetings anyway."

"No John, I hadn't forgotten. There are no major problems. We can go over everything tomorrow."

"Will you have the prototype with you, Fred?"

"Yes," Ross lied, "I expect to pick that up from Martin Quinn tomorrow afternoon, before I meet with you and Tony."

"It's good that you plan to meet with Martin tomorrow. I need to have a copy of your signed contract with Cove Construction. You can black out the dollar amount of course, but I need to see a written contract which addresses the full scope of work, along with completion date information and the like. If you don't have a contract, can you get one signed and make me a copy for tomorrow's meeting?"

"Not a problem," Ross continued to lie. "Will you need anything else?"

"No. That's it Fred. You enjoy the rest of your evening."

"See you tomorrow," Ross replied, before hanging up.

"Fuck. Fuck. Fuck," Fred furiously complained to himself. "Grasso's turning into a real pain in the ass! I've got to catch up with Quinn and get things moving." Despite Ross' coaching, Bay State Fabricators had been unable to give him a price quote which was more competitive than Cove's.

* * * * * * *

Martin was walking across a pharmacy parking lot in Stoughton when he received Fred's call.

"Mr. Quinn, how are you?"

"Good, but don't tell me you need help shoveling your driveway."

"No, nothing like that at all. I want to come to terms with you guys regarding this Seahorse project. Could you stop by my house in the morning?"

Quinn preferred that this meeting be held at Cove's office.

"I have to be at the Hanover Mall tomorrow morning at 7:00. Why don't you come over to my office in Quincy at say, 9:30?" Martin suggested.

"Okay. By the way, how's the prototype coming along? Any chance it will be ready before Monday?"

"No way," Quinn replied, making every effort to sound disappointed.

"I'll see you tomorrow morning at your office. Talk to you later."

The phone line went dead. "Sounds like the plan is starting to come together," Martin thought to himself, as he wrestled two flu medication capsules from several layers of security packaging seals.

By 4:00, and much to Margaret's astonishment and relief, he was home. After supper, he helped Brendan with his homework before settling down to watch television. None of the programs interested him very much. He was just too elated with how the day's events had unfolded. Nevertheless, he felt that the project still had the potential to go off the rails. There were still too many loose ends to tidy up before he would feel comfortable sharing any details with Margaret. The TV line up for that evening included dramas featuring either: paramedics; police officers; lawyers; or a combination of all three. "Nobody ever makes a TV show about engineers or construction workers," he thought to himself and grinned. "I guess our lives are too boring."

7:00AM - Friday February 26, 1999

Quinn did not have to visit the Hanover Mall that morning. It was merely something he had told Fred Ross to make sure their meeting would be held at Cove's office. Since he had nothing scheduled before 9:30, he was able to drop Brendan off at school. Thayer Academy was located two towns away in Braintree and en route to Cove's office. Topics covered during their car ride ranged from Brendan's hockey games that weekend to his schoolwork and examinations which were less than a week away. Unlike the public schools, Thayer Academy had a two week spring break in mid-March. Before the school closed for this vacation, the students had tests in many of their subjects.

"I'll see you later at the rink, Dad," Brendan promised as he shut the Jeep's door.

Sandra had only one phone message for Quinn when he arrived at the office.

"Fred Ross called to say he's running a bit late this morning."

Fred finally arrived at 10:30. Once seated in the conference room, he rolled out a set of plans for the school bus depot project. It was clearly a lame attempt to impress Martin with potential work opportunities.

Soon Quinn had heard enough.

"Is that Seahorse job still going on? Its pace seemed to fade after I prepared the shop drawings."

Ross countered by assuring him it was definitely continuing, except that he still had to finalize a few budget details with John Grasso. With the aid of a legal pad secured in his designer leather executive folder,

Fred explained how much money Cove could make by purchasing the aluminum stock directly from a mill in Pennsylvania. This would deny the fabricating shop any opportunity of a mark-up on those costs. He also suggested dealing directly with the anodizing company, which would apply a protective coat over the aluminum components.

This sort of job cost analysis was typical of Fred Ross. The only thing he knew how to do, was erode any profit a subcontractor or supplier might have. He was full of fanciful ideas and schemes which he felt would make this job incredibly profitable. Once again, Quinn had heard enough.

"Fred, I'm sure there's never been a construction project conceived which you couldn't build on paper – just like that," Martin gestured towards the notes and calculations, "but it's not that easy for me, because I've got to build it for real. It's been three weeks since you've had any monetary discussions with us and from my perspective two things have changed. First, there's now less time available for any contractor to get a share of the $20,000 bonus and second, I've had an opportunity to research the costs a bit more."

"What do you mean? How much do you figure Cove needs to complete this job?"

"$410,000."

"You've got to be fucking kidding me!" Ross blurted out.

"Absolutely not. Maybe we can do it for $400,000 and leave the other $10,000 available if we meet the bonus completion date."

Fred Ross immediately rolled up a set of as-built plans for the bridge, which he had brought to the meeting. He recovered two sets of Martin's shop drawings from his executive leather folder and tossed them across the table.

"You are no longer associated with this project!" he announced, standing up while lifting his belongings.

As Fred turned to walk away, Martin pleaded with him to stop.

"Hold on a minute, you can't leave just like that."

Ross stalled and gave Quinn a look as if to say, "Who's in control now?"

"Why not?" he inquired

"Because you need a rubber band to keep those drawings rolled up neatly. Let me get one from my office."

The expression on Ross' face was priceless. It was obvious he would have relished the sight of Martin back-pedaling in an effort to salvage the negotiations. He did not know what to say or do. More importantly, he was oblivious to the fact that he had already been completely out maneuvered.

Quinn placed a rubber band around the outstretched roll of plans and escorted Ross to the office door. The CEO of RossCon Enterprises left without any further discussion, not even a "Goodbye." Martin was relieved he had arranged to have the meeting at Cove's office rather than at Fred's house. It would have been difficult for the meeting to come to a more decisive end, had Martin been the one who had to leave.

As promised, Quinn called John Grasso and briefed him on the failed contract negotiations.

"This is going to be some meeting when he comes down here this afternoon."

"I wish that I could be a fly on the wall," Martin lamented.

3:00PM - Friday February 26, 1999

John Grasso arrived at Tony Bottazzi's office ahead of Fred Ross. Tony was conscious of his client's displeasure with him for introducing RossCon Enterprises into the program. Although somewhat uncomfortable alone with Grasso, Bottazzi was sure this atmosphere was nothing compared to what it was going to be like, once Ross arrived. When John reported that Fred had fired Martin off the project earlier that morning, Tony knew things had gone from bad to worse. All he could think of was the Polaroid photographs of Quinn and his crew perched on the side of the bridge.

Five minutes later Fred arrived in a buoyant mood, completely unaware of how far ahead of him John Grasso had managed to get.

"Hi Fred!" Grasso exclaimed as he greeted him cheerfully.

Tony's salutation was not so enthusiastic. He was unable to perform with anything close to the same degree of skill. Bottazzi had convinced himself that his best course of action was to speak as little as possible.

"I don't mind telling you Fred," Grasso continued, "I truly believe that this is going to be the best weekend I've had in quite a while. There were times over the past few weeks when I feared this project was going nowhere. But after the week we've just had, I feel there's light at the end of the tunnel. I appreciate what you did with that other engineer, but when we decided at the end of last week, to move forward with Martin Quinn and Cove, it finalized things in my mind. That's why I wrote that letter last week which set out everything."

John paused briefly, so he could study Fred's expression. There was no evidence of any concern.

"By the way, Tony, you got copied on that letter, didn't you?"

"Yes, John. If you recall, you gave us both a copy."

"Well, we had a bit of a snag," Ross reported.

"Don't go spoiling my weekend, Fred!"

"Not at all, John. We had a problem, but I took care of it. Anderson Aluminum can't manufacture the raceway to meet our schedule, so I've brought Bay State Fabricators back on board."

"Stop right there!" Grasso demanded, angrily. "I gave you a very clear letter which set out what everyone would be doing on this project and how nothing was to be changed without my written authorization."

"John, it wasn't like that. When Anderson told me they could no longer meet our schedule, I reacted quickly to get Bay State Fabricators signed up, so we wouldn't lose any more time."

"I don't want Bay State Fabricators to do any work on my project, until I see an original letter on Anderson's stationery which states that they are no longer able to meet the production schedule. Do you understand? There are to be no changes on this project, unless I approve them, in writing."

"I'll get that for you," Ross lied and was about to continue, when Grasso proceeded with his onslaught.

"You were supposed to have a prototype of the design for me this week so I could see it in place on the bridge. Where is it?"

"I don't have it, Cove Construction fucked up."

Neither Tony Bottazzi nor John Grasso could believe their ears. Tony dropped his head into his hands and stared at his feet.

"What the fuck could Martin Quinn be involved in that's more important than my project?" Grasso bellowed.

"He was plowing snow," Ross retorted.

"I just don't fucking believe it, Fred. You were the one who brought this guy into the project. Either get him focused on taking care of what I need, or kick him off the team! Do I make myself clear?"

"Yes, John," Fred acknowledged.

"I promised my company's Director of Northeast Operations that I'd have a prototype attached to the bridge for him to inspect. I told him that, because you promised me that would happen. Do you want me to lose my job, Fred? I need the fucking prototype like you promised and I need it at the bridge on Monday morning!"

Ross was shattered. Not even in his wildest dreams did he expect to be subjected to this sort of beating. Normally he could dance his way around a client's questions, however, this meeting was going from bad to worse. He had expected a bland run of the mill session to finish off his week, but this was ugly and horrible. There was no other way to describe it. "Hopefully, Ian Goodwright can make me a prototype over the weekend," he thought to himself.

"I'll have the prototype for you on Monday morning, John," Ross confirmed. "However, it may not be fabricated out of aluminum."

"What the fuck is it going to be made of?" Grasso demanded. "Wood?"

Fred found himself with absolutely nothing to offer in response to the question. Finally after a few seconds, which seemed like an eternity, John Grasso broke the silence.

"Fred, I'm going to lose my job unless you start doing yours. This meeting is over. Get the fuck out of here and do your damn job."

Ross did not have to be asked to leave twice. When John and Tony could next see him from the third floor office window, he was holding his cell phone to his ear while fumbling at his car door.

"Can you believe that asshole?"

"I don't know what to say, John. I've never come across anyone like him."

"He threw Martin Quinn under the bus without batting an eyelash." Grasso continued. "Plowing snow! The lies just roll off his tongue."

* * * * * * *

Fred's first call was to Eddie Gallagher.

"Eddie?"

"Hi Fred. How's it going?"

"Not too good at the moment. Do you think Martin could be talking directly with Seahorse Communications?"

"I can't imagine that. What gave you that idea?"

"I don't mind telling you Eddie, that I'm being asked some crazy questions all of a sudden, and frankly, I don't know what has caused it. By the way, do you know if Martin's been able to get the prototype made any sooner?"

"I don't think so, but I haven't spoken with him. I'm sure he'll get it over to you as soon as it's ready."

"Maybe not," Ross revealed. "We had a bit of an argument earlier today and I had to walk out of our meeting. We were going over the job costs and he was being unreasonable. I think you and I need to be the ones to agree on a price for having Cove do this job."

"I can't talk about it at the minute. I've got a call on the other line, Fred. I'll have to catch up with you later."

When the phone went dead, Eddie immediately called Martin, who happened to be waiting for Brendan's hockey team to come back onto the ice for the final period of Thayer's game. Reception was always poor in rinks, however, Martin kept Eddie on the line as the signal fluctuated until he got outside.

"I just got a call from Fred. He doesn't seem too happy."

"I think the ass just fell out of his world and he doesn't even really know it. I expect John Grasso will give me a call and bring me up to speed on their meeting. I'm sure it was really something."

"Listen Martin, when are you going to Anderson Aluminum again? I'd love to see their facility. My Liam has a science project for school and I wanted to make him a small generator. I was hoping their shop foreman would be able to help me?"

"I have to go over there tomorrow. Louis Fusco wants me to bring the prototype back to him. Why don't you meet me at the Howard Johnson's, where Route 138 crosses 128? That way you can follow me – it's not an easy place to find if you haven't been there before."

"How about 9:00? Is that okay with you?"

"Perfect. I've got to meet Jose and Manny at Hyde Park at 7:00 to help Rob Hayes. I'll see you after that."

Martin had not even turned to go back into the rink before his phone rang again. When he read John Grasso's number on the caller ID screen, he eagerly took the call. John was ecstatic as he reported the comical details of his meeting with Fred. Grasso was clearly relieved to know that for the first time in over a month, he actually had the upper hand in his dealings with Ross. He also appreciated that it was all thanks to Martin Quinn. "Plowing snow!" he kept repeating and laughing out loud, "Plowing snow!"

"I'll be at Anderson Aluminum on Monday morning to get them under contract to manufacture the raceway," Quinn continued. "I'll keep you in the loop and let you know as soon as I have them signed up."

"Great! Thank you for everything you've done on this job, Martin. I'll talk to you over the weekend."

11:30PM - Friday February 26, 1999

Maria Santos did not know who she could talk to. Her husband had become withdrawn and reclusive since returning home. Nevertheless, he had been emphatic when he instructed her not to help the police or FBI with their inquiries. Consistent with the kidnappers' demands, they had not been contacted until after Xavier's release. Maria could not understand his reluctance to assist the authorities. She lay awake alone, desperately trying to think how she could help him. He rarely slept in their bed since the ordeal, spending most nights secluded in his study. For some reason he prevented her from returning the sledge hammer to the tool shed, choosing instead to place it along the outside edge of his desk. Maria Santos believed her husband had formed a nostalgic bond with the tool which had unlocked the funds used to pay the ransom demand. She also believed that his reluctance to assist the police and FBI was driven by a subconscious desire to put the horrifying episode behind him. Maria was wrong on both counts. Xavier very much wanted to find the kidnappers. His goal, in fact, was to find them before the authorities did. The last thing he wanted was some clever lawyer working the legal system to secure lenient sentences for the perpetrators. He wanted to keep the sledge hammer at easy reach and in plain sight to keep him focused on this mission. Xavier Santos intended using it to recover every last cent of his five hundred thousand dollars.

Maria tossed and turned, oblivious to her husband's plans. Finally she drifted off to sleep, wondering what other secrets were hidden in the rest of the furniture her father-in-law had left.

7:00AM - Saturday February 27, 1999

The jobsite at Hyde Park was covered in at least twenty inches of snow. "Jose and Manny should be here shortly," Quinn reported to Rob Hayes. "I just spoke with them. Their commute from Fall River is messed up. Front-end loaders are working on Route 24, cleaning stock-piles of snow that the plows left behind."

"I appreciate you helping me out. This place is a disaster."

When Jose and Manny arrived, they went to work on the site while Rob helped Martin transfer the raceway components from Jose's truck onto Martin's Jeep Cherokee. In order for the eleven foot long aluminum channels to balance on the Jeep's roof rack, they had to protrude beyond the rear of the vehicle by approximately three feet. Nevertheless, they were strapped down securely and in no danger of sliding off. Rob Hayes enjoyed hearing about recent developments on the Seahorse project and appreciated the opportunity to see the prototype raceway.

"Everything went really well at the bridge on Thursday," Quinn recounted. "John Grasso is relieved the project's finally back on track."

"Good Job, Martin! You deserve a break, given all the bullshit that's gone down."

* * * * * * *

Eddie Gallagher was already at the Howard Johnson's Restaurant in Milton when Martin arrived and circled the parking lot.

"It looks like you're going hang-gliding or wind-surfing," Gallagher observed over the Nextel radio.

"Let's hope we can get this system secured to the bridge without doing either!"

Eddie was glad Martin had suggested meeting, because he certainly would have had problems trying to find the aluminum facility by himself. The two men staggered like penguins as they shuffled across the icy parking lot towards the reception door.

"Hi Martin," Jeff Anderson greeted. "Louis told me you'd be coming in this morning. By the way, I was just speaking with your boss."

"Excuse me?" Martin responded in disbelief.

"I was just speaking with your boss before you arrived."

"Jeff, I want you to meet Eddie Gallagher. He owns 50% of Cove Construction and I own the other 50%. I'm really interested to know who was claiming to be my boss!"

Jeff's face took on a complexion similar to that of the icy parking lot.

"He said his name was Fred Ross and told me you were working for him. He seemed to know all about the job."

Quinn could hardly believe his ears.

"Remember, Jeff, several weeks ago I warned you not to discuss any aspect of this project with anyone? I thought I made it clear that to do otherwise would be a problem. You were supposed to let me know if anyone was making inquiries about similar aluminum sections or material needs. You broke the rules, Jeff! Fred Ross is not my boss and Cove Construction does not work for him. What did you two talk about?" Martin demanded.

"He seemed to know all about the job," Jeff repeated, in an effort to justify his failure to abide by Quinn's prior instructions. "He called this office about twenty minutes ago and introduced himself to me as being in charge of the project. He said that he needed some new prototypes for a meeting on Monday morning. I explained we couldn't make anything at such short notice. I had him speak to Louis so we could furnish the material for him to do his own fabrication. He should be here any minute!"

"We can't be here when he arrives!" Martin warned. "He mustn't see my prototypes. We're going to leave them with Louis. Give Fred any material he wants but make sure that you get a check and do not accept cash."

Martin felt that a cash transaction would be more difficult to link to Fred, should subsequent legal action result from Ross' theft of Quinn's design.

"I'm not going to have anything more to do with him," Jeff decided, "he can deal with Louis. I should never have come near the office this morning. I already told him there was no need to pay until next week!"

Eddie followed Martin back out through Anderson's front door and across the parking lot to remove the aluminum channels off the Jeep. Thanks to a combination of haste and the icy conditions, Martin managed to impale the center of his forehead on the corner edge of one of the aluminum channels which were over-hanging the tailgate.

"Shit!" he exclaimed, staggering backwards in pain. It was now obvious why Eddie had just yelled, "Look out!"

Clutching his forehead, Quinn threw back his head in pain and caught sight of movement high above him. "Can that be the same eagle?" he muttered under his breath. A perfect one inch high impression of the letter "L" appeared in the middle of his forehead. Although the skin was not punctured, he could see in the wing mirror of his Jeep that a bruise would probably remain for several days. The two men quickly removed the aluminum channel prototypes from the roof rack and brought them inside. Louis Fusco approached, completely unaware of the panic which had just descended upon their Saturday morning. Martin hurriedly explained why he and Gallagher needed to leave with such haste.

"We'll call you as soon as we get clear of here," Quinn apologized.

Eddie and Martin managed to get away from Anderson Aluminum before Fred Ross appeared on the scene. They parked their vehicles in a lot one hundred yards further down the road behind a row of tall evergreen pine trees. From this concealed vantage point, they had a perfect view of the factory's main entrance. Quinn left his Jeep and joined Eddie in his SUV. They had not been there more than thirty seconds when Jeff Anderson's car sped off. By the time Martin called Louis Fusco, he had just finished another telephone conversation with Ross. Apparently, Fred was en route and needed better directions than those Jeff had given him.

"Boy was he angry after I spoke to him," Louis explained. "When I told him that he needed to bring a $300 check for the material, he got all upset - claiming Jeff Anderson and he had agreed payment could be made next week. I explained that my boss was no longer in the office and hadn't said anything to me about such an arrangement. Consequently, he was to be treated like any other customer who didn't have an account - C.O.D. I calmed him down by telling him the check would still be on Jeff's desk on Monday morning and he could speak to him about it then."

"Excellent job," Martin congratulated Louis.

"I knew something was wrong as soon as Jeff forwarded me this guy's initial phone call. The dimensions and components he was referencing, related to your earlier design. I suspected he wasn't up to speed, but I figured since Jeff's the boss, then it must be okay."

"Don't worry about it," Quinn reassured him. "This guy couldn't work out how to hook two paper clips together. I dread to think what he's going to make this weekend with the material he ordered!"

At that moment, Ross' white SUV arrived. Ten minutes later it was leaving with several pieces of aluminum 2x4 channel protruding at least four feet through the back doors, which had been partially tied closed with string.

"What an asshole," Eddie muttered under his breath.

"I'm going to call John Grasso," Martin announced. "He'll just love to hear what this weasel is up to."

John could not believe how fortuitous it was they had arranged to visit Anderson's facility. Martin had previously stressed the importance of executing a written contract between the aluminum manufacturer and Cove, so that production could commence. The April 15 completion date was only six weeks away and the raceway still had to be manufactured, anodized, and installed on the bridge. Quinn also needed to make some minor modifications. If his design or calculations were flawed, he would end up with an investment of over $100,000 for the production of nothing other than a pile of useless scrap metal.

Martin wanted so much to be at the bridge on Monday morning to see what Fred had managed to create over the weekend. Nevertheless, he knew his priority was to draft a contract between Cove Construction and Anderson Aluminum. It was agreed that Quinn would remain at Cove's office until Grasso authorized fabrication of the raceway. John would make this call from Jamestown, once his boss witnessed just how incompetent Fred Ross was.

Before leaving the facility, Martin and Eddie went over issues on other Cove projects. Men and equipment were still committed to cleaning massive stockpiles of snow at the Hanover Mall. Even though the storm had ended, the snow removal program was scheduled to recommence later that evening after the mall closed. This operation would continue through the night until Sunday at noon. Organizing this work, as well as making sure there was a crew available for Hyde Park on Monday morning, required some thought.

2:30PM – Saturday February 27, 1999

Megan gazed deep into Tory's eyes. Each breath he exhaled - she inhaled. Each breath she exhaled - he inhaled. They continued to exchange the same pocket of air, oblivious to anything that was going on around them. As he turned his head slightly, she detected a fragrance. The smell was unmistakable - they even used the same brand of shampoo. On his breath she caught a faint trace of the venison he had eaten earlier for lunch. Her favorite dish! What else did they have in common? Suddenly Megan knew that she wanted more - right there and right then.

Tory could sense it too. He gently nuzzled his face deep into the pillow of hair trapped between her neck and shoulder. She smelled so good. She looked incredible. Perfect in every detail - right down to the pedicured toe nails. It did not matter that she was old enough to be his mother. The fact that they were first cousins was also of no concern to Tory. He had no regard for such matters and was sensing that Megan felt the same. They lived eighty miles apart and only got to see each other twice a year. The warm heat from the fire burning inside him raced through his veins. The feeling was overwhelming. Pure animal instinct was taking control of his body. He would take Megan now. She wanted it. He wanted it. It just seemed so right.

Not a word was spoken, yet somehow Megan knew what was about to happen. She arched her back, glanced over her shoulder and prepared to surrender.

"Tory! Cut that out or I'll have to put your leash back on," Shelley threatened.

She had been preoccupied lifting the dog's draft rig from the rear of her SUV and was unaware of his amorous intentions towards Megan. The two Bernese Mountain Dogs abandoned their procreation plans while Shelley apologized to Megan's owner. They had seen one another at previous competitions and events, but had not been introduced.

"No harm done," Megan's owner assured Shelley. "It's all about the birds and the bees."

Tory obediently responded to his master's instruction to heel so that she could put on his harness. Shelley had brought him to Goshen, Connecticut to compete in the Draft Test Trials held by the Bernese Mountain Dog Club of Nashoba Valley. He was an accredited Master Draft Dog (MDD) in recognition of his ability to maneuver a small cart attached to a harness, in similar fashion to what a Clydesdale Horse would pull. Being awarded MDD merit was recognition of both Tory's and Shelley's hard work, however, it was something they really enjoyed doing together. He was glad that a last minute issue at her husband's SCUBA dive shop meant that he could not accompany them. Tory did not need David Swain imposing himself on his time with Shelley. Once the harness was adjusted, the dog gave his coat a quick shake before the draft rig was hitched up. Tory stood attentively, awaiting his master's next command.

9:00PM - Saturday February 27, 1999

Margaret Quinn was not happy when her husband announced that he was going to Hanover to check on snow removal operations at the mall. She knew the toll inclement weather had on Cove's activities, and worried that he was beginning to look weary. Martin had neither the energy nor the desire to get into a discussion regarding her frustration. She was not privy to details regarding the company's lines of credit, delinquent account receivable issues, or any other problematic aspects of Cove's operations. He wanted to shield her from these stressful issues and certainly did not want to share any details of Fred Ross' escapades.

As he drove south on Route 3 to Hanover, Quinn mulled over various scenarios of how he could prevent Ross from causing further problems. He knew that Fred's greed would be a powerful motivator. Martin called his superintendent, Chris Donovan, and took a coffee order for the crew. Even though Quinn was not going to operate any equipment, bringing coffee acknowledged their efforts and showed his appreciation for the long and unsociable hours they were working.

"This Seahorse project has my mind racing to keep ahead of Ross so he doesn't fuck things up for Cove between now and Monday morning," he confided in Donovan as they drank their coffee. "I'm going to take off, but I may stop back later. If you need anything – just call my Nextel."

Traveling north on Route 3, Quinn's mind was again consumed with thoughts of how he would maintain control of the Seahorse project. He decided to spend a couple of hours at The Foxy Lady strip club. Located in Brockton, just off Route 24, it was an easy stop for Martin on his way home any time he needed a quick beer to escape from the pressures of the work day.

By 1:30, he was on his way back to Hanover after having called Donovan and taken another coffee order. The visit to the club had definitely taken his mind off things. The obvious distractions there had a tendency to do that. Ever since Fred Ross announced to John Grasso that Martin was, "plowing snow," the intensity of this whole Seahorse project had shot to another level. Stumbling across Ross at Anderson Aluminum on Saturday morning ratcheted it up even more.

Coffees and donuts were gratefully received and Martin spent some time chatting with the crew. Some of the guys jokingly asked if he had been "thrown out of the house?" Quinn did not get a chance to answer before his phone rang. It was Margaret.

"Where are you?"

"At the Hanover Mall."

"Do you really need to be there?"

"Why don't I just come on home? We won't bother paying the mortgage or sending Thayer Academy their $2,000 for Brendan's school fees this month."

There was silence on the other end of the phone.

After what had to have been at least thirty seconds, Martin asked if Margaret had any other questions.

"Do I have any more questions?" she repeated.

"Well, I've got to pay the bill for this cell phone and then I have to pay the telephone bill at the house. So having both phones connected to one another with no conversation taking place seems pretty foolish to me."

Quinn detected the unmistakable click of the phone hanging up. Then, by pressing the red button on his keypad – neither phone company had a hand in his pocket.

Chris Donovan was not within hearing distance; nevertheless his perception was right on target.

"None of the wives are a fan of this night-time program."

"Whatever," Quinn replied, "I've got to deal with Fred Ross, the weather, fucking Paul Roche trying to screw us out of our money on the Canton job and now this attitude at home!"

"How's our friend, Fred Ross treating you?" Chris asked cynically.

Quinn shared with Donovan, details of the bridge project and Ross' efforts to sabotage Cove.

"This guy just doesn't give up. He's such a fucking weasel," Chris concurred.

"Well I think his run is coming to an end on Monday morning. I'll keep you in the loop. This is going to be a very busy week for me, once Seahorse fires Ross and hires Cove."

The two men talked for over an hour before Quinn left Hanover. He decided to eat breakfast at a twenty-four hour restaurant, before going home. Brendan had an early hockey game that morning, but as long as Martin was home by 6:00, he would have plenty of time to get everyone to the rink.

5:45AM - Sunday February 28, 1999

Quinn called the house as he left Bickford's restaurant in Brockton. Brendan answered the phone and was relieved to hear that his father was only ten minutes away.

"Make sure all your hockey equipment is packed and ready when I get home."

"No problem, Dad."

Brendan had been watching for his father and was first to come out with his equipment bag which he wrestled into the rear of the Expedition. His relief at knowing he would not be late for the hockey game was tempered by his awareness of the tense atmosphere he had just left inside the house. His mother was clearly not happy that his father had been out all night.

Since the snow banks on each side of the driveway made it difficult to open the car doors, Martin reversed the Expedition onto the street so it would be easier for Margaret to get into the vehicle. Brendan loved to sit in the front seat beside his father. If his mother was not traveling, there was no problem. On occasion when she was, he sometimes claimed that seat anyway, which meant Margaret had to sit in the rear (but under mild protest). This morning, however, he was already buckled into the back seat when his mother opened the front passenger door. Martin's Nextel and Verizon phones were sitting in cup holders between the two seats. Margaret reached in, unplugged the Verizon phone from its power cord, dropped it onto the asphalt pavement, and proceeded to stamp on it several times. She then bent down, picked up the largest of the remaining pieces, and calmly returned them to the cup holder.

"Now you won't have to worry about running up a bill on this phone anymore!" she announced triumphantly as she climbed into the vehicle.

They refrained from further discussion during the twenty minute ride to the rink in Randolph. When Martin parked the car, several players were wrestling large equipment bags from vehicles. Margaret took off with one of the other mothers, leaving the Quinn men to get the hockey gear out of the car and into the locker room. Neither of them complained about being abandoned in such a manner.

As Brendan's team took the ice, Martin made his way to the bleacher stands at the other side of the rink. Shortly before the end of the game, the pager attached to his belt began to vibrate. "Surely this can wait until the end of the game," he reckoned, clearing Gallagher's home number off the screen. When the buzzer signaled the end of the game, his pager went off again. This time, Eddie's home number was followed by, "*911." "What's the big panic?" Martin thought to himself. "It's 8:00 on a Sunday morning."

Quinn realized he had no way of making a phone call. His Verizon cell phone was in pieces, many of which were still on the pavement outside their home and his Nextel keypad was malfunctioning. His frustration was eased when he found a public pay phone in the foyer.

"What's up?" Martin inquired, when Eddie answered.

"I got a phone call from my brother-in-law in Ireland. My sister, Pamela, has been missing since Saturday afternoon and they fear she may have committed suicide. They think she overdosed on sleeping pills and waded into the River Shannon, near their home in Limerick. Can you keep your pager on? It looks like I'll have to fly to Ireland, if I get the news we're all dreading."

"I hope that she's safe, but if you do need to go home, there's nothing going on here that I can't handle by myself."

Martin went back into the rink and waited for Brendan to get changed. He looked around, but could not see Margaret. Things were quite hectic with the Zamboni cleaning the ice surface while another thirty teenage hockey players crowded around the doors waiting to skate. It was not too long before Brendan emerged from the locker room.

"Put on your hat before we go outside," his father instructed.

Martin expected to find his wife standing beside the Expedition, since he still had the car keys in his pocket. Margaret, however, had brought the spare keys and was already sitting in the driver's seat with the engine running. He helped his son get the large equipment bag and hockey stick into the back of the SUV, and climbed into the passenger seat.

"Now we'll see how you like it when I drive!" Margaret announced.

Initially, things seemed okay as she negotiated the SUV out of the parking lot. Once on the narrow side street, however, it was like a NASCAR driver exiting pit row. The Expedition lurched forward when she stomped the gas pedal to the floor. Martin did not flinch. In his mind, there was nothing he could do that would lessen the probability of them all being killed, should Margaret lose control of the vehicle. If she wanted to make a statement in this fashion then so be it. They would either all die; not all die; or some scenario in between.

"Whatever," he responded, without any appearance of concern.

As the vehicle raced at seventy miles per hour towards the "Stop" sign at the end of Pleasant Street, he wondered how far into D'Angelo's sub shop the SUV would travel, assuming they managed to make it across Route 28. He never got to find out. Fortunately, the Town of Randolph's Department of Public Works had done an excellent job clearing snow and ice off the town's roads. Margaret was able to bring the vehicle's front tires to a screeching halt, right beside the "Stop" sign.

Martin offered no comment and neither did Brendan. The next six miles were driven within the parameters established by the Commonwealth, as being considered safe for the operator of a vehicle and other users of the State's roads and highways.

Approximately two miles from home, they turned onto Bay Road. One of the oldest thoroughfares within the United States, it has been formally designated as a "Scenic Route." Narrow in spots, it winds and twists around rock ledge outcroppings, trees, and other obstructions. The original post road between Boston and Providence, its layout was first established and surveyed by farmers' livestock rather than civil engineers, as is the practice today. Scars on tree trunks along its route bear witness to drivers who chose to ignore the posted speed limits.

Martin was not really sure what spurred Margaret into having another attempt at destroying their vehicle. Perhaps it was the challenge being taunted by the trees' scars which were grinning away as if to say, "Do you think you can do any better?"

Everyone was thrown back into their seats as the vehicle surged forward again. "Am I going to meet Eddie's sister before he gets over to Ireland?" Martin reflected as trees sped by. He had not shared with his wife the subject of Gallagher's phone conversation. There never seemed to be an appropriate juncture since they left the rink. Regardless, he was now deep in thought trying to work out whom he should thank for the fact that they were all still alive. Should he credit Margaret? She was handling the car really well. Or should the engineers of the Ford Motor Company take credit for the way the SUV was negotiating Bay Road at this speed? Even though it was not an appropriate time to acknowledge it, he did recognized how calm Brendan was during this demonstration. "I guess all the thrilling video games he plays, do have a benefit," Martin mused. After traveling for approximately half a mile at excessive speed, Margaret eased off, much to her husband's relief. A hundred yards later and without any warning, however, she pushed down hard on the gas pedal again. In his mind, Martin questioned the wisdom of the motor industry's practice of providing two sets of keys with the purchase of any new automobile. The car glanced off a snow bank left by a highway plow truck. The vehicle responded by fighting for control and attempting to wrench the steering wheel from Margaret's grip. Fortunately, she was so consumed by rage that nothing was going to wrestle her fingers from the steering wheel. After a few swerves to the left and right, she regained control of the SUV and completed the last mile at a slightly slower speed. The vehicle was brought to an abrupt halt, no more than two inches from the garage door, before its driver disappeared into the house.

Martin remained with Brendan to help him get his hockey equipment out of the car. He also took this time to make sure his son was okay. When he was sure this was the case he went on to solicit his assistance.

"Your Mom's extremely upset at the moment, but you don't have anything to worry about," he began. "Her anger appears to be focused one hundred percent on me. I need your help because I didn't get any sleep last night. I'm going to use the guest room. I want you to hang out in your bedroom to make sure Mom doesn't go into the guest room alone. She's obviously not thinking rationally. If she goes in while I'm asleep, I want you to follow her and wake me up."

"Okay," Brendan responded with concern. "How long are you going to sleep for? Can you help me with my math homework later?"

"No problem. I think I may have to go over to Mr. Gallagher's house this evening, but I'll set the alarm clock for 4:00, so we can take care of your homework."

Martin did not encounter Margaret along his route from the garage to the guest bedroom on the second floor of their home. The door to this room was adjacent to Brendan's and he felt comfortable that his son could easily keep watch. He set the alarm clock on the bedside table, collapsed onto the bed, fully clothed, and immediately fell into a deep sleep.

Quinn was suddenly aware of the impending horror of the situation and was certain he was going to die. The alarm was blaring and he could feel the vibration as the power plant strained to contain the rapidly escalating nuclear reaction. "It has to be a total meltdown of the reactor's core." he feared.

He awoke to discover he was no longer in a failing nuclear power plant. The siren was nothing other than the alarm clock beside his ear. The shuddering of the reactor core was merely his vibrating pager, trapped between his hip and the mattress. His left hand struck the OFF button on the clock as he rolled over to retrieve the pager from its clip on his belt. Gallagher's home number illuminated the screen.

"They found Pamela's body. I've got a flight booked for Monday evening. That will give me time to get the children sent down to their mother for the week, while I'm in Ireland."

Saddened by the news, Martin told Eddie he would drive over to his house later that evening to discuss issues for the upcoming work week.

Quinn made his way downstairs so he could get his Day-Timer from his Jeep, parked in the garage. As he walked through the kitchen he passed Margaret who was setting dinner plates on the kitchen table. He, however, was preoccupied with the fact that he could not find the Jeep's keys. The last time he remembered having them was when he returned home from Anderson Aluminum on Saturday morning. "Perhaps it's open," he hoped, reaching for the driver's door. It was locked. He could see his canvas briefcase on the floor behind the front passenger seat with his Day-Timer poking out. There was even a spare set of car keys inside the bag.

He doubled back through the kitchen but with a new sense of urgency, since he realized that the key to his office in Quincy was also on this ring. Ten minutes of searching around the house yielded nothing. Anxious and annoyed, he took a break to eat. Except for a brief discussion about Brendan's science project, there was scarcely any dinner table conversation.

Subsequent searching for the keys produced nothing. Martin gave up rather than frustrate Brendan who was waiting for help with his math homework. Forty-five minutes later, his son was smiling as he closed his book.

Martin decided this was an appropriate time to share with Brendan what he had decided to do regarding Margaret's behavior earlier that day. His missing keys had reinforced the decision he had made. With everything that was going on, he could not accept they had simply been misplaced. Cove's office keys were on this keyring and his life had recently been the subject of too much turmoil for him to dismiss this latest episode as being merely a bit of bad luck. Since the car was locked and parked in the garage, he believed Margaret had taken the keys. While she was in the family room watching television he took the opportunity to speak with his son privately.

"I'm going to spend the next few days out of the house so things can calm down between your Mom and me."

The young man was clearly upset about this situation, but understood after that morning's phone stomping episode.

"I'll keep in touch with you via e-mail and stop by at Thayer from time to time and make sure you have everything you need. There are too many phones in this house for me to feel comfortable about speaking openly if I call you here."

"I may have a problem reading e-mail because my laptop isn't working properly. I think it may have a virus."

"I'll take your computer with me and give it to Sean Feeney to repair. I'll bring it to you at Thayer later in the week."

They went over details about how they would keep in touch and Brendan put his Apple laptop into its travel case. Martin spent another half hour searching for his keys – but to no avail. By this time it was 8:00 and Margaret had retired to bed. He called AAA for assistance unlocking the Jeep. At 9:00 he was tipping the driver and recovering the spare car keys from his briefcase. Before leaving, he left a note for Margaret explaining that he was going to Gallagher's house and then to Cove's office.

En route to Quincy, Martin called Eddie.

"I need your key to our office. My car keys went missing over the weekend and my office key was on the same ring."

"No problem."

"I hope that's the case," Quinn responded, "but I've not ruled out that they've been taken and not just misplaced."

"What are you going to do about it?"

"After you and I have a beer, I'm going to spend the night at the office and prepare the Anderson Aluminum contract. Tomorrow morning, I'll have the landlord change out the lock."

Martin spent an hour with Eddie before leaving with a key for their office in Marina Bay. His mind was consumed by an analysis of recent events. He found himself questioning the wisdom of being alone at Cove's office under these circumstances. As the traffic light turned green, Quinn realized he was outside Quincy Police Headquarters. He steered the Jeep into the parking lot and went inside.

Cove regularly hired police details to direct traffic when it worked on public streets or highways. In fact, it already had an account established with the City of Quincy. Consequently, Martin had no problem getting the desk sergeant to arrange for an officer to meet him outside Cove's office.

Within twenty minutes, Quinn was standing outside his office, shaking hands with Quincy Police Officer, Rick Willis. Fortunately there was no evidence of any problem inside. Martin made a pot of coffee and the men chatted for a while since Officer Willis was intrigued as to why a police detail had been requested at such short notice.

Energized by the caffeine break, Martin began drafting a contract agreement between Cove Construction and Anderson Aluminum. It was his intention to drive to Canton and get Anderson under contract, immediately after he got authorization from John Grasso. Once this agreement was executed, Quinn knew that no one, other than Cove, could legally complete this project before the April 15 deadline. The contract terms needed to be clear and concise with respect to Anderson's obligations to manufacture the raceway components in what was a very aggressive time frame. He also wanted to make sure Jeff Anderson would sign the contract when they met later that morning. Accordingly, Quinn included a clause requiring that Cove make an advance payment of $25,000 upon execution of the contract documents.

5:00AM - Monday March 1, 1999

Martin had worked through another night without any sleep and at 5:00 decided to dismiss Officer Willis. After completing the Anderson contract agreement, he continued to work on other Cove issues. Since it was the end of the month, invoices needed to be sent to clients in order to close out the company's sales figures for February.

By 7:15, he received his first call of the day from John Grasso.

"I just heard from Mr. Ross. It seems he'll not be ready for the big presentation at 8:00 and has asked that we put it back until 9:00."

"What a surprise!" Martin replied cynically.

Sandra Johnson arrived just as Martin finished the call and he quickly briefed her on the weekend's developments.

"When I get John Grasso's confirmation later this morning, Sandra, I need you to come with me to Anderson Aluminum. We'll both go in your car. I didn't get much sleep this weekend and I don't feel like driving."

As the morning progressed, Martin took several phone calls from John Grasso who kept him informed as to how things were progressing at the bridge. A little before 10:00, Quinn got the call he had been waiting for.

"There's all sorts of shit going on here," Grasso reported. "I'll get back to you later with the details, but Fred's far from happy. My boss, Kevin Shaw, doesn't want to delay the project any longer, so go ahead and get Anderson Aluminum started with the fabrication."

"It's a go!" Quinn announced to Sandra. "Let's get outta here."

Martin asked her to stop at the Dunkin Donuts coffee shop half a mile from Cove's office.

"Do you want a coffee?" he asked, opening the passenger door.

"I'll take a small decaf, cream and one sugar please."

Sandra remained in the car while Quinn went into the shop and took his place in line.

"Twenty dozen donuts, please," Martin replied, when asked for his order.

"What?" paused the young clerk. "Did you say twenty dozen donuts?"

"Yes, twenty dozen. You can mix up the flavors however you want."

"I don't even know if we have twenty dozen," the young girl replied with a baffled look on her face as she disappeared into the back kitchen area.

Martin needed the assistance of two clerks to carry the donuts out to the car.

"It looks like you bought every donut in there!" Sandra exclaimed.

"Just about," replied one of the girls as she lowered her box into the back of the SUV.

Quinn placed the coffees into the cup holders between the two front seats as Sandra reversed out of their parking space.

"What on earth are you doing with twenty dozen donuts? That's crazy."

You'll understand when we get to Anderson Aluminum."

"By the way," she added, "the landlord's office just called me. They've scheduled the locksmith to change the lock on our door this afternoon, like you asked."

"Good job," Quinn acknowledged. "Also, I need you to call Verizon and order a replacement cell phone. Mine got broken yesterday. I'll have to borrow your Nextel until you get the key-pad on this one fixed. I just can't be without a phone. Also, when you speak with the Nextel dealer, order an additional phone for John Grasso's use during this bridge project. I want him to be able to communicate with our company at any time by just pushing a button."

Martin called Jeff Anderson to say he was on his way with a contract and initial deposit check in the amount of $25,000. Jeff confirmed that he would have Louis sit in on their meeting so they could review fabrication details and schedules.

Martin and Sandra paraded into the reception area of Anderson Aluminum, each carrying a large carton of donuts. Sandra had difficulty because one of the top flaps kept obscuring her vision, until finally she managed to keep it closed with her chin.

"What have you got in the boxes?" Jeff inquired, clearly intrigued.

"I'm glad you asked that question," Martin countered. "You see, Jeff, I've been to your office on several occasions and every time I've brought two dozen donuts: one box for your office staff; and one box for the guys out on the shop floor. To date, I've never been offered a cup of coffee during my visits, so that maybe I too could have a donut. I've thought about this and have come to the conclusion that perhaps other clients bring more than two dozen when they visit. So today, I figured we'd celebrate our new venture with a cup of coffee and a donut. I hope I've brought enough!"

"You're crazy," Jeff exclaimed shaking his head. "What are we going to do with all these?"

"Everyone can go home tonight with their own box!"

While Jeff escorted his guests to the staff kitchen, he was relieved to hear that his unsanctioned cooperation with Fred on Saturday morning had not caused too serious a problem.

Louis joined the group as they made their way to the conference room. Confident that they had all heard the last from Fred Ross, everyone got down to the serious business of how to satisfactorily complete the project by its April 15 deadline.

"I'm sure Louis will make it happen," Jeff assured his new client. "He's yet to disappoint a customer in the twenty-five years he's been employed here. Also, there's something else I want to tell you. Last week we ordered all the stock needed to fabricate the support brackets and lower cradle sections of the raceway. It arrived this morning, so we're all set and ready to commence fabrication tomorrow."

Martin was thrilled with this news. It gave him a good measure of Jeff Anderson's commitment to the project and reinforced the decision to bring a $25,000 deposit along with the contract.

Jeff excused himself from the meeting and left Martin, Sandra, and Louis to continue reviewing the technical aspects of the job. Besides, he had everything he needed from the meeting: a signed contract, plus a $25,000 advance payment. His time would be better spent making phone calls to his anodizing subcontractors in order to secure firm commitments from them. He also had to place a call to the Remington Gun Factory. They would be manufacturing the stamp which would label every cover with the name, "SEAHORSE".

Louis Fusco impressed upon Martin the importance of carefully reviewing the design specifications for the extrusion dyes. The Canadian aluminum foundry had a $5,000 charge for each of theses items. If mistakes were made after the two unique dyes were tooled then the best scenario would be that these errors were uncovered before they were used so Cove would only have to pay for their replacement. Receiving specialty sections from Canada that were incorrect as a result of mistakes with Martin's design would be a $40,000 problem, in addition to time lost in the schedule. Consequently it was agreed that Anderson Aluminum would not manufacture any components without first receiving Cove's written approval of their dimensions and specifications. During the meeting, Martin signed off and released into fabrication: 1) the brackets that were to be bolted to the side of the bridge, approximately every ten feet; and 2) the bottom cradle sections of raceway which would span between these brackets. If these two components were correctly manufactured, anodized, and installed in the field, both Seahorse and CellTell Atlantic could install their fiber-optic cables. Cove could then follow up without any urgency and get the top sections and locking brackets in place.

Louis and Sandra reviewed the design plans together. Although Louis had spoken to her occasionally when he called the office, they had not actually met. She had neither been involved with the design nor project management aspects of the fiber-optic job. Martin's decision to have her attend the meeting was to save him from having to drive, as well as to reinforce his company's image with Jeff Anderson. Quinn would be relying on this factory to fabricate $125,000 of specialized raceway system which was of zero value to any other client. If Cove screwed up or failed to pay, Anderson would have very little recourse. Unbeknownst to Jeff, Cove did not, in fact, have a written contract with Seahorse Communications. Nevertheless, Martin needed to have him focused on this project, since anything less would be catastrophic. With their signed contract, Quinn was satisfied he was in control of this relationship. Considering the comparable size of their two companies, it really was a case of, the tail wagging the dog!

At that moment, Martin's Nextel phone rang and John Grasso's number lit up the screen. He excused himself and went to take the call closer to the conference room window where the reception signal was stronger.

"Fred's not going down without a fight," Grasso reported. "He's managed to convince my boss that you don't call all the shots at Cove Construction and his relationship is more with Eddie Gallagher, who he maintains has more of a say in what goes on with your company."

"That's bullshit," Martin retorted.

"I know it is, but when I announced that you were in Anderson's offices this morning, he persuaded my boss that everyone should drive to Canton, so we can all meet."

"It's not going to change anything, John. He has nothing positive to offer. Besides, these people at Anderson don't want to have anything to do with Fred Ross."

"I understand, but Kevin Shaw has already agreed to it. He and I are traveling in the same car with Tony Bottazzi. We're going to get a sandwich before heading in your direction. Fred has to dismantle all his shit off the bridge before he follows us. Is there some place there where we can all sit down and meet?"

"I'm sure Jeff will allow us to use his conference room. I'll go and ask him and make sure it's okay for everyone to land down upon his facility like this."

Martin ended his phone call and stood stunned for several seconds. Fortunately, Louis overheard most of the conversation and was well aware of Ross' character, having recently experienced it first hand on Saturday morning. Quinn relayed Grasso's account of the morning's events at Jamestown during Ross' demonstration.

"I guess this is his last ditch effort to save what has got to be a hopeless situation," Quinn surmised, tempering his language in deference to Sandra's presence.

He had not planned to spend his entire day at Anderson. Sandra had a doctor's appointment that afternoon and it had been his intention to get a ride back to the office with her. Since it was nearly 1:00, he told her she could leave for the day.

"Here Sandra, let's swap Nextel phones before you go," Quinn suggested.

Martin ordered a pizza to be delivered and then got Jeff Anderson's permission to reserve the conference room for Ross' impromptu meeting.

"You're welcome to use it, but I'd prefer not to participate in any meeting with Ross, especially after Saturday's episode," Jeff clarified. "If the Seahorse Communications people want to see our fabrication shop, Louis can give them a tour. But I want to be very clear Martin, keep Fred Ross in the conference room. He's not permitted anywhere else and definitely not on the shop floor."

"Agreed. You and Louis concentrate on taking care of the raceway fabrication; I'll take care of the rest."

Jeff Anderson left the two men to finish their pizza.

"Save room for dessert," Martin joked, "there's bound to be some donuts left over!"

"You don't look like you got much rest over the weekend," Louis observed.

"You're absolutely right Lou, and not just this weekend. Keeping ahead of Ross over the past month, along with everything else I've got going on with Cove has been exhausting. I've got a busy week ahead, but next weekend I should be able to relax. I want to make sure we have the extrusion dye shop drawings reviewed and signed off so that your subcontractor in Canada can get going with its work."

* * * * * * *

After lunch, Martin remained alone and reviewed shop drawings for the various raceway components. It was a little after 3:00 when Quinn overheard Ross introduce himself at the reception area. Anxious to take control, Martin rushed to intercept Fred and led him into the conference room.

"I don't imagine we'll have to wait too long before the Seahorse folks are here," Martin offered as he gathered his Day-Timer and other documents from the table. "Jeff Anderson asked that you do not wander around his facility, but you're welcome to remain here for our meeting. I'll come back when the others arrive."

Martin closed the conference room door and went straight to Louis' office where he called John Grasso to report that Fred had arrived. He refreshed their driving directions and agreed to meet at the rear loading docks so they could talk privately before meeting with Fred.

That was the plan. Twenty minutes later, outside Fusco's office, Martin had just finished introducing Louis to the Seahorse team, when Ross suddenly appeared beside them.

"Fred, you've no authority to be back here," Quinn commanded.

Martin took control, and directed everyone towards the conference room, with Fred Ross leading the way. As they walked through the factory's storage bays of aluminum stock, John Grasso tugged on the back of Quinn's shirt and signaled him to fall back.

"That fucking asshole has been using his cell phone to record our conversations," John whispered. "He left his phone in the car earlier this morning and recorded private discussions Tony and I were having while he was outside speaking with Kevin Shaw. Then he played it back to Kevin along with other recordings and complained we were conspiring against him."

"What a slimy fuck," Martin responded. "I'll make sure there won't be any cell phones operating in this meeting. Besides, he'll not need to play back any recording to recall what was said because I'm going to make it real clear that he's all fucking done!"

As the group filed into the conference room, they were joined by Jeff Anderson who introduced himself to the Seahorse team.

Everyone got seated; however, Jeff suggested that he and Louis Fusco be excused. It was clearly evident he did not want to be involved in any further communications with Ross. "How insightful of Jeff," Martin thought as he looked over at Fred's cell phone sitting on the table.

"Before you gentlemen leave us," Kevin Shaw responded, "perhaps you can confirm that your company can manufacture the raceway within a time frame which will allow Cove to have it installed by April 15."

"It's not going to be easy," Jeff answered, "but I know we can do it. Martin has spent a lot of time with Louis and me, going over what it's going to take from both our companies to get this job done."

"If you're sure that's the case, then I need to get you a purchase order sent out first thing tomorrow, so you can get started," Shaw suggested.

"That won't be necessary," Martin interrupted, "Cove signed a contract agreement with Anderson this morning, at which time I also gave them an advance payment of $25,000 for this order. Before you gentlemen arrived, Jeff confided that he felt so comfortable with our negotiations over the past few weeks, that he went ahead and ordered everything he needs from a mill in Pennsylvania. That material has already been delivered here, so Anderson Aluminum will be starting work on this project tomorrow."

"You can't have Anderson start work on this job!" Fred challenged. "Cove Construction doesn't have a contract with Seahorse Communications. I do."

"Don't you tell me what I can and can't do," Martin snapped back at Ross. "When Anderson has finished manufacturing all the components for this project, I can toss the whole lot into Boston Harbor if I want to!"

Quinn's response silenced Fred. It also silenced everyone else in the room. Was their silence a reaction to the tone in which he had spoken to Ross or had everyone suddenly realized what Martin knew to be a fact? Cove Construction was the only company capable of completing this project before April 15 because, under the terms of their agreement, Anderson could not legally furnish the components to any other party.

It was Jeff Anderson who elected to break the silence.

"Louis and I will leave you gentlemen to go over any other business you need to discuss. For the record, I'm confident we can come through for Martin on this job."

"Thank you," Kevin Shaw replied as the two men retreated.

Martin took control of the meeting as soon as the conference room door closed.

"Before we get started, I think it would be a good idea if we all set our cell phones on the table and turn them off," he suggested.

No one had a problem with this request except Fred Ross who was sitting right opposite Quinn. It was like a scene from an old Wild West movie, except the combatants were reaching for cell phones instead of Colt .45 revolvers. Of the various cell phones set out around the table, Fred's was certainly the slickest. It did not have a leather protective case, nor did it fold closed like a clam shell. Rather, it was a neat, slim model which he carefully appeared to switch off and place back inside the cover of his executive, leather-bound note pad. Martin did not like this maneuver because he could not see if the phone had, in fact, been turned off. Furthermore, Ross could easily turn it back on during the meeting.

"You know," Quinn continued, "I don't mind if any of you think that I'm paranoid, but I want to see the batteries taken out also."

Now it was as if the cowboys were being asked to empty the bullets out of their guns as well! On Martin's command, everyone opened the back of their cell phone and removed the battery. Fred Ross was clearly livid with this second instruction. Even though his hands were complying, he was glaring menacingly at Martin.

The meeting finally got underway with over a thousand dollars of electronic equipment disassembled and discarded on the conference table. It was Kevin Shaw who spoke next.

"I need to begin by saying that I've never been involved in a project, the likes of which I've witnessed today. John Grasso has kept me informed over the past weeks as to how he thought this job was progressing. It wasn't until now that I've had an opportunity to see for myself the conditions he's had to endure."

"My number one priority is the success of this project," Shaw continued, "and from what I can see, it appears that Cove and Anderson have been able to get the raceway fabrication program successfully underway. But there's more to this job and it's those other aspects that I want to focus on. I don't intend to make decisions at this meeting. My goal is to leave today with as much information as I can, so subsequent decisions can be made which are in the best interest of Seahorse Communications and this project."

Discussions continued with everyone attempting to present themselves in the best possible light. Ten minutes into the meeting, Martin's shin was kicked by John Grasso who was sitting to his immediate left. John's eyes glanced over at Fred who was casually manipulating his cell phone battery. From the corner of his eye, Martin monitored Fred's furtive fingering. Very little time passed before Ross had slipped the battery back into his phone.

"What the fuck do you not understand?" Quinn bellowed. "Take the battery out of that cell phone or I'll shove it up your ass!"

Ross complied immediately. Martin remembered what Kevin Shaw had said earlier about not having seen anything like this before. Neither had he!

"I've never had a good working relationship with Martin," Fred explained to Grasso's boss. "My dealings with Cove are normally conducted with Eddie Gallagher. Unfortunately, he's flying to Ireland today for his sister's funeral. I would request that you not make any decisions until he returns and you can have the benefit of his input."

"This is just bullshit," Martin exclaimed before Shaw could respond, "I'm managing this project for Cove Construction. Eddie Gallagher is my equal partner in the company – not my boss. For you to attempt to buy time by bringing up his sister's funeral, is pathetic!"

Shaw realized that the sooner he separated Martin Quinn and Fred Ross the better it would be for all concerned. He never anticipated such a contentious encounter when he conceded to Fred's request to convene the meeting at Anderson. The animosity between Ross and Quinn was palpable.

"I'd like to wrap things up," Shaw announced. "I'm going to give some thought as to how I want this project to proceed and I'll get back to everyone as soon as possible. Right now, I'd like to take a quick walk around Anderson's shop floor."

With that pronouncement, the meeting came to a civil conclusion. After Fred Ross left, Martin looked below the conference table and joked that he was checking for hidden listening devices which may have been planted.

"What a day," John Grasso sighed as he stretched his elbows back behind his shoulder blades.

"What a month," Martin countered.

"I'm glad that I saw all this for myself," Kevin Shaw acknowledged. "Initially I thought John's evaluations seemed too far fetched. But now, I'm so relieved we uncovered Ross' charade before it was too late."

"You can thank Martin for that," Grasso added. "If he hadn't caught on to Fred's scam when he did, this project would have turned into a real disaster."

Tony Bottazzi quietly agreed with all that was being said. Quinn appreciated how awkward he must have felt, since he was responsible for introducing Ross to Seahorse Communications. A decision he had since come to regret.

Jeff Anderson and Louis Fusco returned to the conference room and granted Kevin Shaw's request to tour the shop floor. Martin knew that Louis lived in Stoughton. Conscious that his Jeep was still at Cove's office, he asked Louis for a lift.

"No problem," Fusco replied, "but why didn't you get a ride with Fred? Doesn't he live fairly close to you?"

"Don't get him started," Kevin joked.

"Seriously, Kevin," Martin continued, "before we go back onto the shop floor, we should try to contact Eddie Gallagher before his flight leaves."

"Go ahead," Shaw agreed.

Minutes later, Martin had his business partner on the speakerphone.

"I have Tony Bottazzi; John Grasso; and his boss, Kevin Shaw here with me. Kevin is Seahorse's Director of Northeast Operations. Fred Ross has just left our meeting. I need you to confirm who is running this job for Cove. Fred told them that he has a special relationship with you, which I'm unaware of, and that you have the last word on what happens at Cove. Perhaps you can set the record straight," Quinn suggested.

"I have no special relationship with Fred Ross," Gallagher responded, "and I'm not as familiar with this project as Martin is. He's the one who has been project managing this job from its beginning. Whatever he says goes."

"That seems clear to me," Shaw acknowledged.

John Grasso and Kevin Shaw offered Eddie their condolences before ending the call.

It was nearly 6:30 before the Seahorse folks left for Rhode Island, having taken their guided tour of the factory.

Louis was quite willing to drive to Cove's office to get Martin's Jeep, but Quinn insisted that getting dropped off in Stoughton would be fine. En route, they stopped briefly in Canton at Cove's funeral home project. Conscious that Fred could not drive home from Anderson Aluminum without passing this location, Quinn believed that his construction equipment was somewhat vulnerable to Ross' retaliation. As a precaution, he called the Canton Police Department and scheduled a brief meeting at the jobsite, so he could arrange for a police detail to watch over it that evening.

Before the two men parted in Stoughton center, Fusco remarked that the previous few days had been actually quite entertaining. Quinn headed off in the direction of Stoughton Police Headquarters. Since he was not going to be living at home for the next few days, he wanted to make sure Fred Ross did not bother Margaret. With everything that had gone down recently, it was not at all inconceivable that Fred might try to reason with Martin by going directly to his home. In that event, he did not want his wife to have to deal with such a visit. It was bad enough that the craziness of Cove's work schedule and Martin's extended work hours, had frustrated her to the degree that he had moved out of the house, but to then find out that Fred Ross was involved, would surely rub salt into the wound. As a precaution, Quinn decided to also get a police detail for one night to watch over his own home and make sure that Ross' white Yukon would be intercepted, should it show up. Since his house was situated on a secluded street, there would be no way a car could remain parked for any length of time, without Margaret or one of the neighbors becoming concerned. Consequently, the desk sergeant let Martin call his neighbor, Brad Paterson, to ask permission for the Stoughton Police to park an unmarked car overnight in his driveway. He did not share with Paterson the real reason why he would not be sleeping in his own home. Instead, Quinn told him he was going out of town on business and did not want to worry Margaret about the possibility of a visit from Fred Ross. Brad had no problem with this request, so Martin passed the phone to the desk sergeant, who finalized the arrangements.

Quinn left the police station and went back out to Stoughton center where he had a cup of coffee at Honey Dew Donuts. At this point, he had not slept in over twenty-four hours, during which time he managed to accomplish more than what most people take care of in a week.

"How are you, Martin?" a familiar voice asked.

He looked up. It was his friend, Frank Russo, a Stoughton Police detective. They chatted for nearly an hour, during which time he gave Russo a synopsis of the Seahorse Communications project, culminating with the events of earlier that day.

It was a little after 8:30 when Martin told Frank that he needed to call for a taxi ride to his office in Quincy, where he had parked his car.

"I've got to get going too," Russo announced as he stood up to leave, "I'll make sure that we send a cruiser past your house regularly during the next few days. It sounds as if things are beginning to work themselves out on this bridge project and you should be back living at home before the week is through."

Quinn sat down again after his friend left and reached into his pocket to get Sandra's Nextel phone. He searched in vain remembering the last time he used it was to call the Canton Police Department. "I must have left it in Louis' car," he deduced, slumping further into the seat to take stock of his current situation. "So here I am in the middle of the town where I live; I have no car; no keys to my office; no phone; I've only slept for six hours in the past two days; I'm absolutely exhausted and have yet to organize somewhere to sleep!" While it appeared that he had all Cove's business expertly managed and under control, Quinn's efforts in accomplishing this had certainly taken their toll on his personal circumstances. As he gazed out the window, trying to think where there was a pay phone, he was relieved to see two cabs parked at the taxi stand across the street.

"Thank God," he sighed as he approached the first of the two cars.

Quinn had trouble keeping alert as the taxi traveled north on Route 24. He zoned out briefly, missing much of the trip and could not believe how quickly they had managed to get to his office.

Just as he sat into the Jeep, his pager started to vibrate. It was a Rhode Island number which he did not recognize. As he stared at the screen, the number appeared again. Then a third page came in. This time, a different Rhode Island number with "*911" added. "Who is this?" Martin wondered, automatically reaching for Sandra's Nextel phone, before realizing he had misplaced it.

His pager went off again. And then again! To make matters worse, he remembered that he could not get into his office to use that phone. Earlier in the day, per his request, the landlord had changed the lock on Cove's office door. For the second night in a row, he found himself without a key to his own office! This time, Eddie Gallagher's key would be of no use to him. The pager went off again. It was John Grasso's cell number followed by "*911." Quinn gathered a fist full of coins from the Jeep's console and jogged across the parking lot to the Chantey Pub.

Before he had time to feed coins into the pay phone and dial John's number, his pager went off two more times. Grasso picked up immediately.

"Thanks for getting back to me. Kevin Shaw has been paging you also. We couldn't get an answer on either of your cell phones."

"I have a temporary phone for the next few days," Quinn explained. "I just received several thousand pages in the past five minutes from Rhode Island phone numbers. Your cell number was one of them, so I called you first."

"One of them was my home number," John explained. "Kevin has a proposal for going forward with this project and wants to speak with you before sending his letter to all the parties involved. Although you may not like every aspect, you should find it acceptable how Cove will be compensated. He's waiting in his office for your call."

"I'll call you back after I've spoken with him."

Kevin Shaw answered his phone immediately and explained that he wanted to get everything back on track as soon as possible, since time was so crucial on the project.

"My problem is that Seahorse already awarded RossCon Enterprises a contract to furnish and install this raceway," he continued. "I've drafted a letter which sets out my resolution, but I didn't want to send it out until we had spoken and I had your approval. I needed to come up with a solution that would allow the project to continue the way you appear to have it going, but without further involvement from Mr. Ross and without litigation stemming from my decision to cancel his contract. Consequently, I propose to replace his original contract with a new one, whereby he'll solely monitor progress and prepare weekly field reports for my office. I'll be compensating him more than adequately for this service. This will negate the need for him to resort to litigation now that our original agreement is cancelled. As far as Cove is concerned, I propose to pay you $410,000 for completing the installation of the raceway and a further bonus of $40,000 if you have the work completed in time, so that Seahorse and CellTell Atlantic can install their fiber-optic cables on or before April 15."

"Kevin," Martin began, "I hope if John has been able to get you to understand anything about Cove Construction, it's that we are 'team players.' I understand that without you and John Grasso there would be no project for Cove. What you decide to do with Fred Ross is your business. I'm only interested in taking care of what you need Cove to do. As long as Ross manages to complete his obligations to your company without interfering with my operations, then I've got no problem with your proposal. I understand your predicament."

"I appreciate you taking this approach."

"I'm just relieved the project has been saved by your solution, however, to date you've only been able to see what Fred Ross can't do. Before going any further, why don't we get together tomorrow afternoon at the bridge and I'll bring down Cove's prototype, so you can see how things are supposed to look."

"I'd like to do that. Give me a call tomorrow morning after 9:00 and we can agree on a time that works for us both. I have to finish this letter of understanding and fax it out to everyone. There'll be a signature block at the end for each party to endorse and return to my office. Also, I want to have a meeting at Tony Bottazzi's office on Thursday afternoon, once everyone has acknowledged that they're on board."

They ended their call and Martin reported back to John Grasso, as promised. It was after 10:00 by the time Quinn walked out of the Chantey Pub. Thankfully, his pager had settled down and it looked as if his work day had finally come to an end. All that remained was for him to find somewhere to sleep. He had been awake for over thirty hours and the closest hotel he could think of was the Sheraton in Braintree. Twenty minutes later, he was standing at the reception desk being told there were no rooms available.

"I have an American Express Platinum Card," Martin replied. "I understood that by having this card, I would never be turned away from any hotel." He retrieved the card from his wallet and passed it over to the receptionist. "Why is this necessary?" he thought to himself. "Surely she can see that I'm about to pass out, right here in the lobby." The woman rattled away on her keyboard with three or four short bursts and mulled over options which appeared on the computer screen.

"How many nights will you be staying with us, Mr. Quinn?"

"I'm not sure. Why don't we say, three?"

After processing the reservation, the receptionist returned his credit card and gave him an electronic pass key for his room while explaining some of the hotel's amenities. All Martin wanted to do was sleep!

"Do you need any help with your bags?"

Quinn declined. What was the point? All that he had with him fitted into his canvas briefcase. On Sunday night when he left home he had packed lightly, hastily grabbing some clean underwear, socks, and his shaving kit.

As he pulled the blankets up to his chin, Martin thought about how Margaret was doing. He felt comfortable with the knowledge that the police detail would make sure she and Brendan were safe. "How did I end up like this?" he wondered. Sheer exhaustion prevented him from giving this question any more consideration.

6:00AM - Tuesday March 2, 1999

Martin awoke after seven hours of uninterrupted sleep. "What a gift," he sighed, sitting up in the bed. He picked up his Day-Timer, unclipped the plastic "TODAY" page divider from the previous day, and inserted it in between the two pages allotted for March 2. He had a lot to do before his meeting at the bridge that afternoon and began to prepare a list of tasks, assigning a Cove employee to each.

After a thoroughly invigorating shower he made his first phone call of the day to Chris Donovan. Quinn answered some questions about Cove's ongoing jobs and then told Donovan he wanted to include him in the trip to the Jamestown Bridge. They agreed to meet at Anderson Aluminum at 11:00, so they could load the raceway sections. Chris' truck had a twelve foot long, fully enclosed storage box in the rear, with a roll-up door. It would be ideal for this trip, since it had Cove's name painted on both sides in large print, and was fully fitted out with tool boxes and racks for practically any task the superintendent encountered throughout his work day.

Martin waited until 7:00 and then placed a call to Tom Sullivan. Tom was not only a personal friend, but also Cove Construction's corporate lawyer. With Eddie Gallagher out of the country and all that had gone down the previous day, Martin wanted the benefit of some face-time with Tom. He left voicemail on his attorney's cell phone, for a return call to the hotel room. By 7:30 he was speaking with Tom who was concerned he was calling a hotel and not Martin's home or cell phone. Quinn suggested they meet for breakfast since the Sheraton was only ten minutes from Sullivan's law office.

Before going down to the dining room, Martin called his own office and spoke with Sandra.

"I need you to call Kevin Shaw at Seahorse and schedule a meeting for 1:00 this afternoon at the Jamestown Bridge. Then call Louis Fusco at Anderson and tell him that I need to pick up all the prototype raceway components that I gave him on Saturday morning."

By 8:15, Martin and his guest were giving their breakfast orders to the waitress. Tom had not been aware that Eddie was in Ireland and was glad he had agreed to meet, especially after hearing what had transpired with the Jamestown Bridge project. He was satisfied Martin had solved the problems Fred Ross had created and congratulated him on Seahorse's proposal. He was, however, anxious to review Kevin Shaw's letter before Quinn countersigned it.

"Now what's going on with you and Margaret? How come you stayed here last night?"

Without going into too much detail, he explained to Sullivan how things had gone a bit crazy at home. Tom understood that the schedule Martin maintained over the past four or five weeks had to have taken a toll on the Quinn family.

"Listen. I'm going to have my wife call Margaret later today and make sure that she's okay. If you look after Brendan this weekend, then Kathleen will take Margaret to our farm in Maine on Friday morning for a little break. When they come back on Monday evening, we can all go out to dinner and get you guys back together again."

Martin thanked Tom for his support both as a friend and an attorney.

"Also," Sullivan insisted, "after your meeting today with the people at Seahorse, you need to take a break yourself. Do something unrelated to work and then get some rest."

"Don't worry, I know my limitations. I've already called my uncle. He retired from Boston Edison two years ago and now he helps out at Cove whenever I need him. I'm going to have him drive me to and from Rhode Island, to meet these guys at the bridge."

* * * * * * *

Quinn gathered his Day-Timer and other paperwork related to the bridge project from his room and waited for his Uncle Dan in the lobby of the hotel.

"We need to stop at the mall across the street so I can buy a couple of shirts," Martin explained as his breath condensed in the cold atmosphere of the parking lot. "I can't turn up to meet the Seahorse guys wearing the same one that I had on yesterday."

Dan was an older brother of Martin's father and had immigrated to Boston from Ireland in 1955. His service with the United States Army in Korea made him eligible to become a citizen. In the late 70's and early 80's Martin spent summer vacations from college with his uncle, wife Lorna and their three daughters. Since Dan and Lorna never had a son, he became very close to them all. Years later, when the Quinns decided to escape the troubles of Northern Ireland, Boston was an obvious choice. Dan, Lorna and the girls provided an abundance of assistance with this move and Brendan, who was three when he left Belfast, was treated as if he were their own grandson.

By 11:00 Dan and Martin were reversing into a parking space outside Anderson Aluminum. Chris Donovan, who was already there, had done a first class job of cleaning his truck.

"I just went in and asked for Louis Fusco, but the receptionist told me that he had a dentist appointment this morning," Donovan reported.

"She doesn't know anything about having an order ready for Cove, but she does have your Nextel phone."

Just then, a red Ford Explorer drove into the parking lot. Louis Fusco waved as he brought the vehicle to a stop beside Dan's car. After brief introductions, Martin sent Chris Donovan with Louis to get the prototype, while he retrieved Sandra's Nextel.

By now, Quinn was concerned that he would not get to the bridge in time for the 1:00 meeting he had asked Sandra to arrange. He had no option but to have her reschedule it for 2:00. It upset him that he needed to do so, but accepted the fact that it was more professional than turning up late.

"I can't believe you're calling me to change the time," Sandra responded, "I actually forgot to call Seahorse. John Grasso just called and asked that I contact you to see if 2:00 would work. Kevin Shaw had asked him to follow up when he didn't hear from you."

Martin could not believe what he was hearing. He seemed to be blessed with incredible luck regarding this project. Even when one of his employees messed up, circumstances still worked out for the best.

"Call John back and let him know that 2:00 will be fine," he instructed, resisting the urge to add, "and don't forget!"

Since Donovan had never seen the prototype, Quinn was conscious of the need to explain how it was to be assembled on the bridge. Before they left Anderson's facility, Cove's lead superintendent clearly comprehended how everything went together.

As the Town Car's tires gripped into the slushy road surface, Martin reclined the passenger seat. His uncle was glad he could help and was well used to the craziness that often accompanied Cove's operations. The very first project that Dan worked on with his nephew was the installation of a new septic system for a psychiatric hospital in Pembroke, Massachusetts.

One day, Dan's lunch was interrupted by several staff members looking for a patient who had gone missing. Apparently, a teenager escaped from a secure wing of the hospital. He managed to get into a taxi which had just dropped off a visitor, and left the property before anyone realized there was a problem. Dan often teased Martin about the wisdom of taking on a project at such a place, in case the staff would mistake him for one of the patients! In reality, the hospital's management personnel were excellent to work with and subsequently awarded Cove a job at another affiliated hospital in Westwood, Massachusetts.

During the trip to Rhode Island, Martin shared details of the previous few weeks with his uncle.

"With everything that I've got to sort out on this project during the coming week, it's probably best that I've moved out of the house. This is a very critical project for Cove. If it goes well, we stand to make a very, very good profit."

His uncle was astonished at Martin's profit predictions for this single job. The installation in the field would take three men approximately four weeks. The remainder of the cost was Anderson's manufacturing contract and Martin's supervision and engineering in-house costs.

"How are we going to get you back living at home?" Uncle Dan asked with concern.

When Martin explained Tom Sullivan's plan to have his wife take Margaret to Maine for the weekend, he was relieved that something was being done to resolve the situation.

Chris Donovan kept up with Dan's sedan without any problem and both vehicles eventually came to a halt in the rest area at the northern end of the Jamestown Bridge. John Grasso and Kevin Shaw were already standing on the sidewalk where Martin had previously attached the prototype during Thursday's snow storm. Dan stayed in his car, while Quinn and

Donovan met with the two gentlemen from Seahorse Communications. Ironically, Shaw complimented Martin on his punctuality.

Within minutes, both Cove men were standing on the cable raceway prototype, which had been efficiently secured in place. Kevin Shaw was extremely impressed.

"I'm very much looking forward to this project," he confided. "My secretary should've already faxed the letters of understanding that I spoke to you about last night. I've scheduled a meeting at Tony Bottazzi's office for 3:00 on Thursday afternoon. Please give John a countersigned copy when you see him at the meeting. I'll not be there myself, but I'm confident Cove can take care of things from this point on."

The icy wind blowing from the Atlantic Ocean, underscored the need to keep the field demonstration brief. Once all the components were removed from the bridge and returned to the box-truck, Martin dispatched Chris Donovan back to Boston.

They had not traveled more than two miles when Quinn took a call from Sandra at the office.

"Your patent attorney just called and wants you to contact him. Also, on Thursday morning, the Nextel rep' will drop off your replacement phone and a new one for John Grasso. I should have a new Verizon cell phone for you by that time too. I received the letter from Kevin Shaw and faxed it over to Tom Sullivan's office, like you asked. I just got Tom's response and he has no problem with you signing it."

"Sounds good," Quinn replied, "I'll catch up with you later."

He then placed a call to Arthur Watson, who reported that his Washington, D.C. office had completed extensive searches of the US patent archives. There were no patents either issued or pending, similar to Martin's design. Watson recommended filing a patent application to protect Cove from any litigation. Quinn thanked him for the information and authorized his firm to proceed accordingly.

His uncle understood from what he overheard that his nephew had just received very good news from the attorney.

"Thanks to Ross being an absolute asshole, it now looks as if I'm going to get a patent issued!"

Martin went on to catalog similar instances of recent good fortune, such as walking into Anderson's facility on Saturday morning and being alerted to Ross' covert mission to secure materials for his own prototype.

"Well, hopefully your luck will continue through next weekend and you can get things patched up with Margaret at home," his uncle responded. "Brendan can't be too thrilled about this situation."

"No, he's not. I'm going to call Thayer Academy and get permission to have lunch with him off campus tomorrow. But tonight, I'm going to take my attorney's advice and chill out."

At that instant, the WBZ 1030 radio station was broadcasting a sports report which featured news of that evening's scheduled hockey game between the Boston Bruins and Phoenix Coyotes.

"That's what I'll do," Martin decided, "I'm going to go into Boston tonight and watch the hockey game. I'll call my friend Sean Feeney. I know he'll meet me in there. I can also give him Brendan's laptop computer to repair."

"Good idea," Dan agreed, "but what about driving in and out to the game?"

"I'll get a hotel room for the night in the city. That way I can relax and have a couple of beers without having to drive."

After everything he had been through, especially during the past week, Martin believed he owed himself one good night on the town. He decided to get a room in the Boston Harbor Hotel. It was one of the city's premier landmarks. Located on the waterfront near the aquarium, it featured an impressive sixty foot high open arch in the center of the building. He called 411 for the hotel's phone number and got connected to a woman in reservations.

"Hi, I'd like to book a room for tonight."

"I'm sorry, but we don't have anything available."

This news was inconsistent with all of Martin's recent good fortune and immediately put a damper on his plans. Once again he tried to salvage the situation by playing his platinum trump card that American Express provided.

"I'll take another look for you, Sir."

There was a pause while he listened to the sound of fingers skipping across a computer keyboard in the background.

"I believe we can accommodate you this evening if you'd like to make a reservation over the phone," she continued. "The room is $450, for the night."

Quinn was horrified. It far exceeded what he expected. He had been feeling good about the day, right up until these negotiations.

"Do you have corporate discounts or anything? I own my own company. I just wanted to come into town tonight and watch the hockey game without having to drive."

Once again there was feverish activity on a keyboard, however, this time it went on a bit longer. When the receptionist came back on the line she sounded as if she was whispering to him from underneath her desk. Martin did not clearly hear what she said but the sentence ended with the words, "… $250 and although there's no bed, the couch folds out and there's bed linen in the closet."

"Great, I'll take that."

Quinn did not know what he had replied "Great" to. It was probably a closet in the basement parking garage where the valet drivers threw car keys, but he really did not care. He was going to see the Bruins and would be staying in one the world's finest hotels. Even if it did mean sleeping in the basement or a janitor's closet!

He wrote down a reservation number for future reference, then called Sean Feeney's cell number and left voicemail for him to call back on Sandra's Nextel.

It was 4:00 when Dan parked the car outside the front door of the Braintree Sheraton Hotel.

"Take it easy tonight and make sure you get some sleep," his uncle advised.

Quinn checked out of his room and drove into Boston. The traffic on the I93 Expressway was very heavy, but he had plenty of time, since the game did not start until 7:30. Sean Feeney called back and they agreed to meet at the box office ticket windows inside the Boston Garden. By 5:30 Martin had parked his Jeep in the basement garage of the Boston Harbor Hotel and was riding the elevator up to the front desk lobby. He had managed to cram all his spare clothes and shaving kit into the canvas brief case, along with his Day-Timer and an envelope containing his original signed copy of the contract between Anderson Aluminum and Cove Construction.

He weaved his way through the guests, uniformed valets, and porters in the reception area and stopped at the hotel's front desk. Minutes later, Martin had signed the registration paperwork and was declining an offer for assistance with his bags.

"Your room is on the sixteenth floor, Mr. Quinn. Welcome to the Boston Harbor Hotel. Please enjoy your stay with us."

He thanked the young manager and made his way to a different bank of elevators located just off the main lobby. "Well, I'm not in the basement," he thought to himself.

Quinn studied the polished brass plate on the wall, directing him to his room.

"This is no ordinary room," he acknowledged when he stopped outside number 1608. The entrance was recessed off the hallway with its own alcove and door bell. Only when he stepped inside did he comprehend what the woman had said to him when he made the reservation. She had booked him into the Presidential Suite. Although he did not have access to the bedrooms on either side, there was bed linen in a closet which he could use with the sleep sofa.

Even without access to the two bedrooms, the Presidential Suite was nearly as large as the living space of Quinn's own home. It was divided into three distinct areas and had its own bathroom. The first section was more of a reception area which had a writing desk with a telephone and internet terminal for a laptop computer. This was ideal for receiving business acquaintances and was furnished conservatively to accommodate a small meeting. The next central area was solely for relaxation. It included a large television screen, the like of which Martin had never seen before. The electronic console adjacent to the TV included a twin deck video cassette recorder, a DVD player, and a compact disc player which had a one hundred disc library capacity. Three large leather couches surrounded a beautiful marble coffee table making this place, "Party Central." The third section had a formal dining table with seating for ten, plus a fully stocked wet bar.

All three areas of the suite featured large windows adorned with ornate drapes. They provided a magnificent view of Boston Harbor. Martin simply could not believe it. The sight at night was breathtaking. The lights of Logan International Airport were visible to his left. As he surveyed the view, the glass front of the new federal court house provided a second book-end to the harbor scenery and lights.

Quinn leapt over the back of the couch and grabbed three remote controls. "Good Lord," he thought to himself, "I have remote controls to control remote controls!" He played around with the TV and sound system which combined to saturate the suite with a collage of sports, MTV videos, and sensational rock music. The TV screen could display several different channels at one time and the surround sound stereo system was just amazing. Martin checked his watch and realized he needed to get ready for the hockey game. He took a quick shower and freshened up amidst the marble and gold fixtures of the bathroom. Everywhere he looked exuded wealth and luxury. Quinn was absolutely astonished that he was enjoying all this extravagance at a discount, because he did not want to pay $450 for a regular room!

Before leaving the suite, he retrieved the envelope containing the Anderson contract from his canvas briefcase. There was no way he was going to leave it laying around the hotel room while he was out. Since this document was such an important item in maintaining control of the bridge project, he decided to place it in one of the hotel's safety deposit boxes. If Anderson Aluminum did not perform, he wanted to make sure his copy of the original signed contract was intact.

Upon hearing Martin's request, the front desk manager directed him through a door adjacent to the reception area. An electronic lock was activated as Quinn reached for the handle. He found himself in a room approximately twenty feet by twelve feet, which had all four walls lined with safety deposit boxes. Each safe had two lock escutcheons. One required a master key which was kept by the hotel's management, the second lock was opened using a key, unique to that individual safe. In the middle of the room was a table with two chairs on either side. The front desk manager met Martin by entering the room via a door on his side of the reception desk. He was carrying a leather bound ledger and a small locking file box which contained keys for safes that were available.

He motioned for Quinn to take a seat so they could complete the paperwork which accompanied the issuance of a safety deposit box.

"What size of safe do you think you will need, Sir?"

"I think I'll need this size," Martin replied, pointing to a row of the larger doors behind him. "How much is the fee?"

"That's our largest one, Sir. There's no additional charge to our guests for this service."

Both men signed the log so that the key for box number 215 could be issued. The manager explained that an entry would need to be made in the log every time its contents were accessed. With that said, he opened the upper lock and invited Martin to use his key in the corresponding lower cylinder. Quinn withdrew a steel case with a hinged lid, designed to fit neatly inside the safe.

"I'll leave you alone to conduct your business in private," Jim, the manager, suggested as he gathered his paperwork.

"There's no need to leave, I just want to place this envelope inside. We can lock everything right now."

* * * * * * *

It was no more than a ten minute walk to the Boston Garden, home to both the Boston Bruins hockey and the Boston Celtics basketball teams. As Quinn approached Causeway Street, the sidewalks became more and more packed with fans draped in "Black and Gold" hats, jackets and home-team jerseys, many with the name of current or former Bruins' players.

Sean was already waiting for Martin when he arrived at the box office ticket windows.

"What are our seats like?"

"I don't know. I haven't bought them yet."

"What? I thought one of your company's clients or vendors had given you tickets. I had no idea you were inviting me to a game and you had to pay for tickets," Feeney protested.

"Relax," Quinn responded. "It's not a problem. You've got no idea how insane my life has been over the past month and how lucky I've been."

By now the two friends were at the ticket window, where Martin purchased two premium center-ice seats at $150 each.

"There's no need for this expense," his friend insisted, "we can sit in cheaper seats."

"I'm just doing what my attorney advised," Martin joked, "I was told to relax and take some time out this evening."

Martin had known Sean for nearly ten years, since hiring him as a co-op student at Boston Building Associates. After Feeney graduated with a degree in Civil Engineering from UMass Lowell, he continued to work at BBA. Not only did he have a solid construction and engineering background, but Sean was also extremely talented and knowledgeable regarding Apple computers. During the five years that Martin and Sean worked together, they formed a strong friendship and often socialized at family functions. They shared a lot of common interests, including a healthy distrust and distain for Fred Ross. Quinn knew that Feeney would be delighted to hear all the details about Fred's downfall.

Martin would never have made a habit of paying $150 to watch a hockey game, but their seats were fantastic. They were nicely upholstered and reclined with ample leg room for a totally comfortable experience. The two men did not have to leave in order to get beers or anything to eat since waitresses catered to the fans in this premium section of the arena.

Sean did not know which was more entertaining; Martin's story, or the action on the ice. When the game ended, Feeney insisted on giving his friend a ride back to the hotel so he could see for himself the room Quinn had managed to get at such a huge discount.

A broad smile beamed from Feeney's face as the two men entered room 1608. Soon they were drinking beers, listening to music, and surfing through channels on the big screen.

"Look, that's you and me," Martin joked, pausing on a sports channel which was showing highlights of the game they had just attended.

Sean stayed for about an hour and took photographs of Martin goofing around, posing in various areas of the suite, holding a champagne bottle in an ice bucket. When it was time to leave, Quinn accompanied Feeney down to the parking garage where he retrieved Brendan's computer from his Jeep.

"Don't worry about this. I'll have it back to you before the weekend."

Once back in the suite, Martin turned on an Aerosmith CD that was already in the player. A previous guest had left it behind which Martin recognized as yet another bit of good luck, as the Boston based band launched into "Walk This Way."

It was after midnight when Quinn took some bed sheets from a closet adjacent to the bathroom and made himself comfortable on one of the couches. Although it could fold out to make a bed, he did not bother to do so since the couch was more than adequate, just the way it was. He settled down with his three remote controls and the remainder of a Heineken beer. With the Aerosmith CD playing quietly, he turned off the TV, leaving the night lights from Boston Harbor to wash the ceiling. "What a day," he sighed.

6:20AM - Wednesday March 3, 1999

Half a bottle of Heineken on the coffee table came into focus as Martin opened his eyes. It was dawn outside. His canvas briefcase was sitting on a dining room chair reminding him of the work that needed to be done. He had to prepare for Thursday's meeting at Bottazzi's office. The final design dimensions for the extrusion dyes needed his approval so that Anderson could release this order to the foundry in Canada. Then there were Cove's other projects to be managed and to top everything off, his business partner was out of the country.

Since it was Martin's expectation to be back home by the weekend, he decided to see if the suite was available through noon on Saturday. He reckoned the formal dining table would make a great work area where he could spread out the prototype components and carefully check their dimensions. Although Anderson had begun fabrication of the lower support components using standard sections of aluminum, Quinn had to carefully check the design of the top covers. Once he had approved their shop drawings, these unique sections would be manufactured in a foundry using dyes tooled specifically for this project.

On his way to breakfast, Martin stopped at the front desk where he was able to extend his stay in the Presidential Suite at the same discount rate. At the entrance to the dining room he was greeted by a polite hostess with a South American accent who escorted him to a window table overlooking Boston Harbor. A ferry boat had just docked, bringing passengers from Hingham or Quincy. It was 8:00 and the city was already wide awake and embarked upon its day. After giving the waitress his breakfast order, Martin wrote out a to-do-list in his Day-Timer.

When Quinn returned to his room, he worked down through his list. The first call was to Thayer Academy where he asked to speak to Middle School Principal, Shelley Tyre. He requested permission to take Brendan off campus for lunch and shared with her how he had been living away from home for the past few days.

"I'm sorry to hear that you and Margaret are having problems, but in situations like this, I'm obligated to confirm there are no restraining orders or other legal rulings which would restrict your access to Brendan. I'll have to make a couple of phone calls before I can set this up. If everything is as you are representing, then I would be only too glad to arrange for you and Brendan to have lunch together."

"Thank you, Shelley, please feel free to speak with Brendan. Also, Lieutenant Peter Dorian of the Holbrook Police Department is a good personal friend of the family, as well as one of Brendan's hockey coaches. I'm sure he'll run any checks you need to confirm that this is okay."

Martin's next call was to Cove's office. He gave Sandra a list of files and other items he would need over the next few days and arranged to meet her in Braintree after his lunch with Brendan. Calls to his job superintendents confirmed that Cove's other projects were progressing satisfactorily.

With two hours to spare before he would meet Brendan, he checked out the hotel's health club. Located one level below the reception area, this exclusive facility also featured a day spa and hair dressing salon. A friendly receptionist confirmed Martin was a guest in the hotel and then went through the various amenities, which were also available to non-residents who paid a substantial membership fee. Quinn explained his schedule had changed unexpectedly so he would be staying in the hotel for the remainder of the week, but did not have swimming trunks or pool sandals.

"Not a problem. We've a nice selection of each available for purchase. Also, when you come in, there's no need to worry about bringing towels or robes from your room. Everything you need is here. If any of your guests want to join you in the health club, we also have complimentary swimwear for their convenience."

Ten minutes later he was making his way to the Jacuzzi via the showers. Quinn had no desire to use any of the exercise equipment in the fitness room, however, relaxing in the Jacuzzi and swimming a few laps in the pool was certainly appealing. "So this is how the other half lives," he thought to himself as he took off one of the hotel's white monogrammed robes and stepped down into the bubbling jets of water. "What a way to start a day. Memo to self: begin every day in the health club!" There was even a breakfast area set discreetly off to the side. Some guests were reading the morning newspaper while they enjoyed fresh orange juice and coffee. Before taking a shower, Quinn spent twenty minutes in the sauna. By the time he was leaving to meet Brendan, he was thoroughly refreshed and extremely pleased he had made the decision to extend his stay.

En route to Braintree, Martin thought about how messed up things had become with Margaret. It was obvious from Sunday's driving exhibition that she was extremely angry. "But about what," he wondered. The only possible reason he could think of, was the number of hours he was away from home working. Given all of Quinn's financial obligations in addition to those of Cove Construction, he had no other choice. But then, he had shielded her from much of the detail surrounding the operations of the company. All he wanted was the business to be a success so that it would provide adequately for his family. As he approached Thayer Academy, he recalled happier times with Margaret and Brendan when they first visited the school campus three years earlier. Recent events, however, meant that he had to rely on Shelley Tyre to see his own son. Quinn recognized how his insight and intuition had helped him keep ahead of Fred Ross; however, he was seemingly oblivious to how his actions were causing so much discord in his family.

He drove into the parking lot of the middle school which was located two hundred yards along Hobart Avenue beyond the main high school. Nestled in peaceful tree lined surroundings, this campus was an extension of the prestigious private prep' school. The traditional red brick and sandstone buildings were proud testaments to the institution's development, since its opening in 1877 with trust money bequeathed by General Sylvanus Thayer. A native of Braintree, General Thayer was a respected academic and soldier. He held the post of Superintendent of the United States Military Academy at West Point from 1817 until 1833, when he resigned following a disagreement with President Andrew Jackson.

As Quinn walked towards the main door, he appreciated how fortunate Brendan was to be a student at this elite school. The Middle School's administrative assistant greeted him when he entered the main office.

"Ms. Tyre is just finishing a meeting at the high school. She called to let you know that she's on her way," Ms. Kelly explained in a polite and professional manner.

"Not a problem, I'm a little bit early actually."

Martin could see across into Shelley Tyre's office through its open door. It was not common practice for the principal of such a prestigious school to share an office. Shelley chose to share hers with her best friend. Apparently, the one hundred and five pound Bernese Mountain Dog's attendance had not been required at the high school meeting! Consequently, he had chosen to catch up on his sleep. His tail gave a friendly wave upon hearing his master enter the building. Tory was the calmest and gentlest of creatures, adored by the students and even featured as a member of staff in the school's yearbook photographs.

"Sorry for running late," she apologized unnecessarily.

Shelley Tyre gestured for Quinn to follow her into her office. She closed the door so they could conduct their discussions in private and without interruption.

"I'm very fond of Brendan, as I am of all the students, but your son is a very nice young man. I'm truly sorry Margaret and you are not getting along at the present time, however, I'm delighted to see you are keen to make sure that Brendan's life continues as normally as it can, during what must be stressful times for all of you. Please understand I will assist you in any way I can to make sure his experience here at Thayer does not suffer. I'll make sure the teachers are aware of his current family situation and take it into consideration when reviewing his classwork and homework assignments."

Martin thanked her and explained how his aggressive schedule over the past month had caused problems at home. As soon as he mentioned the bridge project at Jamestown, Rhode Island, Shelley gave a huge smile.

"That's where we live," she interjected, "my husband operates a SCUBA diving school and shop in Jamestown. What a coincidence!"

When he heard this, Martin's eyes welled up. It was obvious the last few weeks had been even more stressful than he himself had perceived. But it was more than that. He realized that despite all the adversity and turmoil in his life, he was not being left to overcome it by himself. He closed his eyes and turned his head towards the floor while he wiped away tears with a pinching stroke of the forefinger and thumb of his left hand. Shelley lifted a box of tissues from a shelf behind her chair and offered them to him.

"I know how you must be feeling," she confided, "I know what it's like to be in a relationship that's not going too well. It's got to be a very tough time for you."

Martin reached out and took a tissue from the box.

"Why don't I send word to Brendan's classroom so that he can get released ten minutes early?" suggested Shelley. "I'll be right back, Tory will keep you company!"

She closed the door behind her, leaving Martin alone with the dog. Tory appeared to have understood every word of the conversation. He glanced over in Martin's direction with a reassuring expression, as if he and Shelley had an understanding that anything overheard during meetings in her office was not to be repeated.

"Well I hope that your project goes well," Shelley announced upon her return.

Tory got out of his bed and stood beside his master when he realized that Martin was getting ready to leave. She affectionately scratched the back of the huge dog's head while they waited for Brendan to arrive.

"Please don't hesitate to call me if you should need anything else," Shelley offered as they parted.

It was no more than a five minute drive to Bugaboo Creek, a Canadian-theme restaurant. The hostess seated Martin and Brendan below a giant trophy head of a black bear which sang a little song at regular intervals. Other animated characters throughout the dining room occasionally took a turn at entertaining the younger patrons.

During lunch, Martin assured Brendan the Jamestown project was at last coming together since Fred Ross had been exposed and could no longer be a threat to Cove. He cautioned that there still was a lot of work to be done on the job and under very critical time constraints. Brendan was relieved to hear that the Sullivans were helping to get things sorted out on the home front. By the end of lunch, they were both glad to have caught up with each other's news from the previous few days.

* * * * * * *

Sandra was already waiting in the car park of Barnes & Noble when Quinn drove in. As he approached, she opened the tailgate of her SUV to reveal a large cardboard box containing a sample bracket, some files related to the bridge project, as well as paperwork pertaining to other Cove jobs. Underneath she had arranged the top and bottom sections of a four foot long sample of the aluminum raceway, which were too long to fit inside this box.

"Here are some phone messages," she said, handing over an envelope containing the slips. "Two of them are from Tony Lopez, returning your calls from earlier this week. I told him I would be seeing you today and explained that you were using my phone while yours is getting repaired."

Tony Lopez was a good friend who worked as an account representative for one of the region's largest asphalt and ready-mixed concrete suppliers. Cove was one of his clients and Martin knew that Tony would be amused to see where he had recently taken up residence.

Martin headed back to Boston and had just merged onto I193 when he received a telephone call from Rob Hayes, at the pharmacy jobsite.

"I'm sorry I didn't get back to you sooner, Martin. I got a bit confused with the different cell numbers you were leaving. Your messages said that you're staying at the Boston Harbor Hotel. What's all that about?"

"It's pretty crazy," responded Quinn, "you've got to check out my new digs. Do you want to come in and have a beer this evening after work? Just ask for me at the front desk. If I'm not in my room, I'll probably be in the Jacuzzi in the health club. If that's the case, just come on down and let them know you're my guest and they'll give you swimming trunks, towels, and a bath robe."

Upon his return to the hotel, Martin checked in with the girls at the guests' business office. They had made some phone calls as he had asked and also printed out two faxes. One of them was from his company's insurance agent, Helen Costa. Quinn had asked her to confirm that Cove's policy was adequate for the bridge project. Apparently operations in the vicinity of marine structures required additional classes of insurance coverage, which the policy did not provide. Also, the general liability coverage limits needed to be increased from $2,000,000 to $5,000,000 in order to comply with Seahorse's contract terms. Martin very much appreciated having her as his insurance agent and made a note in his Day-Timer to call her the following day.

Quinn then went across to the front reception desk and requested access to his safe deposit box. He did so for no other reason than to raise his profile in the hotel by engaging and interacting with the staff. He was intrigued to see how much assistance one could receive while staying in the Presidential Suite. Of course he could send his own faxes and make his own calls, but he was a firm advocate for working as a team. He enjoyed the challenge of enlisting the assistance of as many hotel employees as possible.

It was the tall front desk manager, Jim, who responded to his request to open the safe deposit box. Once in the private annex off the main lobby, Martin took this opportunity to share his concerns regarding the hotel's security.

"I don't mind telling you, Jim, that I'm a bit concerned over the lack of security in the hotel."

"You shouldn't have any reason to worry, Mr. Quinn."

"Well, I'm staying in the Presidential Suite and of all the rooms I would have expected this one to be the safest. This must not be the case, however, because the mini-bar refrigerator has a lock on it."

"Oh, that's not because of any security concerns Mr. Quinn," Jim assured him earnestly and without any indication he realized Martin was joking. "That's to stop children from gaining access to the alcohol."

"Thank you for clearing that up for me."

"Not at all, security is something we take very seriously here at the Boston Harbor Hotel. We have undercover personnel patrolling the hotel, as well as our uniformed staff members."

He thanked Jim for his explanation and was left to privately access the contents of his safe deposit box. Martin had only been joking, but it was obvious the young man took pride in both his job and the hotel. Quinn admired this character trait. When he was finished, he pressed the call button on the wall so they could both witness the closing of the box and complete the log book entry.

Back in his room, he spent some time examining and measuring the prototype sections which Sandra had brought to him. He made review notes in the margin of the shop drawings so he could discuss his thoughts later with Louis Fusco. After a while, he decided to go down to the health club.

By 5:00, he was relaxing in the Jacuzzi, mulling over issues which he thought would be raised at Thursday's meeting in Tony Bottazzi's office. Quinn's thoughts were interrupted by a familiar voice. It was Rob Hayes, decked out in a fresh monogrammed bath robe.

"Good afternoon, Mr. Quinn," he announced, in the politest accent he could muster. "Is everything to your satisfaction?"

"I believe one of the fresh towels in the changing room may have a wrinkle in it, but other than that, everything appears to be fine," Martin joked.

The two men relaxed in the spa tub while Hayes was brought up to date on developments with the Seahorse project. Martin also recounted the reservation negotiations which resulted in his occupancy of the Presidential Suite, at a discount rate. Revived and refreshed after their health club session, they decided to eat dinner. Martin wanted to return his shower slippers, swimming trunks, and other toiletries to his room and Rob welcomed this opportunity to see where his friend was residing.

"It's nearly the year 2000 and I can't believe the problem I'm having communicating with the rest of the world," Martin confided as they rode up in the elevator. "I'm using our office manager's Nextel while my own phones are getting replaced. But nobody has this number and I'm sure I'm missing a lot of calls."

"We've become so dependent on these foolish phones."

"Thank goodness for my pager," Quinn acknowledged.

"This is incredible!" Hayes exclaimed as they entered Suite 1608. "You've got the most awesome view of Boston Harbor."

"If you can believe it Rob, the whole experience is actually too good. To be honest, I find it hard to settle down and sleep at night. The atmosphere is too exciting and with everything that's been going on, my life seems to be running on overdrive. Even when bad things happen, they just seem to trigger better experiences."

Before going into the lounge, they stopped at the front desk where Quinn requested his phone calls be put through to the bar and not his room. He was expecting a return call from Police Lieutenant Peter Dorian whom he had asked to follow-up with Shelley Tyre to confirm that there was no restraining order to prevent him from seeing Brendan. Quinn and Hayes accepted menus from the barman, but indicated their preference to eat in the restaurant, so Martin asked the barman to forward his calls there. Having noted the room number written on the bar tab, as well as

Quinn's generous tip, he had no problem with this request. Just as they were being seated, Martin's pager vibrated. It was Lieutenant Dorian. Quinn excused himself and returned to his room, so he could make the call in private.

As soon as he opened the door to his suite, he saw the orange voice-mail light flashing on the hotel phone. Martin was irate. When he checked the message, it was from Peter Dorian. He returned the call and finally managed to speak with his friend. The conversation finished with the lieutenant accepting Quinn's invitation to come into the hotel for a beer, after his shift ended at 10:00.

Martin headed back down to the lobby and straight to the front desk.

"Good evening, Mr. Quinn."

"Good evening, Jim, I need you to have the manager on duty come and see me in the restaurant, please."

"Is everything alright?"

"Not really, but I have a guest waiting for me. Please have the manager come and see me when he or she gets a chance."

Martin and Rob had just finished their salads when a neatly dressed young lady approached the table and asked which of them was Mr. Quinn. She was impeccably presented and appeared to be a very capable ambassador for the hotel. Martin stood up and the young woman introduced herself as Assistant Manager, Caroline Hunter. Quinn thanked her for coming to see him so promptly and asked her to join them so he could explain his problem.

"Ms. Hunter, I don't want to use the language that first comes to mind to describe how I feel at the present time. I'm staying in your Presidential Suite, however, I feel like calling for a limo' so I can pack my belongings and head to the nearest discount motel. I believe a stay there would be less stressful than what I'm experiencing here!"

"I'm truly sorry to hear this. If I can't correct this problem and take care of your needs one hundred percent, then I'm not doing my job. Please explain why you are so disappointed and what I need to do to regain your trust."

Quinn relayed how his phone calls had not been put through to the bar as requested causing him to miss an important call from a party he had been trying to reach all day. He refrained from explaining how his own cell phone problems had led to his reliance on the hotel staff.

"I have no idea how this mix up happened, but I can assure you it will not happen again. Is there anything else we can do to make your stay more comfortable?"

"Well, now that you ask, there is something. I have some large aluminum components in my room that are part of a project I'm working on. I would like to place them on the dining table without scratching the polished finish. Perhaps you could have Housekeeping cover half the table, but leave the end closest to the window clear for my books and files. Also, the cord on the phone at this end of the suite is not long enough for it to be placed onto the dining table. Could you please replace the cord between the wall jack and this phone, so I can use it where I'll be working? Oh, and one last thing. I need an alarm clock for my room."

"I'll make sure all this is taken care of within the hour," Ms. Hunter promised, pushing back her chair. "Also, please let me know immediately if there are any other issues. Here is my card and this is the direct phone line to my desk. Now, I'd like you to enjoy dessert and coffee this evening with our compliments."

* * * * * * *

After Hayes left, Quinn returned to his room. The sound of the Aerosmith CD playing in the background greeted him as he entered the suite. He had to walk into the room about twelve feet and pass the bathroom door before he could look over to his right towards the formal dining area. A table cloth was neatly folded over on itself and covered the half of the table closest to the wet bar, while a phone sat at the other end. An alarm clock radio was placed next to a lamp on one of the two side tables that were positioned where the corners of the couches met to form a horseshoe layout in front of the entertainment system. "It's like having my own genie," he smiled to himself. "All I have to do is ask for wishes and they're granted."

He arranged the cable race way components in an orderly fashion on the table and then got a tape measure and the Vernier calipers from his canvas briefcase. "This is a perfect work area," he thought aloud as he transferred his Day-Timer and other files from the small writing desk onto the dining table adjacent to the phone. Five minutes later, everything was as he wanted. Without realizing, Quinn became engrossed in shop drawing review and careful inspection of the various raceway components. On this project, Martin elected not to follow the standard industry practice of having the subcontractor or manufacturer prepare its own shop drawings. He was not comfortable with Anderson's ability to do so within the tight time constraints of this job. Consequently, Cove Construction prepared the shop drawings. By doing this, however, the company was assuming more liability in the event of an error. Nevertheless, Quinn believed this was the best course of action since he needed to keep control of the design and it had to be completed quickly. His concentration was interrupted by the door bell ringing.

"Not too shabby at all," the police lieutenant observed as he entered, "I'm very impressed."

"Look, Peter," Martin instructed, opening the closet next to the bathroom, "even in the midst of all this luxury, I have to use plastic supermarket bags to carry my belongings!"

"This is such a spectacular view. If I ever get thrown out of my house, I know exactly where I'm going to come - even if I can only afford it for one night."

Dorian walked over to the table, lifted one of the four foot long aluminum channels and balanced it in the palm of his hand.

"So this is what you've been working on for the past month."

Martin took a few minutes to explain how the system worked and then showed Peter the letter from Seahorse Communications indicating how much Cove would be compensated for the project.

"We should make at least $250,000 for just three weeks work in the field. I'm concentrating on the most important task at the minute. Once I sign off on these drawings and release the order into fabrication, all the difficult work will have been completed. After that, I'll just be hanging out at Narragansett Bay, enjoying the view and making sure my crew gets the job done on time."

Quinn got two beers from the refrigerator and the friends relaxed in front of the big-screen TV. He turned down the volume on the CD player and surfed sports channels until they found a hockey game. Peter was a good friend, not just to Martin, but to the whole Quinn family. They had met through their children's hockey program. Peter's son, Mark, was the same age as Brendan and they had been on the same team for several years. Dorian was one of the coaches and was loved by both parents and children alike.

"If Brendan's at practice tomorrow evening, I'll let him know that his dad is doing alright. Now, what's going on with you and Margaret?"

Martin explained how overwhelming his recent work schedule had been and the stress it caused at home.

"It's going to be hard to give up life here in the Presidential Suite," Quinn joked, "but I hope to be back home by Monday at the latest."

Peter declined the offer of a second beer.

"My primary reason for coming in tonight was to make sure you're okay. I can see that's certainly the case, but don't hesitate to ask if you need anything."

"Thank you, Peter. With all that's been going on recently, one thing I've come to appreciate, is how fortunate I am to have good friends."

The brief visit ended shortly before 11:30. Martin gathered blankets from the closet to make up his bed on the largest of the three couches. He fell asleep with the TV playing in the background.

12:50AM - Thursday March 4, 1999

Brian Molloy was a small-time drug dealer who made a living in the Boston suburbs of Allston and Brighton, using product supplied by Xavier Santos. It had not been his intention to visit the Cocoa Bean that evening, because he owed its owner $20,000 for merchandise previously furnished. Over the past week, Molloy had been unable to avoid Santos' phone calls and with no apparent means of paying the debt, he kept well away from the nightclub. At least until that evening. Quite unexpectedly, Molloy's brother Jack repaid $30,000 he had borrowed. Brian could not believe his luck, but knew better than to ask his brother how he had earned the money. All he could think about was putting an end to his supplier's menacing phone calls.

Far in the distance he could hear the rhythmic pounding beat of a Rob Zombie song. As the noise volume increased so did the agonizing pain, throbbing in concert with the demonic drone. Duct tape prevented him from spitting out the rolled up hundred dollar bills. These muffled his frantic attempts to empty his lungs and alert the oblivious drunken patrons who were dancing elsewhere in the building. Somehow he had found himself in the basement of the Cocoa Bean with Xavier Santos towering above him, leaning on the handle of a ten pound sledge hammer as if it were a gentleman's walking stick. The 6-mil clear polyethylene sheet spread out on the cellar floor made it difficult to get a proper grip as he tried to lean forward on his elbow. It had only taken one blow of the sledge hammer delivered to each of his knee caps to pulverize them beyond recognition, mercifully causing him to lose consciousness.

Earlier that evening when Brian followed his gut instinct and decided to repay Xavier, he unwittingly sealed his own death warrant. President Ronald Reagan could not have envisioned the type of horrendous consequences which Molloy was enduring, when he extolled the virtues of trickle down economics. The money his brother, Jack, gave him earlier that afternoon had, until recently, been hidden inside the false bottom of an ornate footstool. Santos placed his left foot on the outstretched wrist in an effort to steady the elbow joint as he brought the sledge hammer down upon it. Molloy passed out again.

Brian knew that giving up Jack's name as the source of the money would not save his own life. As he regained consciousness, he realized that relief from pain was only seconds away when he saw Santos threading an EVOLUTION-9 suppressor onto the muzzle of a 9mm Glock pistol. The last sensation Brian Molloy experienced before his life ended was a faint smell of cedar, given off by the roll of hundred dollar bills stuffed inside his mouth. Santos recognized the distinctive aroma when he had been given the money an hour earlier, even before checking to see their dated serial numbers.

5:00AM - Thursday March 4, 1999

Quinn was wide awake after only four hours sleep. He recalled a brief interruption during the night by a Blu-Blocker Sunglasses infomercial which prompted him to turn off the TV. He had arranged to meet Tony Lopez at 6:30 for breakfast in the health club. With at least an hour to pass before then, he finished reviewing the final shop drawings for Anderson. His mind was fresh and he wanted to be able to report to John Grasso that everything was released into production. By 6:15 he was satisfied with his review notes and modifications which he had made on the five 81/2 X 11 shop drawings. He placed them neatly aside before gathering his swimming trunks, toiletries, and a change of clothes. Fortunately, the hotel's prompt laundry service was compensating for his limited wardrobe.

That morning, his elevator did not go directly to the health club, but stopped on the first floor. The doors opened to reveal Tony Lopez.

"Mr. Quinn!"

"Good morning, Mr. Lopez," replied Martin as the two men shook hands.

Although good friends, they re-enacted their established routine of greeting each other formally using last names.

"It looks like you've got everything you need for your morning workout," Martin observed, tugging on Tony's black gym bag which had a New England Aggregates logo on the side.

"I just took this out of its plastic wrapper this morning. It was given to me last year at our company's annual golf tournament. I couldn't very well walk into the Boston Harbor Hotel with a used gym bag."

"I'm impressed," Quinn grinned.

After swimming a few laps in the pool, the two men retired to the Jacuzzi. Each enjoyed a glass of freshly squeezed orange juice as Martin recounted how he came to be living amidst such lavish opulence. They split their time between the Jacuzzi and the breakfast area where they enjoyed fresh fruit, cereal, and coffee, before heading back to the locker room.

While he was getting dressed after his shower, Martin could hear two men discussing their recent court room appearances. They were standing nearby so it was impossible not to overhear their conversation.

"The pre-trial conference only took a few minutes," stated the heavier of the two gentlemen. "I told the judge my client would plead down and pay the $40,000 fine, but wasn't prepared to do any prison time."

"What did he say?"

"He indicated that it was a decision for the District Attorney's office, but also pressured the young ADA by drawing our attention to the court's heavy schedule and back-log. Five minutes later, I had a deal for my client with no prison time."

"Excellent!" commended his colleague.

At that point, Martin decided to interrupt.

"Excuse me," he began, addressing the larger of the two men. "You wouldn't happen to be an attorney by any chance?"

It was hardly a shot in the dark. Apart from the subject matter of their conversation, there were also the designer suit pants, the "GG" monogrammed dress shirt pocket, gold cuff-links, and spotless black wing-tip leather shoes. Furthermore, the hotel was no more than a ten minute walk from the new Federal Court House. Martin reckoned that they were non-resident health club members.

"Yes, I am an attorney, why do you ask?"

"I might need some help on a matter."

"Well, I hope you don't need my help, because I'm a criminal defense attorney," he retorted, reaching out to shake hands and introduce himself, "George Grey."

"Hi, Martin Quinn. Not to worry, if you can't help, maybe you can refer me to a colleague. Why don't you give me a call and perhaps we can schedule an appointment?"

"I'll call you later today when I have my calendar in front of me," responded Martin's new attorney friend. "Do you have a business card?"

"I'm sorry, I don't have any with me," Quinn apologized as he turned to Lopez, "but you can call me here at the hotel. Tony, do me a favor and write out my name and room number on the back of one of your cards for George, please."

Martin wanted to create an impression with this stranger that he had people to take care of even the most menial of tasks, such as giving out contact information.

"What's your room number?" Lopez asked, while writing Martin's name on the back of one of his own business cards.

"1608," Quinn replied, before Tony handed it to the attorney.

"Thank you Martin, I'll call you later from my office," the attorney replied, as he placed the card in his front breast pocket and continued adjusting his collar and tie.

This whole encounter had been spontaneous on Quinn's part. His prime motive for engaging Grey was his belief that if this attorney was paying the exorbitant fees to be a member of the health club, then he was probably a prominent person in the Boston legal community. Appreciating the benefit of having influential contacts, especially within the justice system, he reckoned that his residence in the Presidential Suite endorsed this introduction. He was confident that Grey would be intrigued enough to reach out and contact him. Quinn did not share society's caustic evaluation of lawyers. They were very often vilified - not just by stand-up comics, but also by business professionals, frustrated by the invoices associated with their legal services. Martin believed that a good lawyer was no different from a good plumber, a good electrician, or even a good construction laborer. If they provided a quality service, then they should be properly compensated. Why should any individual take time out of his or her day to resolve somebody else's problems, without getting paid to do so?

Soon after George Grey and his colleague left the locker room, Martin and Tony did so too. As they stood in the main lobby of the hotel, Lopez repeated his fascination at Quinn's recent sagas and suggested the two men meet the following week for a beer.

"What are you doing tonight, Tony?"

"I have to go to a wake. My great aunt passed away on Monday."

"I want to have some people over to the hotel this evening for dinner. I've got a meeting in Rhode Island this afternoon so I don't intend on eating until at least 8:30 or 9:00. Why don't you come over after the wake?"

"That would be great, but I'll be with my sister, Nicole. We're going to the funeral home in Medford together."

"Bring her along too. I'll count you both in. We'll have cocktails in the Presidential Suite before dinner. Just get over here whenever you can," Quinn insisted, as the two men parted.

* * * * * * *

Martin brought down the revised shop drawings, which he wanted to fax over to Anderson Aluminum, to Jennifer in the guests' business office. She made several entries in her notebook as he went through his to-do list for her.

Upon his return to the suite, Quinn was greeted by Steven Tyler and Aerosmith in the background, as well as the voicemail light flashing on the hotel phone. He turned down the CD and retrieved the message. It was from George Grey, who had left his direct number for a return call and indicated that he would be in his office until 11:00. Conscious that his residence in the Presidential Suite was likely to end on Saturday, Martin decided to return the call immediately.

"George Grey," the voice answered.

"George, it's Martin Quinn. Thank you for getting back to me. I got your voicemail."

"Hi, Martin, you said that you'd like to get together. Do you want to grab a sandwich at lunch-time today?"

Martin could have done so; however he did not want George to think his schedule was so light, he could agree to the first time that was suggested. Besides, if Grey wanted to meet the man in the Presidential Suite, Martin did not want to make it too easy.

"Lunch-time doesn't work for me today."

"I have an hour open at 4:00," Grey countered.

"I'm traveling out of state this afternoon," Quinn explained truthfully. "Can you meet for lunch tomorrow?"

"That works for me," the attorney replied.

"Why don't we eat here at the hotel," suggested Martin, "say 12:30."

"I'll meet you in the Bistro restaurant just off the main lobby."

"Looking forward to it, George - see you then."

His next call was to Chris Donovan to tell his superintendent that he wanted him to attend the 3:00 meeting in Bottazzi's office. Quinn also instructed him to bring the new cell phones that Sandra had ordered.

"Chris, have you got anything planned for tonight?"

"What's today," Donovan thought out loud. "Thursday. No, tonight is free. Why do you ask?"

"I'm going to have some people over for dinner this evening. I'd like to invite you and your wife."

When the conversation with Donovan ended, he picked up the fax he had received the day before from his insurance agent, Helen Costa. After a quick review, he called her to discuss it further. Helen thoroughly explained the details, and also the cost of modifying Cove's insurance coverage so it would be compliant with the terms of its contract with Seahorse, as well as Department of Transportation regulations.

"How come you're staying in the Boston Harbor Hotel?" she inquired when they had finished talking business.

"Helen, you've no idea how lucky I've been recently. I've actually been staying in the Presidential Suite all week, but I can't put everything down to luck. People like you have been an incredible help."

"I'm only too happy to help. This particular insurance issue is something I happen to be more familiar with than perhaps other agents might be. Since our office is in Hingham, a lot of our clients happen to own boats."

"Would you and your husband like to come in for dinner this evening at the hotel? I'm having a few people over and both of you would be more than welcome."

"That's really nice of you to offer, Martin," she replied in a disappointed tone, "but Justin and I already have plans for this evening. Now I'm upset because the Boston Harbor Hotel is one of my favorite buildings. It looks so majestic with that arch which opens up to the harbor. Thank you for being so considerate. Perhaps another time?"

"I'll probably be checking out this weekend. So why don't you come in tomorrow morning for breakfast. I'll have the hotel send a car to your office."

"I can't put you to that bother, Martin."

"Not at all, if you only knew my lifestyle at the moment, then you'd realize that it's not any bother at all. Far from it. I'll have a car at your office tomorrow morning at 7:45. I apologize for it being so early, but I already have a lunch appointment. The car will have you back at work by 10:30."

Quinn spent some time ordering concrete manholes and sewer pipe for one of Cove's jobsites, as well as preparing for his meeting later that afternoon. He only had one copy of the letter of understanding that John's boss, Kevin Shaw, had sent out on Monday evening. Martin did not want to return his original, so he brought it down to the business office and had Jennifer make some copies. He countersigned one of them and placed the original in his safe deposit box with the Anderson contract. This letter, coupled with the Anderson agreement, locked up Cove's control of this project. He then returned to his room to finalize his preparation for the meeting at Bottazzi's office.

There was something about the Presidential Suite which was beginning to bother Martin, but he had a problem identifying exactly what it was. Everything looked fantastic. The view of Boston Harbor was spectacular. The hotel staff took care of all his requests and ever since he had the discussion with the assistant manager, they appeared to be even more attentive to his needs. As he looked around, he suddenly realized what it was. The music! The CD player had only one disc by Aerosmith, which was playing repeatedly at a low volume. He reached for the remote control and turned it off, wishing that he had brought some of his own CDs from home when he left on Sunday evening.

He then called Jeff Anderson to confirm that he and Louis had received his fax with the marked up shop drawings.

"I spoke to the foundry in Canada about an hour ago," Jeff reported. "They've committed to putting us into their production schedule within the next fourteen to twenty-one days."

"That should work fine because we don't need the top cover sections on the job until after we have the fiber-optic cable in place. Seahorse's primary concern is that we have supporting brackets and lower raceway sections in place to receive fiber-optic cable on or before April 15."

"It's going to be close," Jeff acknowledged, "but I think we'll make it. What bothers me is the anodizing. There are only a few facilities that can work on sections longer than ten feet."

"Well, we have to get it done. You gave your word to Kevin Shaw on Monday afternoon. Don't keep any problems to yourself. Let me know immediately if you have an issue, so we can work on resolving it together. That's very important."

At lunch-time Quinn felt like getting some fresh air. He took a brisk walk around the historic Faneuil Hall area before stopping at the "Black Rose" bar for a sandwich and cup of chowder. As he walked back to the hotel, Martin speculated as to how Fred Ross would conduct himself during the meeting that afternoon. His concentration was interrupted by the doorman of the hotel.

"How are you today, Mr. Quinn?"

"Fine, thank you," replied Martin as he entered the main lobby.

He had only been in the hotel for two days and yet many of the staff knew his name! "How funny is that?" he mused. "They must make it their business to keep on top of who is in the high priced suites. If they only knew, that I'm in the Presidential Suite because I didn't want to pay full price for a regular room!"

* * * * * * *

Chris Donovan was already in the parking lot of Bottazzi Associates when Martin arrived. He sat into Donovan's truck and quickly inspected the three new phones. Quinn also signed payroll checks which he had instructed Sandra to send as well.

"Why don't we put my new phones into the Jeep," Martin suggested. "I'll not need them in the meeting. We'll just bring this Nextel for John Grasso."

Tanya welcomed the two men as they stepped out of the elevator and into the reception area. At that moment, John Grasso came walking down the hallway.

"I thought I heard you. Come on back, we're going to meet in Tony's office."

Martin introduced Chris Donovan as Tony stood up from behind his desk to greet them.

"Well, we're just waiting for Fred Ross to arrive," Grasso began. "He just called to say he was running late because of traffic."

"He should have been coming south on I95 like we just did," Chris thought aloud, "we didn't hit any traffic problems."

No one seemed surprised by Chris' observation.

"There's something we can take care of while we're waiting," Martin suggested. "John, during this job, I don't want you to have any problem communicating with me or any of my crew. So I got you a Nextel phone that's programmed into our system. You'll now be able to speak with anyone in our company by just pressing a button."

"I'm impressed," Grasso replied as Quinn opened the box containing the new phone.

"It has two modes of operation. There's a regular cellular service and since you already have a cell phone, we've opted for the cheapest plan, with the fewest minutes, if that's okay."

"That's fine; I can't believe that you did anything like this."

"The second mode is similar to a two-way radio. You just have to scroll down the list of employee names and select who you want to speak with, by pressing this button on the side. There's no dialing required. Just release the button after you've spoken, so the other party can reply."

Quinn decided to demonstrate Grasso's new phone by having it communicate with Donovan's. The new Nextel made an annoying squelching noise, the like of which Martin had never heard before. More importantly Chris' phone remained silent. He tried again, but with the same result.

"Well, this isn't a great endorsement for Nextel," Quinn vented.

"Sandra mentioned that the rep' had problems programming the phone when he delivered it," Donovan offered.

"Why did she take it from him if it wasn't working correctly?" Martin asked with frustration.

The failed demonstration did not diminish Grasso's appreciation of the gesture. As Martin struggled to return the phone and its accessories into the original packaging, Tanya announced over the intercom that Fred Ross was in the lobby.

Ross entered and apologized for running late. No one made any effort to respond and John Grasso took control of the meeting.

"Well, let's get started. I need your countersigned copies of the agreement letter. Tony gave me his copy before you guys arrived."

Martin took Cove's countersigned letter from his briefcase and handed it to John.

"My attorney has given me a list of concerns which he advises be resolved before I sign it," Ross announced.

"Look, Fred," Grasso responded sternly, "Kevin Shaw gave me explicit instructions before I left to come here. Only people whose company has countersigned his letter are to be included in this meeting. If you're not part of this meeting, then you'll not be involved in the project going forward. The terms of this letter are not negotiable."

"There are only three points that need to be addressed," Fred protested.

John interrupted, before he could continue.

"Fred, stop! I don't have time to keep repeating myself. I personally hope that you don't endorse it. You've had it since Tuesday and haven't represented until now that you had a problem. Kevin Shaw was very clear with me this morning. If I have a countersigned letter from you, then you can remain in the meeting. If I don't, then I'm to ask you to leave. You and your attorney can take it up with Seahorse's legal department. You'll have plenty of time to devote to the matter, because you won't be involved with this project."

Fred did not say another word. He retrieved a pen from a pouch in his executive leather folder, endorsed his copy of the agreement letter, and handed it to John Grasso.

"Thank you," John acknowledged. "With that issue resolved, I want to set everyone straight on how Seahorse Communications wants this job to be run. We are the ones who will be paying for this work to be completed, therefore, it's important everyone understands that it needs to be done in the manner we decide. Everyone will have a role to play in this project and no one is to operate beyond their specific tasks without first obtaining my written permission. Tony Bottazzi's company has been, until now, the primary point of contact for the State of Rhode Island and the bridge's owners. I want this situation to remain unchanged. The State will have inspectors visit the job from time to time. Should they have any questions or issues, then you are to have them communicate with Tony's office. Cove will be responsible for manufacturing the raceway system and installing it on the bridge. Fred, your company will be preparing weekly status reports and forwarding them to my office each Monday morning. Has anyone any questions about anything I've just said?"

"John, I have an issue, if you don't mind," Martin interjected, looking directly at Ross. "I want to ensure that Fred does not communicate with my crew in the field. By all means he can visit the site and walk back and forth across the bridge all week if he so chooses, but if he has any questions for my company, then I want him to direct those inquiries to me, and only me."

"I would assume your company will have a superintendent on the project," Ross responded indignantly. "Shouldn't he be able to answer any questions I might have?"

"No, Fred. While my men are working on this bridge, it is imperative they are not interrupted. There's boat traffic below and vehicular traffic, two feet away, driving by at sixty miles per hour. I don't want them being unnecessarily distracted. I will give you a weekly report, in writing, every Friday morning and you can call me at any time if you have other questions. I'll also be directing my men not to engage in any discussions with you."

Martin could see John Grasso smiling as Ross was beginning to realize just how limited his involvement was going to be. The meeting continued addressing logistical issues pertinent to all parties, other than RossCon Enterprises.

Prior to concluding the meeting, John solicited input from the assembled team. Tony declined the invitation and so did Fred. Quinn could not determine whether Ross genuinely had nothing to contribute, or if he had finally realized that no one wanted to hear anything he had to offer. Martin could not let the proceedings end without messing with Fred, one more time.

"I have a final item regarding insurance," Martin began. "It's important that any entity working on this job comply with Federal Department of Transportation regulations related to operations being undertaken in the vicinity of navigable waterways. This bridge has considerable boat traffic below and falls within the jurisdiction of the Department of Transportation. Regular contractor's insurance is not adequate. So I'm confident John, that you'll make sure Fred's insurance agent provides you with proof of such coverage, before you allow him to visit the bridge on your company's behalf?"

"I don't need any special insurance," Ross protested, "I won't be doing any work. I'm just observing as a consultant."

"I don't make the law," Quinn responded. "Even a ball-point pen striking a boat passing below the bridge would cause all sorts of problems. Once the attorneys realize that Cove is the only one with valid insurance, it will become embroiled in lawsuits, regardless of its culpability. If you don't have proper insurance, I won't tolerate you visiting the work site and I'm sure John Grasso isn't going to expose Seahorse Communications to this liability either."

This had not been a good meeting for Fred, which was clearly evidenced by the expression on his face. John requested that everyone either have their insurance agent forward proof of insurance directly to his office, or provide a notarized affidavit that they would not visit the bridge during the project. The term, "as useful as tits on a bull," seemed to be the most appropriate simile to describe Ross' involvement, Martin thought to himself. He did not feel sorry for Fred in the least. He could have been part of a tight team on a high profile project which had the potential to reward everyone, more than adequately, for their efforts.

Greed had turned everything upside down for him. He was isolated and despised by everyone involved and had absolutely no credibility.

When the meeting ended, Fred was the first to leave. Martin, John, and Chris chatted with Tony Bottazzi for a few minutes before going out into the parking lot. As Chris Donovan said goodbye and got into his truck, Quinn turned to Grasso.

"Listen John, I need to ask you something and I'm not going to take 'no' for an answer. This week, I'm staying at the Boston Harbor Hotel and tonight I'm having a few friends over for a small dinner party. I'd like you and your wife to be my guests. You won't need to worry about driving in and out of Boston, because I'll get you a room."

"That would be awesome, let me call Amy right now and see if she's up for it."

"You'll have to use your own phone," Quinn joked as he waved the box containing the malfunctioning Nextel.

Grasso smiled as he dialed his wife's number. Two minutes later, he was giving Martin the thumbs up sign.

"I'll take care of your reservation. Just check in at the front desk and give me a call when you guys have settled into your room. We'll have cocktails in the Presidential Suite before dinner."

"What do you mean? Who do you know in the Presidential Suite?"

"Me! That's where I'm staying this week."

"What the fuck!" John exclaimed. "How come you're in the Presidential Suite? How much is that costing?"

"Less than your room, but it's too long of a story to go into now. I'll explain everything tonight."

On the drive back to Boston, Quinn made several calls including one to his recently recruited personal assistants at the hotel guests' business office. Alison confirmed the numbers for his dinner party, reserved a room for the Grassos, and arranged for extra beers and sodas to be brought to his suite.

When Quinn entered the Presidential Suite, he found additional ice coolers stocked with Heineken and Amstel beers, as well as a selection of soft drinks. There were additional glasses, fresh bar towels, and a generous selection of chips and snacks. He turned on the Aerosmith CD, opened a beer, and headed into the bathroom to take a shower.

7:55PM - Thursday March 4, 1999

The first guests to arrive were Tony Lopez and his sister, Nicole. Martin welcomed them and offered his condolences on the passing of their aunt. He recalled seeing Nicole at a New England Aggregates function some years earlier, although they had not been formally introduced until that evening. She had dark hair like her brother, was very attractive, and probably in her mid-thirties.

Chris Donovan arrived on his own with news that his wife was laid up with a head cold. John and Amy Grasso completed the group shortly thereafter. Everyone was extremely impressed by Quinn's choice of hotel accommodation.

"So is this going to be Cove's new world headquarters?" John Grasso surmised jokingly.

"No," replied Martin. "This is just the construction office for your Jamestown project! I'm going to arrange for a boat to pick me up at the dock below and bring me around to Narragansett Bay each day."

"If that's the case, I'll have to spend a lot more time out of the office supervising this project."

For the next hour everyone relaxed and listened to Martin and John recount various comical episodes involving Fred Ross. The raceway prototype components and shop drawings were spread out over the dining table from when Quinn had worked on them earlier that morning. Every now and again, he or John lifted one of the pieces to demonstrate some aspect of their story. The girls divided their attention between these tales and the fabulous view of Boston Harbor.

"Why do you need so many phones?" Amy Grasso asked, gesturing towards the four cell phones sitting on the dining table.

"One of the Nextel phones was supposed to be for your husband," Martin began. "Since Seahorse doesn't have Nextels for its employees, we got one for John to use while we're working on the Jamestown project. When we gave it to him earlier this afternoon, it wouldn't work properly."

"Good idea," commended Tony Lopez. "I've never heard of a contractor furnishing its client's project manager with a cell phone."

"Cove's not like any other contractor and we regard Seahorse Communications as a very important client," Quinn emphasized.

"That only explains one of the four phones," Nicole Lopez observed.

"Well, that other one is a replacement for my regular cell phone which got dropped and smashed. This one is an exchange for my old Nextel phone because its key pad went on the fritz a few weeks back. It took them nearly a week to make the swap, so I've been using our office manager's Nextel for the past few days. That's the fourth one."

"If anyone was to come in here right now they'd think that they had walked onto a movie set," Amy remarked. "It seems quite exciting to be up here in the Presidential Suite with all these cell phones, pieces of aluminum, and technical drawings scattered across the table!"

"I love America," Quinn replied. "Come on, let's go eat!"

A smartly dressed maitre d' greeted the party and escorted them to a secluded table in a quiet corner of the dining room. The service and attention to detail by the staff was first class. No one's wine glass was permitted to run dry. Each dinner course was beautifully presented and tasted every bit as good as it looked.

Martin enjoyed this opportunity to get to know John Grasso outside the work environment. He was intrigued to discover that John had actually worked extensively in Boston several years earlier, overseeing fiber-optic cable installations with another employer. Grasso's schooling was also fascinating. Seemingly, his education since high school had been primarily in acting. As a keen student of mime, John had studied with one of the world's best artists and had even worked as a circus clown! He managed a rock band on the side but was finding this to be too much work, now that the band was beginning to get established. Quinn had never encountered anyone who had come into the industry via such an unusual route.

By 11:30, Martin's guests were drinking coffee, trying to fight the effects of the late hour and sumptuous meal. Not everyone finished dessert. This was no reflection on how it tasted, but rather how good the prior courses had been. Tony Lopez was the first to thank Quinn for his hospitality.

"I have a morning full of meetings and the first one starts at 6:30," he explained.

"You're working yourself too hard. You need to take a leaf out of my book."

"We all don't have the luck of the Irish like you," Tony replied.

Nicole also thanked Martin for dinner and expressed her genuine enjoyment with the whole evening.

"I've got an early start in the morning, myself," Chris Donovan added. "Why don't we share the elevator?"

The three guests left Quinn and the Grassos to finish their coffees.

"What about a night-cap back at the Presidential Suite?" Martin suggested.

"Sounds good to me," John agreed.

"You guys can go ahead, but I really have to call it a night," Amy declined, "I'm exhausted."

After a brief detour outside to the boat dock so the Grassos could each smoke a cigarette, they made their way to the elevators.

"Good evening, Mr. Quinn," greeted the front desk manager as they walked by.

"Good evening, Jim."

"Everyone seems to know you by name," observed John as they stepped into the elevator.

"I can't say enough about the staff. I had a little issue earlier in the week with my incoming phone calls. Once that got corrected, it's been nothing short of first class all across the board."

The elevator stopped at the fourth floor. John escorted his wife out and told Martin he would join him shortly.

Ten minutes later, Quinn and Grasso were relaxing in the Presidential Suite as John sipped a brandy while Martin nursed a Heineken beer.

John Grasso very much appreciated the invitation into Boston and was clearly relieved to know that his project was on schedule and in good hands. The meeting at Tony Bottazzi's office earlier that afternoon sealed the deal for all concerned. Now the job could continue without any further disruption from Fred Ross. As he surveyed the array of raceway components laid out on the dining table, Grasso recalled when Quinn first brought the sample bracket to Bottazzi's office. Later that morning, when Martin started taking measurements at the bridge using the Vernier calipers, he knew then and there, he had the right man for the job. It was his sense of relief on that occasion which put him off guard during his initial dealings with Ross, but that was all behind him.

"I hope you understand if Cove is able to pull off this job before the April 15 deadline, there'll be a lot more work coming its way from Seahorse."

"Thank you John, I know we can do a good job for you, not only on this project, but on anything else that you give us."

A little after 1:00, the two men called it a night, and John Grasso returned to his room. Quinn tossed some blankets onto the leather couch and was fast asleep, almost before his head hit the pillow.

4:30AM - Friday March 5, 1999

Martin found himself wide awake at 4:30. "This week has been hectic," he thought to himself. He was averaging about four hours of sleep at night, which recently seemed to be more than adequate. His mind was working overtime in a million different directions. There was the fiber-optic bridge project for Seahorse. Then there were the issues with Cove's other jobs. These required more management in winter months due to inclement weather conditions. There was also the discord at home with Margaret. Even though this had landed him in the lap of luxury, he knew this was no way to live. It was just ridiculous. He recognized that it had to be tough on both Brendan and his mother. Hopefully Tom Sullivan's wife would bring Margaret to Maine. Quinn reminded himself to call Tom later that morning to confirm this arrangement. Finally, there was Eddie's sister's suicide. Martin had never experienced a week like it.

It was too early to follow up with phone calls to people who conducted business within the accepted constraints of Eastern Standard Time, so Martin made a few phone calls to friends and family members in Belfast, Northern Ireland. He also sent a fax to his former boss, Graham Simpson. They had kept in touch regularly, so Martin composed a short note on hotel stationery. He knew his friend would be impressed because a few years earlier when he and his wife had visited Boston, they commented on the beautiful hotel, which they had previously seen featured on a television documentary in Northern Ireland.

Quinn got dressed and went down to the front desk where he asked Jim to fax the one page note to Simpson's office in Belfast. When the young man returned the sheet, along with the report page indicating that it had been sent and received, Martin tipped him $20.

"That's quite unnecessary," Jim protested.

"Not at all, you've been a great help all week and I'll probably be checking out tomorrow morning."

"Well I hope you'll come back and stay with us again real soon, Mr. Quinn."

Martin began to tidy his paperwork and job files while choosing not to turn on the Aerosmith CD again. Since he was not a fan of morning television, he decided to listen to "The Hillman Morning Show," with Greg Hill and Lyndon Byers on WAAF 107.3. When he turned on the stereo receiver, it was tuned into 100.1; an oldies rock 'n roll station. He hit the forward search button each time the tuner stopped on a station as it moved along the frequencies. The console had a digital display which identified each station it found. When Quinn heard a disco tune from KISS 108, he realized it had skipped past 107.3. He corrected the problem by hitting the search button to move back down the FM bandwidth. The dial stopped at 106.3, a soft-rock station which was broadcasting an annoying rendition from Kenny G. Martin again hit the search button to move higher on the FM dial, but the system returned to the KISS 108 disco station without stopping at 107.3. The radio receiver did not have a dial that allowed the user to tune into a specific station, but it did have another set of buttons so the operator could move through the FM frequencies at 0.1 increments. Martin repeatedly hit the lower button as the dial counted down until it read 107.3, but this only resulted in a gentle hiss from the speakers and absolutely no trace of a radio broadcast. He continued to play around with the expensive sound system for another five minutes without any success. Similar efforts with the alarm clock radio also proved futile. Then he remembered what the hotel's assistant manager had said to him earlier in the week. "Please let us know immediately, if you have a problem with any of the services provided by the hotel and we will take care of the issue." Martin lifted the phone and called the front desk.

"Yes, Mr. Quinn?"

"Jim, I have a problem with the radios in my suite. They're not picking up WAAF 107.3. Is there someone in hotel maintenance who could check this out?"

"I'll have a technician from our Engineering Department take care of this for you right away, Mr. Quinn."

Martin hung up the phone and continued to work on both the alarm clock radio and entertainment system. Minutes later, he answered his door to a gentleman dressed in a gray technician's lab coat and carrying a leather and canvas tool bag. The visitor introduced himself as Sam from Hotel Engineering.

Sam was clearly better equipped to deal with the problem than Martin was. Apart from the tool bag, the lapel pocket of his coat had different electrical testers neatly clipped onto the top seam. He also had a leather pouch on his trouser belt that contained a small flashlight along with a Leatherman folding tool which appeared to encompass every gadget and blade ever developed. Nevertheless, fifteen minutes later, he too had failed to get Greg Hill on the air!

"I need to go and check the connections to the antenna on the roof," he explained, standing up to stretch his cramped back. "This is very puzzling. Are you sure that the radio station you want to listen to, broadcasts at 107.3 on the FM bandwidth?"

"Absolutely, it's my favorite radio morning show."

"This seems strange," Sam repeated, "I'll be right back."

Martin could not help thinking how funny it was that he was staying in one of the city's most expensive hotel rooms, yet could not listen to his favorite radio station. He believed he knew some folks who would share his sense of humor in this situation. "Surely Greg Hill and his colleagues would see the funny side of this."

The DJs routinely gave out the station's phone number for listeners to call in and contribute to the show. Martin could not remember that number, and not being able to listen to the station was an obvious disadvantage. He believed the telephone number ended with the four digits that corresponded with "WAAF" on the phone keypad. He could not, however, remember anything else.

He picked up the phone and dialed 411 for Directory Assistance.

Quinn did not recognize the number he was given, nevertheless, the phone line clicked and began to ring. An automated voice answered. Martin had been connected to the radio station's main switchboard, not to the broadcast studio. It was only 6:00 and obviously too early for a live operator. He listened to various instructions on the menu, hoping to hear how to get connected to the on-air DJ. No such option was available.

He hung up and called 411 again, but the operator informed him that this was the only listing she had in her system for WAAF.

After redialing the main number, he navigated through the automated prompts and by chance ended up on Lyndon Byers' voicemail. Martin left a brief message explaining that he did not have the regular call-in phone number and had a funny story to share with the morning show, should this voicemail be heard during the broadcast. He left his name and the main phone number for the hotel along with his room number.

He had no sooner finished with that phone call when Sam returned to continue working on the stereo system's radio receiver.

"Everything appears to be okay on the roof," he reported, kneeling down again in front of the hi-fi equipment. "I left my assistant up there to make adjustments to the antenna mast while I observe things down here.

I need to talk to him using my two-way radio, but I'll keep the volume down so I don't make a nuisance of myself, Sir."

"You're not bothering me in the least, just go ahead and do your best to get this sorted out."

Quinn had a mental picture of Sam's assistant struggling on the roof of the building, trying to maneuver a giant set of rabbit ears. While he appreciated the hotel's response to even the most insignificant of his needs, he was beginning to find the whole scenario extremely amusing. Not wanting to miss any of the entertainment, he called down to Jim at the front desk and asked for breakfast to be sent to the suite.

"Did our engineering staff correct the issue with your radio, Mr. Quinn?" the young man asked, conscious that it had been over an hour since the problem was first reported.

"We've had no luck with WAAF; however, we're now able to speak with the control tower at Logan Airport!"

"Good Lord - that's crazy!"

"I was only joking about the airport, Jim, but your engineers are still working on the problem."

"My shift here at the front desk ends in ten minutes at 7:00, I'm going to come up and see this situation for myself. If we need to get anyone else involved, I want to let my boss know before I leave. In the meantime, I'll get breakfast sent to your room."

"Thank you Jim," Martin replied and hung up the phone.

Sam was busy adjusting the radio tuner and talking back and forth on his two-way radio with a "Hector" who was obviously on the roof. Quinn was interrupted by a call from Chris Donovan. During this phone conversation regarding various Cove issues, Sam was summoned by Hector. It was clearly his intention to return because his tools and testing equipment remained laid out on the floor, and there was still no broadcast from WAAF.

Quinn reckoned Rob Hayes would share his amusement at the morning's events, since he was present earlier in the week when the assistant manager insisted the hotel would take care of his every need. Hayes was bemused at how a simple problem could trigger such a response.

"Any other hotel would probably have told you to listen to another station," Hayes offered. "Not the Boston Harbor Hotel, though. These folks aren't going to settle until you're able to hear Greg Hill and his friends!"

"I'll keep you updated on their efforts," Quinn promised.

It was certainly obvious that Martin's phones were operating normally again because he missed two calls during his conversation with Rob Hayes. He found himself arranging the various cellular and Nextel phones neatly on the formal dining table, which was beginning to become his "communications center." Although the two-way feature of the Nextel, intended for John Grasso, did not operate correctly, its regular cell phone mode did function.

At that instant, he had another idea as to how he could contact the folks at WAAF. Boston had an all news radio station, WBZ 1030, which regularly solicited listeners to call in with news tips and traffic problems. "Surely, they'll pass this information along to their industry colleagues," he thought as he looked up their number in the phone book. Quinn used the hotel's land-line, so the station's caller ID would confirm the origin of the call.

"WBZ 1030 News Room, this is a recorded line. What is the nature of your call?"

"I have a news story for your station, but I have one condition. I want you to share the coverage with Lyndon Byers at WAAF."

"Is it a sports story?" the reporter asked, thinking it involved the former Bruins hockey player.

"No. It's not a sports story. I'm staying in the Presidential Suite of the Boston Harbor Hotel. My name is Martin Quinn. I'm going to hang up on this call now. So if you're interested in hearing any more of my story, you can call me back."

He hung up the phone and then decided to call John Grasso. Martin believed that he also would be entertained by the efforts the hotel was making to tune in his radio!

"John, you've got to come up to the suite, it's starting to get pretty crazy here this morning and all because I couldn't tune the radio into my favorite morning show!"

"Are you serious?"

"Yes, you've got to come and see this!"

As Martin hung up the phone, his door bell chimed. He opened the door and was greeted by: the room service valet, complete with breakfast laid out on a cart; Jim, the front desk manager from the night shift; and Sam, the engineering technician who was returning from the roof.

"I was just speaking with Sam about your problem, Mr. Quinn," Jim began, stepping back to allow the breakfast cart to get pushed through the doorway. "He's never encountered anything like it before. Every other station appears to be coming through without any problem. Why 107.3 is not getting picked up by the entertainment system in your suite is truly baffling."

"Come on in, Jim, and see for yourself."

Sam was already back on his knees in front of the hi-fi system. Martin thought how ironic it was that this equipment was referred to as an "entertainment system." It was certainly living up to its name that morning!

"Jim, are you all set and finished with your shift?"

"I am. Why do you ask, Mr. Quinn?"

"Well, I need a little help for about fifteen or twenty minutes, if you can spare the time."

"I've no problem staying around if you need something," Jim replied. "What would you like me to do?"

"Let me take care of your colleague here," Martin continued as he tipped the room service waiter and took control of the breakfast cart, parking it beside the large dining table.

"I need some help with my phones. I'll take care of the room's land-line, but I want you to answer any of these if they ring. I'll set you up over here at the coffee table," Martin suggested as he gathered up the three Nextel phones along with the Verizon cellular phone and laid them out for Jim to monitor.

"If anyone calls on the regular cell feature, answer the phone, find out who it is, and ask the party to hold for a minute. I'll either take the call or tell you to let them know that I'll call them back. You'll probably need to take notes," he explained to the young man, as he lifted a legal pad and pen from where he had been working earlier.

"What's all this stuff?" Jim asked pointing to the various fiber-optic raceway components set out on the dining table.

"If I told you what all this was for, then I'd have to kill you!" Martin joked.

Quinn wanted his new assistant to focus his attention on the bank of cell phones.

"If someone calls on the two-way radio mode of these Nextels, the calling party's name will come up on the screen. If I'm on another call and can't talk with them, just press this button on the side of the phone and tell them to, 'stand by for Martin.' You can use their name if you're able to read it off the screen. If I'm not involved on another call, then I'll most likely speak with them myself."

"I've never used one of these before, Mr. Quinn, but they appear to be simple enough," he acknowledged as his new boss demonstrated using two of the Nextel phones.

"I really appreciate you helping me out this morning," Martin continued, slipping $40 into his hand, "I only need about fifteen minutes of help here and I should be all set."

"Thank you, Mr. Quinn," Jim acknowledged, sitting forward on the couch to rearrange the pen and note pad.

Martin had just poured himself a glass of orange juice when the door bell chimed again. He answered the door to a somewhat bewildered John Grasso.

At the same time, Jim was speaking to Rob Hayes on one of the cell phones.

"Please hold for Mr. Quinn," Grasso could hear the young man ask.

Martin took the phone from his new assistant and beckoned John to enter. Rob Hayes wanted to schedule a meeting at his jobsite because he had just found out that the electric utility company intended to relocate a transformer.

"I'll see you at 2:00 on Tuesday," Quinn confirmed while recording the appointment in his Day-Timer.

John Grasso knew what a normal hotel room should look like at 7:00 in the morning. It should be quiet and peaceful – certainly not like this. While Martin was busy on one line, he had a member of the hotel's staff taking a message on another. Then there was a technician speaking on a two-way radio to someone else, while making adjustments to the hi-fi equipment. Grasso did not like what he saw and it showed on his face.

"Hey John," Martin began, motioning towards Jim as he handed back the cell phone, "I need to introduce you to my new Director of Communications!"

Grasso appeared baffled.

"Things got a bit too hectic, so Jim is helping out by covering my incoming calls."

"Good morning, Jim," Grasso offered.

"Sam over here is working on getting my radio tuned into WAAF 107.3," Quinn continued. "He has another technician making adjustments to the antenna on the roof. That's who he's talking to on the two-way radio. They've been working on the problem since 5:30, with no success."

John did not seem very comfortable with the whole scene into which he had just entered. Martin could not understand why that was the case. "What's bothering him?" he wondered. "Last night Grasso was very relaxed and obviously entertained by everything I had to say. But this morning's show is proving not to be the hit that last night's performance was."

Quinn was about to elaborate on his problems with the radio when the room's land-line phone rang. He excused himself and turned towards the dining table to answer it.

It was the WBZ news reporter.

"Is this Martin Quinn?"

"Yes it is."

"This is Paul Murphy with WBZ. What's your story?"

"You agree to share it with Lyndon Byers at WAAF?"

"Sure, if that's what you want."

"Well, I've been staying here in the Presidential Suite of the Boston Harbor Hotel for the past week," Martin began. "The hotel and its staff have been absolutely first class and have taken care of everything that I've asked for. This morning, however, I decided I'd like to listen to my favorite morning radio program, the 'Hillman Morning Show.' Even though there's thousands of dollars worth of electronic entertainment equipment here, it's unable to pick up WAAF."

While Quinn was explaining his story to the reporter, he happened to glance behind himself just in time to see John Grasso quietly guiding Sam and Jim out into the hallway. Distracted by his conversation with the reporter, Martin was unable to comprehend why Grasso was taking control of the hotel staff and giving them instructions that were contrary to his.

"Is that the story?" the reporter asked.

"It sure is," Quinn responded indignantly. "Have you any idea what it costs to stay here in the Presidential Suite?"

Martin was upset and this must have been evident from the tone of his voice. It was not anything the reporter had said which bothered him, but rather what was going on in the suite. "John is my guest," he thought. "So why is he taking charge of my room like this?"

"That's no story!" blurted the reporter before hanging up the phone.

"Fuck him," Martin muttered at the response as he turned to go after Grasso and the others. He ran across the suite and opened the door to the hallway. He had not brought his magnetic door card to operate the lock and consequently could not travel any further than one step beyond the threshold without locking himself out. Quinn stretched forward into the hallway as far as he could, while keeping his right foot wedged against the door jamb. This was just far enough for him to be able to look beyond the alcove and see John, Sam, and Jim stepping into one of the three elevators at the end of the corridor. If any of the men heard Martin exiting his room in pursuit, they made no attempt to look back in his direction.

Quinn's heart started to race. A thousand questions suddenly rushed through his mind. Something was going on, but he could not fathom what it was. There was definitely a marked change in John Grasso's behavior. This was a man who had relied on him so much over the past month.

Now he was ordering hotel staff around as if he owned the place. Who was John Grasso?

He quickly retreated back into the Presidential Suite and locked himself inside. Leaning back against the door, Martin paused and surveyed the hotel suite. In an instant everything became terrifyingly clear. John Grasso was not who he had been claiming to be and his sudden change in behavior was triggered by his mistaken belief that Martin had uncovered his true identity. "It must have been the combination of my four phones, plus technicians working on the hi-fi system and the roof, that rattled him," Quinn surmised. It had been just four days since Grasso discovered that Fred Ross had been surreptitiously recording his conversations using a cell phone. "He must think that I've taken over where Ross left off and that the Nextel I tried to give him yesterday was bugged which was why it wouldn't work." Martin continued rationalizing Grasso's actions. "Did John suspect that the entertainment equipment in the suite had been bugged, causing it to malfunction? Is he afraid that all our conversations yesterday evening have been recorded? Does he think that his own hotel room is bugged too?"

Quinn had to acknowledge that he had given John Grasso good reason to be concerned. John's behavior, however, was giving Martin even more reason to be concerned. He was suddenly convinced there was something sinister about this whole fiber-optic project and was overwhelmed by the horrifying realization that Seahorse Communications was being operated by an organized crime syndicate. "Why would one of the biggest communication companies employ an actor to be a project manager?" he tried urgently to reason. "How did my company get involved with Seahorse Communications?" Cove had no experience working on bridges or with fiber-optic cable installations. This was a project that CellTell Atlantic could not get permission to undertake in the State of Rhode Island. If that wasn't crazy enough, Cove was going to be compensated far in excess of any previous project. Once Fred Ross had been removed from the equation, it seemed to Martin that money was really not the primary concern in any of the decisions that Seahorse made. They appeared to be totally goal driven and did whatever needed to be done, in order to ensure that the project stayed on track. He had no idea how Fred Ross got involved with Seahorse. It had to have been a combination of greed and his ability to lie and lie and lie again. "Grasso must have been assigned to oversee Ross, and then me. How could I have been so blind to the sort of people I was getting involved with?"

Martin continued to interrogate himself. He was now in a complete state of frenzy, fueled by a high octane mixture of torment and disgust. "What the hell am I going to do now? How long do I have before two goons come down the hallway and just throw me out the window?" Quinn's mind clicked into overdrive, frantically trying to process a thousand different scenarios. "It's obvious that Grasso has full control of the hotel. But why wouldn't he? An organization like his would be diversified and spread throughout all facets of society and commerce." He recalled how John had told him the previous evening that he had already installed fiber-optic cable in Boston. Until that morning he believed Grasso was his guest, but clearly this was not the case. The manner in which John had taken control of the hotel staff was alarming, even though it was Quinn's suite and he had tipped them generously throughout the week.

Martin had to think fast. First, he needed to secure the room. There were three ways into the suite: one door from the hallway and one from each of the two bedrooms on either side. All three opened into the room. He wedged two of the aluminum sections of raceway between the handles and floor at each of the bedroom doors. The pile on the carpet helped secure these braces tightly in place. He then wedged the back of one of the dining room chairs against the handle of the hallway door in a similar fashion. When they were all locked and secured, he closed the drapes on each of the three large windows overlooking Boston Harbor. Now he had to find a safe way out of the hotel.

Quinn had never been involved in anything like this in his life. Who could he trust? Why had Seahorse Communications singled out Cove Construction for this project? All sorts of questions continued to bombard his mind as he rationalized that this crime syndicate had obviously targeted the telecommunication industry as one that it wanted to infiltrate. He believed that in the twenty-first century, the fiber-optic infrastructure would be similar to the railways of the twentieth century and canals of the nineteenth century. It was possible to monitor all information flowing between every user on the infrastructure, whether it was a telephone conversation, SMS text message, e-mail, or any other format. Even if the exact contents of the transmission were not monitored, the volume of communications or variation in the pattern could be significant. There was no better industry to control.

Martin remembered a conversation he had some weeks earlier, at one of his construction projects, with an engineer for AT&T. Cove had been scheduled to excavate a public highway in order to work on an existing water main. Prior to starting excavation, the law requires that all relevant underground utility providers are notified, so they can mark the location of their buried services. The AT&T engineer cautioned that if Cove damaged the fiber-optic cable, it would be liable for the loss of income until it was repaired. He explained that this one cable generated over $75,000 of sales revenue every minute! Quinn knew that these communication companies were entrusted with the transmission of a staggering volume of data. Access to such information would be of major interest to organized crime. Certainly anyone who interfered with their agenda would be swiftly and severely dealt with. He needed to get out of the hotel to somewhere safe and this had to happen immediately.

His frantic and terrifying evaluation of the situation was interrupted by a phone ringing. He ran over to the coffee table and shuffled through the pile. He recognized the number. It was Rob Hayes.

"Hi Martin, I need to change the time of next week's meeting, on this transformer issue."

"We can talk about that later. Things have gone very, very wrong for me. I think my life's in danger!"

"What's going on?" Hayes asked in a concerned tone.

"I don't really know, but I need you to call me at this number every thirty minutes. If I don't answer, then I want you to contact the police."

"What will I tell them?"

"Just tell them what I asked you to do and let them know when and where I was when we last spoke. I'm in the hotel now, but it's no longer safe. I've got to work on a plan for getting out of here alive. I'll talk to you later."

Quinn decided to contact his own corporate attorney, Tom Sullivan, as well as George Grey, the attorney he had met in the health club on Thursday morning. He was scheduled to have lunch with Attorney Grey but that could no longer happen. He had Grey's direct phone number and got straight through to his desk. Unfortunately, he was not in his office so Martin left voicemail asking for a call back as soon as possible.

When he called Sullivan's cell phone, he did get an answer. Tom was in his car and on his way to work. Alarmed by Martin's tone and plea for help, he disregarded any plans or appointments that he had for the morning.

"Stay in your room and relax," he instructed. "It shouldn't take me too long to get into Boston. I'm already on Rte. 3 in Braintree. I'll call you as soon as I get into the lobby."

As the call ended, Quinn detected the sound of a helicopter approaching. He carefully peeped out past the edge of the heavy drape, thinking it might be the WBZ traffic helicopter that had been dispatched following his call to the newsroom. Although it did not display the news station's logo, it was hovering level with the window. Quinn pushed back the drape, making him visible to the pilot. The aircraft moved closer to the hotel and held a position approximately one hundred feet from where he stood. Martin quickly grabbed a pen and pad and wrote the word "HELP" in the largest letters that would fit on the page. The window was designed to open no more than six inches. This was just wide enough for him to wave the note pad outside, with the word "HELP" facing the pilot. The black helicopter moved closer and hovered for about fifteen seconds in front of Martin. Suddenly it banked down to the right and sped off towards the Federal Court House.

Quinn quickly closed the window, drew the drapes, and retreated into the room. "Have I made a terrible mistake?" he thought. The helicopter initially seemed to offer a way of communicating his predicament to the outside world, since he could no longer be sure whether or not his phone conversations were being monitored. His efforts to signal the pilot, however, appeared to have been counterproductive, spurring him to react in a more sinister fashion. "The helicopter must have been sent to check out the rear of the hotel and my room was definitely the target. Who sent it?" he questioned as his heart raced even faster. "If it was sent to check me out, then I'm dealing with some seriously connected people! I definitely need to get out of here fast," he concluded in a complete state of panic.

The hotel phone rang and Martin was relieved to hear attorney Grey's voice.

"I just got your voicemail. Is there a problem?"

"My life's in danger. A project that I was working on has gone seriously wrong. Can you come over to the hotel this morning so I can explain?"

"My schedule is open, so I can run over and see what's bothering you."

"Thank you, George," Martin replied and hung up the phone.

Quinn ran around the room checking the three doors and make-shift braces he had put in place to secure them shut. He also adjusted the drapes to make sure they were completely closed. A phone call from Chris Donovan invaded the chaos of his luxurious fortress.

"Chris, something has gone very wrong with the Seahorse deal. I need you to go over to Thayer Academy Middle School this morning and introduce yourself to Shelley Tyre, the Principal. Brendan has early dismissal today because it's the last day of classes before spring break. I don't want him to leave the school alone. I want to make sure you're on campus to keep an eye on him. I don't think we've been dealing with a legitimate company over the past few weeks. Something changed dramatically this morning and I don't want to take any chances. I need to know that if I call your Nextel you can confirm Brendan is safe. Also, if at any time you fail to communicate with me, I want you to take Brendan somewhere safe and contact the police as well as Tom Sullivan, our corporate attorney."

Quinn gave Donovan the cell and office phone numbers for Tom Sullivan and reiterated his instructions regarding keeping in contact every thirty minutes. He then called Thayer Academy and got to speak with Shelley Tyre.

"Shelley, it's Martin Quinn."

"Hi Martin, what can I do for you?"

"I think I'm in trouble. It involves the bridge project that I spoke to you about the other day. I'm sending one of my company's superintendents over to the school to keep an eye on Brendan. His name is Chris Donovan. I told him to report to your office and you would set him up so that he could keep watch over Brendan during the school day without either being noticeable or a problem for you and your staff."

"This sounds serious. Are you sure any of this is warranted?"

"I hope not, but I don't want to take any chances."

Martin gave Shelley his Verizon cell phone number and explained that having Chris Donovan go to the school was just a precaution until he got a handle on what was going on.

Quinn gathered his belongings, folding plans and hastily bundling them into the canvas briefcase along with files related to the Seahorse project. Once that was done, he paced back and forth in the room like a caged animal, trying to go over the sequence of events which had led to his life unraveling so rapidly. He was annoyed with himself for not spotting any signs that should have alerted him to problems with this whole operation. His thoughts were interrupted by the hotel phone ringing. It was George Grey.

"I'm down here in the lobby. We can chat over a cup of coffee in the restaurant."

"I'd rather not, George. Why don't you come up to my room? It's safer here."

After a brief silence, the attorney responded.

"Okay, I'll be right up. You're in room 1608, correct?"

Two minutes later, Grey was ringing the doorbell of the Presidential Suite. Martin checked through the security peep-hole before removing the dining chair from below the door handle. Once inside, George was stunned by what he saw. He was alarmed not only by Martin's disheveled appearance and the room's drawn drapes, but also by the sight of heavy sections of metal fortifying the doors at either end of the suite. Grey was an intimidating man, probably six foot - four inches tall and at least two hundred and sixty pounds. He did not look like a person who backed down from anyone or anything.

"What the hell's going on?" he demanded.

"I got involved in a project with people who I had no business dealing with. I only realized it this morning. The project manager, who I've been working with for the past two months, took over the hotel an hour ago just like he owned it. Until now, he's relied on me for everything, but all that stopped because he thinks I'm recording his conversations."

"What would have made him think that?" George asked.

Martin responded, continuing to speak rapidly and barely pausing to take a breath.

"He came into my room earlier this morning and saw me with four cell phones. Plus I had two technicians from the hotel working on the stereo equipment. I can't blame him if he does suspect that, because both of us had dealings with another individual who had been secretly recording conversations with his cell phone."

"Stop a minute! This isn't making things any clearer for me to understand. Why have you barricaded yourself in this room and what help do you want from me?"

"George," Quinn began again, reaching for his wallet in the back pocket of his pants, "you don't know me. So why don't I begin by showing you my driver's license and giving you a comfort level as to who I am before I begin again."

He handed the attorney his license and then walked over to the dining table where he began rummaging through the papers in his briefcase. He quickly located the letter from John Grasso's boss, Kevin Shaw, which confirmed the award of the bridge project to Cove.

"I'm a fifty percent stock owner of Cove Construction," he continued, trading the letter for his license. "We were recently awarded a $450,000 contract to complete a project that will take approximately three weeks in the field with four men and yield a profit in the region of $250,000!"

"Where's the problem?" George asked cynically, while studying the two page letter.

"It was all too good to be true. Cove is just a small company that's been operating for barely two years. We never have margins like this on our jobs. We've never completed a fiber-optic installation in our lives, nor worked on a highway bridge. It all came together extremely fast in the past few weeks. I thought I was in control of everything until this morning when I realized that is not the case. I think I'm dealing with some organized crime syndicate or some other very powerful and sinister group of people."

George Grey handed back the letter with a concerned expression.

"I don't know who I can trust and who I can't," Quinn continued. "I figured since you're an officer of the court, I can trust you. I also called my company's corporate attorney and he's on his way to the hotel as we speak. Between the three of us, we need to come up with a plan to get me safely out of this hotel. I truly believe that my life is in danger."

"I can get you out of the hotel safely without any problem," George insisted. "So pack up your belongings and meet me in the lobby."

Martin stalled while he considered the attorney's instructions.

"Listen, Martin, regardless of who you believe is going to do you any harm, I've got some very solid connections. If you want my help, then meet me downstairs."

Grey was interrupted by the hotel phone.

"Martin, it's Tom Sullivan. I'm in the lobby."

"I'll see you in few minutes. I have another attorney with me. His name is George Grey and he's coming down right now. Look out for him. He's about six foot - four, and he's wearing a beige overcoat with a brown scarf."

"Okay," Tom replied.

"Get your things together and meet me downstairs," George repeated with authority. "What's your attorney's name again?"

"Tom Sullivan."

As soon as Attorney Grey left, Martin replaced the chair below the door handle and hastily gathered his belongings. He performed a thorough final sweep of the suite before placing the four phones in his briefcase. After peering through the security peep-hole, he removed the chair and exited. Quinn jogged down the hallway and pushed the elevator call button. Seconds passed, though to him it seemed like hours. One set of doors opened revealing an empty car. He quickly entered and pushed every button below the sixteenth floor. When it stopped on the fifteenth, Martin stepped out to let it continue without him, one level at a time. After waiting a few seconds, he summoned another. Again, much to his relief, it too was empty. Quinn was confident he had delayed the elevators so as to impede anyone in pursuit. He jumped inside, pressed the lobby button and slumped back against the wall as the car descended to the ground floor. Martin hastily pushed through a party of guests whose comments suggested they had been waiting longer than they should have expected. Turning to his left, he saw Tom Sullivan and George Grey talking together in the middle of the lobby. He quickly made his way towards the pair who suggested that they all go to the restaurant for coffee.

"I have to take care of a couple of things first," Quinn insisted.

Just then, Martin saw Helen Costa in the distance, walking towards the front desk.

"I had a breakfast appointment with Helen Costa," Martin continued, "that's her over at the reception desk. I think it would be safer if she didn't join us this morning. There's no reason for her to be seen associating with me in the hotel."

"I'll go over and explain the situation," Sullivan suggested.

"I had the hotel send a car to pick Helen up this morning. Make sure that they bring her back to Hingham," Quinn instructed.

Helen turned as Tom approached. She could see Martin beyond and smiled in recognition. The smile dissipated as Sullivan began speaking, but she did look anxiously in Quinn's direction a couple of times during their conversation. Then both Tom and Helen spoke with a receptionist who was obviously being asked to organize the return trip to Hingham. Their brief encounter concluded with an exchange of business cards. Helen gave Martin a little wave as she headed towards the front door of the hotel.

"What a nice lady," Tom remarked upon his return.

"I know," Martin agreed, "I feel bad messing up her morning like this."

"Let's go and sit down in the restaurant," George Grey suggested.

"There's one more thing. I need to get into my safe deposit box. There are contracts in it that I want in my possession immediately. I'll be right back."

Quinn took off, followed by Sullivan, who motioned for George Grey to stay put. At the reception desk, Martin requested access to his safe deposit box and was courteously directed to enter the door to his right. As the two men approached, the electric lock buzzed. Inside, they were joined by the pretty receptionist with whom they had just spoken.

"If you don't mind, Sir, I need to see a photo ID," she began.

They were interrupted by one of the phones in Martin's briefcase. He excused himself and hunted through the bundle to retrieve the one that was ringing.

"Is everything okay?" Rob Hayes asked.

"So far. Call me in another half hour. I'm still here at the hotel."

"Will do."

Martin put the phone back in his briefcase and returned to the business at hand.

"What's your name?" he asked the receptionist as he handed over his driving license.

"Cheryl."

"I only need to get one item out of my safe deposit box this morning. You don't need to give me any privacy," he informed her, while signing the access log against the entry she had just made.

"Certainly, Mr. Quinn," she replied, opening the upper lock of box number 215.

Using his own key in the lower lock, Martin opened its door to reveal the removable metal drawer.

"You know the reason I'm taking this out is because I can no longer trust the hotel's security."

"I'm very sorry to hear that, Sir."

"It's not your fault, but I do have reason to believe that my life's in danger. That's why I have my attorney here with me this morning and that's why I need you to do me a favor, Cheryl."

The color drained from the young woman's face as he shared his fears with her. He recovered the envelope which contained the contract between Cove Construction and Anderson Aluminum as well as the countersigned letter of agreement from Seahorse. Quinn was afraid Cove would have nothing, if he did not have these original documents in his possession. He first checked the contents of the package to make sure everything was intact and then placed it carefully into his briefcase.

"I'm going to give you a Nextel," Martin began as he retrieved Sandra's phone from his bag. Using his own Nextel, he then made sure the obviously concerned girl understood how to use its two-way feature.

"I'll be in the restaurant with my two attorneys. I want you to contact me every thirty minutes to make sure I answer and tell you that everything is okay. If I don't respond, contact hotel security and the police. Also, let me know if anyone comes looking for me at the reception desk."

Tom Sullivan had yet to have an opportunity to spend time with Martin and discuss his concerns. All he could do was assure the young lady that everything would be fine and she should have no reason to be concerned.

"I also need you to let me know if anyone asks you to give them access to my safe deposit box, Cheryl. Can you do this for me?"

"Yes, Mr. Quinn," she replied nervously as Martin and Tom left to rejoin George Grey.

The three men negotiated the busy lobby traffic as they made their way to the restaurant located at the rear of the hotel.

"Three for breakfast?" asked the hostess.

"Yes, thank you," replied George Grey.

She led the men to a table in the middle of the room and placed a menu on each of three place mats.

"We need somewhere more private, please," Martin immediately insisted as he scrutinized the other guests in close proximity to the table. Everyone was a suspect now. Quinn did not know who to trust. Also, he did not want to be sitting with his back to the restaurant entrance.

"May we sit over there by the window in the corner?"

"Why certainly, Sir. Angela will be your waitress this morning. Please let me know if anything is not to your satisfaction."

Quinn positioned himself so he had a clear view of everyone entering and leaving the restaurant. He could also easily observe everything that was happening outside the hotel on the boardwalk, where ferry boats were unloading commuters coming into Boston from Hingham, Quincy, and Logan Airport.

"You look exhausted," Tom Sullivan observed. "I thought I told you to get some rest at the beginning of the week. How on earth did you end up staying in here?"

"I don't know where to start."

"Why don't you begin by telling us why you believe that someone is out to do you harm?" Grey suggested.

As Martin began to speak, the waitress arrived and took a coffee order. Although Quinn was adamant he was not hungry, Tom Sullivan insisted that she bring a selection of muffins. Before she could write anything down, Quinn spotted his cousins' husbands walking towards the table. He was so startled at seeing them that he did not think to ask how they came to be there.

"Adam, David, how are you guys? Let me introduce you to Tom Sullivan and George Grey."

Quinn was unaware Sullivan was expecting to see the new arrivals, since he had contacted Margaret immediately after receiving her husband's call. They both feared Martin was having a breakdown of some sort. She, in turn, reached out for help from his cousins, who subsequently dispatched their husbands to the hotel. He was relieved that two men he trusted had come to help him.

It was George Grey who put an end to the niceties, insisting Quinn explain why he felt his life was in danger. Martin relayed how Seahorse Communications had contracted with Cove Construction to install the specialty aluminum raceway on the Jamestown Bridge, despite Fred Ross' devious efforts to the contrary. He attributed this initial good fortune primarily to the relationship fostered between himself and Seahorse's project manager, John Grasso.

"Until this morning, I was extremely proud of how I had managed to get Cove awarded this contract, but now I realize that I was foolish and naïve."

Martin expanded on his conspiracy theories, and concluded by describing how everything came to a head after he had invited John Grasso to witness the circus which spontaneously developed when the stereo equipment malfunctioned.

"How did you manage to get yourself into the Presidential Suite in the first place?" David asked. "Wasn't a regular room good enough for you?"

"It's just typical of how my life has gone recently. I ended up staying there because I didn't want to pay $450 for a regular room. My efforts to negotiate a cheaper rate resulted in getting the Presidential Suite for only $250 a night!"

No one bothered to question the logic of this explanation. Quinn continued for more than an hour recounting details of his dealings with John Grasso, while remaining vigilant for Seahorse's agents, who he feared may have been trying to infiltrate the area. On one occasion he prevented four businessmen from taking a table within ten feet of where he was sitting. Quinn felt that he could not be too cautious. If they were not actually there to do him harm, they may have been sent over for surveillance. Although the men were willing enough to sit elsewhere, they were not too happy about it. Tom Sullivan helped by supporting his request of the four strangers. Martin had resolved to exercise extreme caution and could no longer trust anyone unless he had an established relationship with that person, prior to the Jamestown project. Everyone had become a suspect.

His thought processes and efforts to bring the group up to speed with his situation were punctuated with calls from Rob Hayes and Chris Donovan, who checked in periodically as instructed. They were definitely a source of comfort which he very much needed. Even people walking back and forth outside the window of the restaurant alarmed him. If Martin caught their eye at all, it fueled his paranoia with concern as to why they were looking in his direction. He was also cognizant of the fact that the layers of heavy winter clothing made it easy to conceal a weapon.

Suddenly George Grey became the target of Quinn's anxiety. Could he be trusted? These fears dissipated when he rationalized that even though the attorney was practically a complete stranger, he was exhibiting concern and an apparent understanding of Martin's predicament.

"If you truly believe that your life is in danger and you need protection, then I can get you all the help you need," George offered, in response to what had just been relayed. "Before I was an attorney, I was employed by the sheriff's department. My duties included working closely with the FBI and other police departments while setting up safe houses for witness protection programs. I have a lot of contacts who can guarantee both your safety and your family's."

"One step at a time," Martin cautioned. "First of all I'm going to get out of this hotel, but only with the help of people I know for certain that I can trust. You all should abide by the same rule."

"What do you mean?" Grey asked. "You need to be more specific."

"I only want you to rely on people who you have known and worked with before any of this happened this morning."

"Is all this really necessary?" Tom Sullivan asked. "Why won't you leave with any of us?"

"I'm not leaving here unless I'm accompanied by my friend, Peter Dorian. He's a lieutenant in the Holbrook Police Department. Since he doesn't have jurisdiction in the City of Boston, I'm going to insist that he's accompanied by a Boston Police officer he can personally vouch for."

Martin was interrupted by a phone call from Chris Donovan.

"I'm here at Thayer Academy and Brendan is safe. I've spoken with Shelley Tyre and explained your concerns. Brendan has classes until lunch-time and then some sort of school performance in the main assembly hall. The school has an early dismissal today. Everything will be wrapped up by 2:30. I'll be staying in my truck that's parked in the corner of the middle school parking lot. I'll keep an eye on Brendan when he goes over to the cafeteria at the high school. I'll also be able to go into the concert this afternoon, so you've no reason to worry."

"That's good. We can decide later what to do at the end of the school day. Keep in touch, Chris."

Martin then went back to answering Tom Sullivan's question.

"I know Peter Dorian can take me to his police station where I'm certain I'll be safe. After that, I can regroup and decide what my next course of action should be. There's no reason to expose any of you to more risk than I may have already."

Tom realized there was no point continuing with the argument. He could see Martin was distressed and adamant regarding whom he would allow assist him, from this point on.

Quinn recovered Lieutenant Dorian's pager number from his Day-Timer, and while he waited for the call to be returned, Adam and David made fruitless attempts to convince him that there was no need to take such precautions.

"Peter, thanks for getting back to me so quickly. My life's in serious danger. I need to get to your police station where I can gather my thoughts and plan the next move."

"What brought all this on?"

"It's too long a story - just trust me. I don't feel safe at all and I've got very few people I can turn to for help. You're one of those people, Peter. I need you to be cautious too. Do not come into the hotel unless you're accompanied by a Boston Police officer. Don't trust any Boston Police officer. Make sure that you only contact a colleague who you know personally and trust with absolute certainty. The people I've been dealing with recently on this fiber-optic project are extremely well connected. Please don't take any unnecessary risks."

"This sounds a bit over the top, but I'll come and get you out of there, if that's what you want. What's your room number again?"

"I'm not in my room anymore. When you come into the hotel, you need to go straight through the main lobby to the restaurant. I'm with two attorneys and my cousins' husbands."

"I can be there by 11:30. You'll need to be ready to leave immediately."

"I'll be ready," Martin assured him and ended the call.

"Lieutenant Dorian will be here in about an hour," Quinn reported.

George Grey repeated his offer of assistance.

"This is what I used to do up until a few years ago. I've some very good contacts in the FBI and other law enforcement agencies. I'll give Tom one of my cards, should you decide to take me up on this offer."

For the next hour, the four men tried to reassure Quinn. While affording them the courtesy of respecting their opinions, Martin held steadfast to the assessment that his life was truly in peril.

"These people are extremely well connected and very goal driven," he repeated. "I understand exactly what their agenda is. Knowledge gives them power and money. Controlling the country's communications network gives them access to all their clients' information. Their customers are private individuals, corporations, as well as government agencies. I'm sure their influence doesn't stop at the US border. They're certainly not going to let the likes of me screw anything up on a program that's as extensive as this."

There was nothing any of the four could say that would allay his fears. Quinn was adamant that he had stumbled upon a giant hornets' nest.

"Seahorse has access to every aspect of our lives. Plus they'd never comply with the levels of judicial controls and legal oversight which regulate electronic surveillance. They know what television shows we like to watch. They can track every keystroke on our computers. They can monitor every transmission over the Internet. Listen to our phone calls. Track our physical movements using any video camera being operated with an Internet link. There's just no hiding from these people. Now I come along and disrupt their program!"

"But why would these people want to monitor us?" Adam asked. "What would be the point?"

"I doubt under normal circumstances any of us would warrant such attention," Quinn agreed. "But my situation is unique in that I've spooked one of their people. I imagine their normal surveillance targets would be stock brokers and banks so they can get ahead of what's going to happen in the market. If you see a public company's board members buying or selling their own shares, it certainly gives you an idea as to what those insiders believe is going to happen with the stock price. The scenarios and benefits are endless."

He continued to receive regular check-in phone calls. Brendan was safely in his last class before lunch and all the emergency controls that Martin had implemented, appeared to be holding up. Thankfully too, none of the guests in the restaurant had blown his or her cover and attempted to kill him. The same could be said for the people passing back and forth outside the window. Martin was wise enough, however, to understand that this did not mean the threat was any less. It was important that he not become complacent.

Without any warning, Quinn's brunch party was interrupted by

Lieutenant Dorian shouting his name. He looked up and saw his friend standing at the entrance to the restaurant. Neither he nor the large gentleman standing beside him was in uniform.

"Martin, it's time to go. Now!" Peter announced, marching towards the table.

Quinn stood up, gathered his cell phones, and placed them into the canvas briefcase.

"Is that a Boston Police officer? Have you known him for some time?"

"Enough of that," Dorian responded abruptly. "You asked me to get you out of here safely and that's what's going to happen. We're going to do it my way. We have to leave right now."

"I've got to go," Martin informed the group as they all stood up. There was no need to explain since it was obvious to all from the way Lieutenant Dorian had taken control.

"Tom, can you please close out my hotel bill? They already have my credit card on file from when I checked in," Martin asked.

There was no time for the obligatory farewells that go along with such parting of company. Peter placed a hand on Martin's shoulder and guided him towards his colleague who had remained at the hostess' station.

The two plain-clothed police officers escorted Quinn briskly through the lobby, followed by David and Adam. Once outside, Peter led the group towards two unmarked police cars. They were double parked fifty feet from the front door of the hotel, with their tail lights and reversing lights flashing.

"I'll take it from here, Michael. Thanks for your help."

"Take care, Peter, and you too, Martin," replied the Boston Police detective.

Quinn scarcely had time to thank Peter's colleague before he found himself in the back seat of the unmarked cruiser which was parked closest to the curb. Adam sat in the front passenger seat as they sped along Atlantic Avenue before crossing under the elevated expressway, to travel south on I93.

"David and I both drove into Boston in his car this morning," Adam explained, "so he's going to follow us - but at a much slower speed!"

"Sorry," Dorian apologized. "Force of habit, I guess."

"I can't thank you enough, Peter," Martin began, leaning forward between the two front seats. "I'll be so relieved once we get to your police station."

"You're all set now, Martin. You can relax."

"I wish that was the case," he contradicted. "You've got no idea how powerful and influential these people are. They control everything."

He revealed his theories to Dorian about how he had stumbled upon an organized-crime syndicate, intent on gaining control of the telecommunications industry. His presentation was interrupted by phone calls from both Chris Donovan and Rob Hayes. Since Donovan was still keeping watch over Brendan, Martin wanted him to continue checking in, but explained to Hayes that he no longer needed to do so.

"I'm with a good friend who's a police lieutenant. I'll call you in a couple of days. Thank you for looking out for me. You're a good friend, Rob. I really appreciate it."

If Quinn had paid more attention while they were traveling south on Route 24, he would have realized they were not heading to Holbrook. Dorian drove past Exit 20 which would have taken them there via Randolph. It was not until the car turned into the parking lot of Martin's doctor's office that he realized what was happening.

Panic engulfed Quinn. He had known Peter Dorian to be an intelligent and respected police officer. His cousin's husband, Adam, had seen active service as a Marine during the Desert Storm conflict in Saudi Arabia. Neither of these two men was a stranger to danger. Quinn had not expected such a cavalier response to his request for help. They appeared to completely disregard his assessment of the danger that threatened both his life and his family's. "Why do they think that a visit to my doctor's office is going to be any help?"

As Peter brought the car to a halt, Martin's Verizon cell phone rang. He recognized the number as Eddie Gallagher's and answered the call.

"Eddie, there's no fiber-optic bridge project. Cove should never have been involved in this."

"What do you mean?" Gallagher replied. "What's going on?"

"I'll explain later. Talk to Tom Sullivan, he'll bring you up to speed. I was with him until half an hour ago."

"Who was that?" Adam asked when the phone call ended.

"My business partner, Eddie Gallagher. He just got back from Ireland. His sister committed suicide last week and he had to go over for the funeral."

"What are we doing here, Peter?" Martin demanded, avoiding any further distracting questions from Adam. "This is wrong."

"Your doctor asked that we let him give you a quick check up. It's standard procedure in cases like this. It won't take any time at all."

Despite Quinn's protests, Peter Dorian marched him through the front door of the building and into the waiting area on the first floor. Dr. Dean shared this office with several other general and family practitioners. As usual, there were at least a dozen patients waiting for their appointments. Unlike previous visits, however, Martin did not have to join them. The receptionist had obviously been expecting him, because she immediately motioned for the three men to come into the consultation area. They were met by a nurse who escorted them into a private room to await the doctor.

"I think I'll have you bring me to all my appointments from now on," Martin commended Peter. "There've been times when I've sat out in that waiting area for nearly an hour!"

A short time later, the three men were joined by David Heinz, who had followed them from the hotel in his own car. The consultation room had not been designed to accommodate so many people, but the four men chatted as if it were the most normal place to hang out on a Friday afternoon. A gentle knock on the door heralded Dr. Dean's entrance into what was already a congested space. David, being the last to arrive, had to shuffle to his right along the wall. As he entered, Michael Dean proffered a hand to greet his patient.

"Hi Martin. If it's okay, I'd like to ask you a few questions."

"Go ahead, Doctor."

"Can you tell me how many hours of sleep you've been getting recently?"

"I've probably been averaging three or four hours a night over the past week to ten days. Last Saturday and Sunday night, however, I didn't get any sleep at all."

As he leaned against the wall, Dr. Dean continued to write notes in a patient file which he had placed on the counter.

"Can you tell me what today's date is?" he asked, without looking up.

"Today is Friday, March 12," Quinn replied promptly.

"Martin, if I was to say to you, 'People in glass houses should not throw stones.' What would you understand from that statement?"

"Well, let's imagine I was coming to you to get treatment for alcoholism and during this treatment program, we were both at lunch together in a restaurant. If I started to laugh and make jokes at the expense of a diner at another table who was obviously under the influence of alcohol, then you might make such a statement to me."

"That's fine, Martin," the doctor replied as he closed the file. "Please excuse me for a couple of minutes, gentlemen. I'll be right back."

Peter, Adam, and David tried to make small talk with Quinn, who was preoccupied with something else as he thumbed through pages in his Day-Timer.

"I just gave the doctor an incorrect answer to his question about today's date. How could I have messed that up? I was off by a week. Look, I had a meeting yesterday at Tony Bottazzi's office. Here it is marked in my Day-Timer. I can't believe I messed that up!"

"Don't worry about it," Dorian reassured him.

"I guess it was a good idea to come in and get checked out. At least he can confirm I'm not under the influence of drugs or alcohol," Quinn conceded.

The doctor returned after twenty minutes.

"Okay, Martin, I want you to take a few days off and get some rest. I wasn't able to get you a place in Pembroke Hospital, but I did manage to get you into Westwood Lodge."

"That's okay," Quinn replied. "They're both owned by the same company. It shouldn't make any difference which one I check into."

"How do you know that they're owned by the same company?" Dr. Dean asked in amazement.

"My construction company has only been operating for two years, but I've already completed contracts at both facilities."

Martin could tell from the expression on the men's faces that they found this somewhat amusing.

"It's a small world, isn't it?" Quinn added.

All three onlookers nodded their heads in agreement as the doctor made more entries in the file.

Dr. Dean's plan to have him sign into a psychiatric hospital appealed to Martin, and he could tell that everyone was relieved by his apparent compliance. There probably was no safer place for him to hide while he collected his thoughts and decided what his next move should be. "It's perfect. How much of a threat could Grasso and his colleagues believe me to be if I'm locked up in a mental hospital?" he thought to himself.

"Martin, I'll bring you to Westwood Lodge, but I want to take the cruiser back to the station and pick up my Jeep," explained Peter Dorian. "Do you mind waiting here with Adam and David until I return?"

"Not at all, Peter. If that's okay with them, then it's fine with me."

Everyone agreed, which left Quinn with his two cousins alone in the consultation room. He continued to elaborate on various details of his escapades over the past few weeks. While they were talking, Martin received another call from Eddie Gallagher.

"Eddie, it's not good to be calling me at this number. It's probably not a secure line. I'm getting taken somewhere safe. I'll contact you in a couple of days. In the meantime, you need to speak with Tom Sullivan."

"I'm on my way to his office now. I'm just getting out of the airport as we speak. What's going on?"

"It's not safe to discuss it over the phone. I really can't talk right now," Martin insisted.

He ended the call and then phoned Chris Donovan.

"Chris, I don't want you to give Brendan any cause for concern. Just follow his school bus home and make sure that he gets into the house okay. You can call it a day after that. You probably won't be able to contact me for much longer."

It took Peter Dorian an hour to switch vehicles, during which time Adam and David engaged Martin in casual conversation in an effort to distract him from thinking about the Seahorse project.

"I'm all set," Peter announced when he entered the room with Dr. Dean following behind. "Although I'll need directions to Westwood Lodge."

"That won't be necessary," Martin interrupted. "I know the way."

"Are you sure?" Dorian asked.

Even though he was talking to Martin, it was obvious that Peter was looking directly at Dr. Dean for an answer too.

"Sure I know the way, Peter, I worked there last year. I don't doubt that my actions have given you guys cause for alarm, but I'm convinced my life is in danger. I respect Dr. Dean's decision that I may be overreacting and unnecessarily paranoid. If he believes that spending a little time in Westwood Lodge will help him formulate a better diagnosis, then that's fine with me. Their staff will confirm I'm not under the influence of drugs or alcohol and sooner or later you'll all come to realize that I've good reason to be concerned for my well being."

The more Martin thought about it, the more he came to appreciate what an excellent place Westwood Lodge would be for him to hide during the next few days. With his construction background and knowledge of the facility, he was confident he could escape if there was a problem. It surprised both the doctor and the police lieutenant, just how receptive Quinn was to the idea of psychiatric treatment.

They all thanked Dr. Dean, before making their way to the parking lot. It was not common practice for four adult men to simultaneously exit from one of the private consultation rooms. Quinn was conscious of the looks that various members of staff shot in their direction. Some were aware of the circumstances, but others seemed quite puzzled.

Adam and David's parting was somewhat awkward, but Martin was confident that soon each would understand he was not as crazy as they thought. Peter thanked them also as he and Martin walked towards Dorian's red Jeep.

En route to Westwood Lodge, Quinn realized he was still in possession of the original contract agreements and other material, which he felt should not be brought into the hospital.

"Not a problem," Peter responded to his request, "I'll keep everything safe until you get out. Also, just call me when you're leaving and I'll come and pick you up."

Martin emptied his pockets and put everything, including his wallet, car keys and wedding ring into his briefcase. He was intent on making it as difficult as he could for Seahorse's agents to recover these contracts or other items which would assist them in their quest to harm either him or his family.

5:50PM - Friday March 5, 1999

CC This looks like a very nice place," remarked the lieutenant, responding to Martin's final directions as they drove through secluded, tree-lined streets of the affluent Westwood suburb. The twenty acres of Westwood Lodge Hospital sat inconspicuously within a residential neighborhood of beautiful homes. The main building was hardly visible from the street, set back in its grounds and concealed by mature trees and landscaping. Dorian would have driven past the gate, but for the navigational assistance of his passenger.

"It's seen better times," Martin continued. "Back in the 1960s it was a favored refuge for Hollywood movie and television celebrities."

Dorian privately acknowledged that Quinn's grasp of reality appeared to be more than solid. He grinned as he reflected that although he had been raised in the area himself, it was Martin who was giving directions to the hospital, as well as providing a brief history of its most notable patients throughout the years.

Peter was right to stop and question the irony of the situation. Martin was correct in his trivia about the hospital, which he had picked up while working there. It was easier for the celebrity patients to receive private treatment at Westwood Lodge, where they were far away from the press and society reporters who hounded them around the movie studios in Hollywood. Many of their problems stemmed from alcohol or substance abuse. Once they were cleaned up, they could take a quick European vacation and then have their agent book them appearances on the talk-show circuit.

As the two men walked towards the main entrance, Martin studied the building. An impartial and candid observer would have to admit that the maintenance budget of recent years had not been adequate. Even though Westwood Lodge was an architecturally beautiful structure, it needed a complete exterior paint job as well as cosmetic repairs to the masonry finishes.

They introduced themselves to the receptionist who invited them to sit while she summoned one of the admission nurses.

"When you're ready to leave here, just give me a call and I'll be right over," Peter reiterated.

"Thank you," Martin replied as the admitting nurse entered from a door adjacent to the reception window.

"Peter!"

"Mary, how are you? I had no idea this is where you worked. Martin, you're in good hands. Mary O'Donnell is a neighbor of mine," Dorian explained. "Martin's a good friend and his doctor suggested that you guys look after him for a few days. I was only his chauffeur today; there was no need for a police escort."

"That's fine. We'll take good care of him," Mary assured her friend as she directed Quinn towards the doorway she had just come through.

Martin thanked Peter again, shook his hand, and then followed Mary O'Donnell out of the reception area. They proceeded down a corridor for about thirty feet and through an open door on the right, into her office.

"Please take a seat. I've already started a file with the information I got from Dr. Dean," Nurse O'Donnell began, as she sat behind her desk. "Since yours is a voluntary admission, and not court ordered, you sign your own papers and agree to a minimum of seventy-two hours of observation and treatment."

"I've got no problem with that and you being a friend of Peter Dorian carries a lot of weight with me. But I'll only sign the papers on condition that no drugs or medication are prescribed during my stay here."

"I'm afraid the hospital cannot agree to such a restriction. We must reserve the right to administer any treatment which we deem necessary in the event a patient may be a danger to himself or others."

"Okay. That's understandable. I have no problem agreeing to that qualification, provided I'm never left alone in the sole company of one member of the staff. If there are always at least two present, then there's less risk of a contentious situation developing and the hospital subsequently only having one employee's account of the events."

Mary O'Donnell finished filling out the admission paperwork and passed it across the desk for him to sign. Before doing so, Quinn wrote a lengthy rider in the margin of the document, qualifying the terms upon which he was agreeing to enter the hospital. When he was done, he stressed how glad he was to be entering Westwood Lodge.

"I feel this is the ideal location for me to take some time-out and get rested," he confided. "It's a very complicated story, but I found myself in the company of people who I had no business being involved with. My life is in considerable danger. It's extremely important no one is able to track me down while I'm here. I've given Peter Dorian all my belongings. I have nothing with me that can be used to help identify me."

Martin suddenly noticed his gold wristwatch. Panicked that it was still in his possession, he immediately unbuckled the strap and gave it to the nurse, noticing that it was 6:05 as he did so.

"I'm sorry, but I can't take property from our patients," she explained, gently pushing Martin's hand back without taking the watch.

"I really don't care what the rules are here," he protested. "I'm not entering the hospital with any item that can connect me to the outside world."

With that said, Quinn placed the watch among some pens and pencils which were in a mug on her desk. Mary chose not to argue. The admission paperwork was completed without further discussion, at which time she suggested that they go down to the ward.

It was no more than fifteen paces along the corridor from Nurse O'Donnell's office to another door, which had a narrow wired security glass observation window above the handle. Mary peered through before swiping her plastic ID card in an electronic reader on the wall adjacent to the lockset. Martin followed her through the open door and along another corridor, where the floor was pitched with a gentle ramp. There were no other doors except for one at the opposite end. Quinn and his escort had approximately fifty feet to walk. There were no windows, and the florescent light fixtures which illuminated the white walls were each housed within a steel mesh grill. The brown carpet had a short man-made pile running perpendicular to the slope which provided traction on the gentle gradient.

"You know that you're breaking the rules of our agreement already. The one about me always being in the presence of at least two employees."

"Sorry Martin, I don't have anyone to call on. It's Friday evening and we're already on our weekend staffing schedule."

"Relax," he assured her, "Juicy Fruit."

Quinn was sure she would understand the, "Juicy Fruit," reference. It was a Will Sampson quote from the movie, *One Flew Over The Cuckoo's Nest*, in which he played the part of Chief, a Native American psychiatric patient.

Mary O'Donnell gave no indication she understood Martin's comment as she opened the door at the bottom of the ramp. They were now in a main hospital corridor and proceeded towards a pair of double doors about thirty feet from where they had entered. Each door had a wired glass security panel. This time, Nurse O'Donnell made no attempt to open either of these doors. Rather, she pushed a call button to their left and waited as another staff member came to meet them. Quinn surmised it was hospital policy not to enter this ward with a new patient, unless authorized by the staff on duty. This reduced the risk of anyone entering if another patient was hiding behind the door or was involved in an altercation with the staff. Consequently, access was granted only when conditions were conducive.

"Emily, this is Martin," Mary announced.

"Hi Martin," responded a young woman in her late twenties or perhaps early thirties. "We've got your room ready."

"Take care, Martin and get some rest," Nurse O'Donnell advised, leaving him in the custody of her colleague.

Emily was indistinguishable from any of the patients, except for an ID badge clipped to her belt. Her name and photograph were etched into the plastic.

As the door locked behind them, Quinn followed her into the ward. It was laid out in the shape of the letter "L." They had entered at its "toe" and as they walked towards the corner or "heel," they passed some patients' rooms on their left. The wall on their right was blank for the first twenty-five feet until they passed a TV room. It was separated from the ward by floor-to-ceiling panels of wired security glass. Consequently, neither the programs nor anyone watching TV was ever out of sight from the staff. Two patients were engrossed in a Bugs Bunny cartoon. Quinn could see beyond them that the exterior windows had security grilles on the inside of the frame. The nurses' station was located directly ahead, where the ward turned to the left. There was a little spur to the right at this corner. It was the width of the corridor, but no deeper than the TV room. A warning notice affixed to an emergency exit at the end, advised that it could only be opened by a member of staff. There were two public pay phones in this alcove. The one further down and on the right was in its own private phone box. The one opposite, outside the nurses' station, was mounted on the wall. There was a chalk board beside it for phone messages. Right opposite Martin and Emily as they made the turn, was a reception window and door to the nurses' station. As they proceeded further into the ward they passed a common reading area on their left. It was furnished with a mixture of couches, easy chairs, and coffee tables. Molded plastic conference-type chairs were stacked neatly in the far corner.

"You can see we have a TV room back there or if you just want to relax and read a magazine or book, you can sit out here. Tomorrow we'll fix you up with a locker," Emily explained, pointing to a bank of about twenty small lockers with combination locks, situated below a bench along the wall facing the TV room.

Quinn smiled as he compared the hospital's lockers to the Boston Harbor Hotel's safety deposit boxes which he had been using up until that morning. Just beyond the reading area was a small, narrow kitchenette which could be accessed from the corridor. As they passed, he could see a refrigerator at the end and a counter running its full length on the right side. His host explained that there were always snacks, fruit, and juices available for the patients. Martin declined her invitation to get something to eat and drink. He was anxious to get to his own room and away from the parabolic security mirrors, strategically located throughout the ward, suspecting there were cameras hidden behind them.

They stopped at the second to last door on the left side of the corridor. Emily pointed out the men's restroom, right opposite, before opening the door to Quinn's room. About fifteen feet further along at the end of the corridor was another door with an electronic reader mechanism and a "Fire Exit" sign. There was also a notice indicating that this door could only be opened by a member of staff. To the left of this exit was a small alcove which accessed the last of the patients' rooms. All the doors of the patient rooms had a twelve inch square observation window with wired security glass. As he entered his new accommodation, Quinn understood that there could be no expectation of privacy. "Well, it's certainly not the Presidential Suite," Martin acknowledged privately.

The room had a single bed, a wardrobe, and one wooden chair. The walls were plainly painted a light shade of blue and a metal grille was secured to the inside of the window frame, making it difficult to see the hospital grounds beyond.

Just then, they were joined by a tall, slim gentleman in a tweed sports coat, who introduced himself as Dr. Theo Shield. He extended his hand to greet their newest patient. His left hand held a manila file jacket which had Quinn's name typed on a label affixed to a corner tab. He peered at Martin above neat gold-rimmed glasses perched halfway down his long narrow nose. The arms of the glasses disappeared into a mop of curly gray hair, which he appeared to have given up trying to groom a long time ago. Quinn found himself checking to make sure his first visitor was wearing a staff ID badge - which was, in fact, the case.

"I'm one of the doctors on duty this evening. Dr. Andreus Kaskarelis will be looking after you during your stay with us and I'm sure he'll meet with you on Monday morning during his rounds. Do you think you need any medication to help you sleep or relax?"

"No thank you, Doctor."

"Very well then, I'll leave you alone to get settled," responded the doctor as he closed Martin's medical file and left.

"If you need anything, just come and see us at the nurses' station.

There's additional bed linen and blankets in the corner closet of the TV room."

"Thank you, Emily."

"I'll close this, so you can get some rest," she suggested, shutting the door behind her.

Martin sat on the bed and surveyed his new surroundings. All edges of the wooden bed frame were rounded off, minimizing the risk of injury. His fingers gripped six inch long slots along the side of the frame which were obviously provided to facilitate restraint straps in the event that a patient needed to be subdued. There were no sharp edges on the wooden chair either. A white, plastic, two gallon trash bin sat in the corner and an institutional grade box of tissues had been placed on the window sill. This also had no sharp corners or edges and did not protrude more than two inches beyond the wall. "If only the same effort could be made to make the rest of the world this safe," Quinn reflected while looking around to see if there was any evidence of surveillance equipment in his room. He satisfied himself that there was none. Nevertheless, he recalled seeing at least two parabolic mirrors in the ward, which he believed concealed cameras.

He unbuttoned his blue dress shirt and hung it around the back of the chair. After slipping off his shoes and socks, he removed his jeans. It was Martin's habit to sleep naked, however, since he had not had the pleasure of meeting his fellow guests, and given the nature of his new residence, he climbed into bed still wearing a tee-shirt and underpants.

As his head sank gently into the pillow, Quinn appreciated that he could not have expected a better outcome to the day, considering how it had started. Westwood Lodge was the safest place for him to hide from John Grasso and his associates. "Would Dr. Dean have sent me here, had I correctly answered his question about the date?" Martin wondered.

"Here's another example of a mistake contributing to something positive in my life."

Within minutes, he was fast asleep.

7:30AM - Saturday March 6, 1999

Quinn could recall at least two occasions during the night when he awoke to see a member of the staff looking through the wired glass security window of his door. He felt really refreshed having had one of his best night's sleep in over a month. He lay in bed and reviewed the situation. "Dr. Theo Shield," he thought to himself. "Is that a code name for someone who's supposed to be protecting me? If you take away the letter 'o' from his name, you are left with 'The Shield.' Has George Grey got me set up in an interim safe house?" He tried to analyze the crazy sequence of events which had led to him waking up in a mental hospital. A month earlier his life had been bland and predictable. He identified the initial incident that triggered the slow spinning motion, which gradually increased into the chaotic tail-spin of the previous day's episode in the hotel. It was the first meeting with Fred Ross in Eddie Gallagher's kitchen. "That was the beginning," Martin decided as he reviewed the previous five weeks of his life. The whole fiber-optic bridge project and its related events had taken on a momentum of their own. Once Quinn got on board, he adjusted his own actions and reactions to compensate for the gradually increasing inertia of the spinning process. He recognized specific incidents that accelerated it: his first meeting to show John Grasso the sample bracket at Bottazzi's offices; his realization that Fred was up to no good when the shop drawings were taken away from Tony Bottazzi; his decision to contact Grasso directly and share with him his concerns for the project; seeing Ross sneak out of Anderson Aluminum with material to make his own prototype; the show-down meeting in Anderson's conference room with all the cell phones dismantled around the table; his patent attorney's success at protecting the design; Eddie's sister committing suicide; moving out of his home and ending up as a guest in the Presidential Suite of the Boston Harbor Hotel; the frantic events of the previous morning at the hotel; the good fortune of having Tom Sullivan help him escape, as well as Attorney Grey, with his experience and law enforcement contacts; and finally, the rapid exit from Boston in Peter Dorian's cruiser. Each event added its own acceleration to the spin. Martin was finally flung off the ride and had landed abruptly in a psychiatric ward!

He could hear people coming and going past his door. Occasionally, it sounded as if they entered or exited the ward through the door at the end of the corridor, near his room. Both the men's and women's bathrooms were located across the hallway. He could overhear conversations which indicated the patients would soon be leaving the ward to get breakfast in the dining room. Quinn had absolutely no desire to join them, deciding that more time was needed to assess the current situation before he would feel comfortable leaving his room. Even though he had managed to get himself into the security of the psychiatric hospital, he did not want to underestimate the resourcefulness of the people he was trying to avoid. If there were closed-circuit security cameras in the hallways and other areas of this hospital, then John Grasso's people could tap into them. Quinn was resolute that, for the present time, it was best for him to remain confined to his private room.

Martin got out from under the bedclothes and sat on the edge of his bed. The carpet pile tickled the soles of his feet as he stretched back his shoulder blades. "I really did have a good night's sleep," he thought to himself again, while reaching over to grab his jeans. He did not want his decision to sequester himself in this room to adversely affect his health and fitness. Before putting on his shirt, he did twenty, one-armed push-ups with each hand as well as sit-ups and other exercises.

Quinn lay back on the bed and began to get his mind accustomed to his new surroundings. He could not trust anyone. Understanding where he was and gathering information about the hospital and its staff was critical to maintaining an advantage during any encounters. He also understood how important it was to keep his body and mind active. To do that, he needed to work on both physical and mental exercises. He had already taken care of a short physical workout and resolved that at least once every hour he would walk around his small room several times. But he needed to come up with something to keep his mind occupied.

As he looked around, Martin decided he would survey and mentally record every aspect of the room's dimensions. This activity would keep his brain working and draw upon talents and skills developed during his twenty years in the construction industry. The room had a plain solid ceiling. Had it been a suspended ceiling with a grid, Martin could easily have estimated the foot-print dimensions to within a couple of inches of its actual size. The carpet on the floor had no pattern and therefore could not offer any dimensional reference for this task either. If a twelve inch square vinyl floor tile had been used, this task would have been relatively simple.

When it came to the height of the room, he did not have much to go on either. The wall was smooth and painted a solid pale blue. His knowledge of standard commercial door sizes in North America limited his door's height options to either six foot - eight inches or seven feet. Martin did not have to stand next to the door to see that it was most likely six foot - eight inches high. He continued to survey the room and estimate the dimensions of all its components and layout. How long was the window? What was the height of the window sill off the floor? How deep was the window sill?

Quinn spent the next few hours engaged in this activity, keeping track of different dimensions in his mind. He also surveyed the ward as much as he could, through the observation window in his door. Steel blinds on the exterior window hindered any efforts to study the hospital grounds. Their manufacturer obviously gave more consideration to security than aesthetics. Of one thing Quinn was absolutely certain - he was no longer residing in the Boston Harbor Hotel.

Without his watch, Martin was unable to keep accurate track of time. It was some time mid morning when a knock on his door announced the arrival of a nurse.

"Hi, my name is Angela Curran and I'm a staff nurse."

A heavy-set middle-aged woman entered the room, dressed in a medical laboratory coat which matched her white pants and practical flat heeled shoes. A light green hair band accented her blouse and kept shoulder length brunette curls off her face. In her left hand, Angela was carrying a tan colored plastic box, similar to what a fisherman would use. She did not have a fishing pole, so Martin doubted the box contained fishing tackle or bait.

"How are you feeling today?"

"Fine, I had a really good night's sleep."

"That's what we like to hear. Now, I need to take a blood sample."

"As long as you don't administer any medication or drugs, Angela, then I don't have a problem with that."

It had not gone unnoticed by Quinn that his request to never be left in the company of only one staff member had been ignored. He could live with this violation, provided there was no attempt to administer drugs without his permission.

"Thank you, Martin," she replied, opening the fishing tackle box which she had placed on the bed. It contained an array of syringes, vials, and other items used to recover blood samples. She lifted the upper tray completely out of the box to reveal more supplies, including rubber gloves and alcohol swabs. This lower section of her case also contained a plastic receptacle for discarded syringes and other bio-hazard trash accumulated in the course of her work.

"I made it a condition of entering the hospital that I don't have to take any medication or drugs against my will."

"Not a problem," replied Angela as she went about her business of writing labels and preparing to take three blood samples. "No drugs will be administered."

"I'm very happy to be in here. It's probably the safest place I could have found at such short notice. I realized yesterday morning that I was involved with some very dangerous people. I don't expect anyone here to believe me, but I understand your need to check my blood to make sure I'm not under the influence of drugs."

"I'll need to take three blood samples because the lab will be running several tests. I also have a short questionnaire for you. It's a standard list of questions we ask patients to help us develop an accurate analysis of their health."

Several minutes after entering his room, Nurse Curran was fastening the latches on the top of her plastic fishing tackle box. Martin took this opportunity to get as much information as he could. Her watch told him that it was 10:15 and labels she had placed on the specimen tubes confirmed the date as March 6, 1999.

"I understand you haven't been out of your room this morning for breakfast. Is there any reason?"

"I can't trust anyone or any situation with which I'm not familiar. I don't know anyone in the ward and after everything I've gone through recently, I'm not prepared to take the risk of leaving this room until I feel it's safe."

"You've nothing to be worried about and you really should go and get a snack from the kitchen."

As far as he was concerned, Angela Curran had not done anything to convince him that she could be trusted. So why would her security assessment be of any value?

"I appreciate your concern, but for the rest of my life I'll have to keep looking over my shoulder."

"Well, I've everything I need for the present time. I'll leave you alone, Martin and let you get some rest."

He returned to the task of surveying his room. A little later, while doing some physical exercises he lifted the box of tissues from the window sill. A note on the side of the box read, "NOT FOR RESALE." The product had obviously been packaged for use in hospitals, hotels, or other commercial businesses. On the underside of the box, he glanced at the product's specifications which indicated they were two-ply tissues, each nine inches long, by eight and one half inches wide. Quinn realized he could use these tissues to create a more accurate method of taking measurements throughout his room. By folding the eight and one half inch edge diagonally along the nine inch edge, he now had an accurate measurement of one half inch. Folding a tissue long ways into three equal columns, gave him an accurate measurement of three inches. Various geometric scenarios yielded different fractions of either the nine inch or eight and one half inch dimension. Armed with half a dozen folded tissue measuring instruments, Quinn reworked his survey of the room and compared his estimated dimensions with those calculated using the "tissue method." Without having anything to write with, this activity kept him occupied until what he assumed to be lunch-time. Trying to recall his prior estimates and compare them with his more recent measurements was just the type of challenge that Martin needed to keep his mind occupied. Once again, he was conscious of activity and conversations outside his room as other patients were getting ready to leave the ward for lunch.

Quinn lay down on his bed to rest. Prior to doing so, he placed the folded tissues between his mattress and the bed frame, for future use.

12:10PM on Saturday March 6, 1999

A s the two boys led their parents towards the departure gates, Grey side-stepped a luggage cart overloaded with suitcases and golf clubs. They had been late checking in, nevertheless, the obliging ticket agent managed to seat him and his wife at a window, with their two sons immediately in front, in the next row. All four were looking forward to ten days of fun and relaxation on the sunny beaches of the British Virgin Islands. George surreptitiously felt the large bundle of hundred dollar bills zipped inside his jacket pocket and smiled. He complimented himself on his choice of vacation resort. The British Virgin Islands used United Stated dollars as its currency, yet all of its commerce was conducted beyond the jurisdiction of United States' authorities. There would be no trace of his lavish cash transactions and hence no reason to ever have to explain the source of the income needed to cover this family treat.

12:45PM on Saturday March 6, 1999

Shelley adjusted her seat belt and appeared to pay attention to the flight attendant's instructions; however, her mind was elsewhere. She was looking forward to spending the next week relaxing and exploring the tranquil waters of the British Virgin Islands. At first, when her husband suggested this venue for their spring break vacation, she had not been too keen on the idea. As time went by, she warmed to the plan - especially after the previous week. Martin Quinn had certainly given her plenty to do and think about during the last days of term. Did he have any real reason to believe that either his life or his son's was in danger? She was left with mixed emotions after receiving Margaret Quinn's call, late on Friday afternoon, reporting that her husband had been admitted into a psychiatric hospital. While Shelley felt relieved that her student was probably in no danger, it did concern her that his father was so troubled. It reinforced the wisdom of her decision to help get Brendan out of Massachusetts for two weeks. Hopefully, Martin Quinn's condition would improve before his son's return from Seattle. Perhaps her young student's parents would have reconciled their differences by then also.

This was not the only couple for whom she had such aspirations. Her own husband, oblivious to the flight attendant's demonstration, was leaning against the window engrossed in the latest edition of In Depth SCUBA. Shelley and David had known happier times. Her recent decision to leave Thayer Academy and accept a similar position at a school closer to their home, did not meet with his approval. This new job would pay substantially less and force him to give serious consideration regarding the viability of continuing to operate his SCUBA diving store and training center. Shelley, however, felt that the Thayer commute placed too much strain on their relationship. It had been a difficult decision to make, but she knew it was one that had to be made for the sake of their marriage. She studied the body language of the couple seated in front of her and how it suggested that they were happy together. "What's their secret?" she wondered. "They must be married at least fifteen years if those two boys are their sons."

1:40PM on Saturday March 6, 1999

M artin was wakened from his nap by a knock on the door. A casually dressed gentleman entered the room and introduced himself
as David Harrington. Quinn sat up and welcomed his guest.

"I'm a psychologist and I'd like to have a little chat with you, today."

"That's fine, but you'll have to bear with me while I confirm you
are who you say you are. I've been through some extremely crazy times
recently, which have made me realize that my life's in considerable danger.
People like yourself, who I've never met before, need to earn my trust. I
hope you can appreciate that, David."

Martin's latest visitor leaned his six foot - two inch frame back against
the wall opposite the bed and folded his arms. His left hand gripped
the corner of the patient file that Mary O'Donnell and Dr. Shield had
previously started. He had short blonde hair and looked to be in his mid
forties. The gray shirt he wore had its top button open, revealing a black
turtleneck underneath. Pleated pants in a dark shade of gray were kept
up with a designer black leather belt. As he listened to qualifications for
future communication, Harrington lifted his right heel out of its wine
colored penny loafer, keeping the ball of his foot in the middle of the
shoe, while he gently rotated his ankle.

"Okay, how can I put your mind at ease?"

"I'm going to ask you some questions about Westwood Lodge."

"What sort of questions?" David inquired, sliding his right foot back
into its shoe so that he could stand up straight.

"Questions about the buildings and grounds outside."

"I may not be able to answer them correctly," Harrington warned.

"Well, then it's going to be difficult for you to gain my trust. You have a file for reference, plus a team of people you can rely on to furnish you with information about me. Unfortunately, I don't have any resources. If you want to come in here and spend time with me, then I need to verify that you are who you say you are."

"I rarely work here in Westwood. I'm just filling in for a few weeks. I normally work at another hospital in Pembroke."

"That's okay; I'll ask you some questions about that location instead."

Harrington had never been through such an interview before. He had intended to be the one asking the questions, however, this had now become a clear example of what happens when you allow "the lunatics to run the asylum."

"David, in the grounds of Pembroke Hospital there's an outside basketball court. If you were standing in the middle of this court, looking over at the main hospital building with your arms outstretched and pointed to each of the basketball nets, what would you be able to see that is directly in front of you and right next the hospital building?"

Harrington's silence underscored the puzzled look on his face.

"Do you understand my question?" Quinn challenged.

"Yes, I'm just trying to think what it is that I would be looking at."

"It's not something you're going to be able to work out by giving it more thought. You either know the answer because you're familiar with Pembroke Hospital or you don't know the answer because you're not familiar with that facility."

"I don't know the answer. What is it that I would be able to see?"

"A fenced-in area for children who are patients in the hospital, so they can go outside and play. There's a sand pit, a swing set, and a slide."

"I don't usually go around to that side of the building."

"I'm sorry, David, but you've failed the test. That side of the building is where most of the staff park their cars. I can't keep asking you questions until you finally get one correct. You know nothing about this hospital and probably less about the one in Pembroke. I'm afraid you're not anyone I'm prepared to trust. We can talk about the weather or how Boston's sports teams are playing if you wish to hang around, but my room isn't very big and I've no plans to leave it at the present time."

"I think it would be better if I left you alone to get some more rest," the psychologist responded. "I'll stop in and see you again, maybe tomorrow."

Harrington had hoped his first meeting with this patient would have had a different outcome, but it was obvious to both men that there was nothing more to be said.

Martin lay on the bed, closed his eyes, and reflected on the meeting. Once again he had been touched by good fortune since his working knowledge of both hospital locations had certainly prepared him for this encounter. Nevertheless, he did not want to discourage future visits. He enjoyed the social interaction, and would rely on these occasions to gain information. Harrington's watch had indicated that it was 1:55. Quinn resolved to utilize the staff, patients and any of the amenities to his advantage. He would not allow his confinement to deter him from this mission, but rather, use it as a motivator. As he drifted off to sleep, his mind shifted to consider the problem of surveillance cameras in the ward.

Quinn had no idea how long he had slept. From the shadows on the ground outside, he estimated it to be about 3:30. As he stepped back from squinting through the metal blinds, he looked around and smiled to himself. "So this is home."

Martin had neither eaten nor had anything to drink since Friday morning. He began to wonder how he could get a drink of water that he would know for sure had not been drugged. The problem was compounded by the fact that he did not want to leave the safety of his room. He went over to the door and peered through the wired glass of its observation window. It was difficult to identify the staff, some of whom did not wear medical coats or uniforms. "That's the problem with some crazy people," he thought to himself, "they look the same as everyone else!" Had it not been for the ID badges, Quinn would have had difficulty knowing whom to ask for assistance. He identified two male employees and waited for an opportunity to call one of them over to his door.

"Hi, my name is Martin."

"Hi Martin, I'm Warren."

Warren was in his early thirties, about five foot - nine inches tall, with dark hair. His choice of apparel was more casual than David Harrington's. He wore athletic shoes which Quinn believed were a practical choice. His firm handshake and broad shouldered physique projected a persona of confidence and strength.

"Could you do me a big favor? I can't leave this room because my life is in danger. Is there any way you could bring me half a cup of water from the kitchen?"

"Not a problem," Warren agreed with a puzzled look on his face. "I'll be right back."

He returned, less than a minute later, with a ten ounce, clear plastic cup, half filled with water.

"Thank you, Warren."

"You know there's really nothing to be worried about if you come out of your room."

"I'm sure your intentions are well meant, but my life is at risk. The people I need to avoid are very powerful and influential. I'm quite happy to stay right here in this room for the time being."

Warren did not push the issue any further and went on his way. Besides, he had other patients in the ward to look after, whose intentions were the exact opposite. They wanted out. Patients like Martin had to be a pleasant change of pace for him.

Quinn placed the cup of water on his window sill, not knowing whether or not it had been drugged. He returned to the observation window of his door and kept watch on the corridor. After spotting the other male staff member, he quickly opened the door to catch his attention and introduce himself.

"Hi Martin, I'm Norman."

Quinn observed that this gentleman must have been decorating at home because even though his hands were scrubbed clean, there were still small traces of white latex paint and plaster on the edges of some of his finger nails. Norman was of similar stature and build to Martin. His six foot tall frame weighed about two hundred pounds. From behind, he could have been mistaken for Quinn, except for the short blonde hair. He reckoned that Norman was, like himself, about forty years of age.

"I really need your help. I can't leave this room because I have reason to believe that my life is in serious danger. Could you please get me half a cup of water from the kitchen?"

"Sure, I'll be right back."

He returned to find Martin holding the plastic cup of water that Warren had given to him earlier. Quinn took the second cup from Norman who was clearly puzzled why he had been sent on this mission.

"Norman, may I ask you a question?"

"Certainly."

"Do you trust the guy you're working with here this afternoon?"

"Warren? Sure I do, why do you ask?"

"Well, I've never met him before today, so I have no idea if he can be trusted. He brought me this water ten minutes ago, but I don't know if it's safe to drink."

Martin poured the drink he had just received into the cup that Warren had brought earlier. He then repeated the process back and forth, several times, thoroughly mixing the contents. When he stopped, both cups contained an equal volume of water. Quinn then handed one of them back to Norman.

"You see, I never met either you or Warren before today. Because of what I've recently gone through, I need people to earn my trust. If you have no problem drinking your cup of water, I can assume that neither of you has tampered with it. Then I can drink mine."

Norman was somewhat bemused. He had been transformed from hospital employee, to room service butler, and finally into some sort of guinea pig for Quinn's water quality testing program. Fortunately, he was familiar with the symptoms of paranoia, so Norman drank the water without any reservation. Martin then downed his first drink in over thirty hours.

"Thank you for helping me with this."

"You know you really need to come out of your room."

"I'm not ready to do that yet - maybe later."

"Okay, just take your time and come out whenever you feel up to it."

Martin checked to make sure his test subject did not go directly to the men's restroom across the hallway. Instead, Norman went to catch up with his colleague, Warren, to let him know what had just happened.

Once again he lay down on his bed and gave some thought to his next problem: the cameras in the ward. "Surely John Grasso's associates at Seahorse could tap into these circuits and track me down," he rationalized. "They've probably worked out where Peter Dorian took me after leaving the hotel. If they don't already know where I am, then it's only a matter of time."

Quinn drifted in and out of sleep until he became aware of activity in the ward. From what he could overhear, visitors were leaving and his fellow patients were heading to the dining room. Even though he had not eaten in over thirty hours, he was not particularly hungry. When he thought about it, he realized that he had not eaten anything on Friday. His last proper meal was actually on Thursday evening. In addition to not eating, he had not used the bathroom since leaving the hotel. So as not to dwell on the subject, he tried recalling the layout of the hospital from when Cove worked there the previous year. After a short while he fell asleep again.

He awoke to a gentle knocking on his door and Norman standing in the doorway.

"How are you doing in here?"

"Fine thanks. I can't remember the last time I was able to get as much rest."

"Well, I hope you can remember getting more to eat than you have in the past twenty four hours. You haven't come out of this room since you arrived. That means you haven't had anything to eat, nor have you used the bathroom, and that's not healthy. Why don't you come with me and get a snack from the kitchen?"

Martin knew that he could not remain confined to his room indefinitely, but he was still concerned about the risk of mingling among patients and hospital staff. Any of them could be an agent for John Grasso's people and he was not even sure who those people were. All he knew was that they were both dangerous and powerful. Then there was also the issue of the surveillance cameras.

"Okay," he conceded, "but I need to conceal my identity. My life is in danger."

"That's fair enough, though you really don't have anything to worry about while you're here."

"You have no idea what sort of people are out to get me," Martin countered, standing up while holding the open collar of his dress shirt over his mouth and nose. "For the rest of my life, I'm going to have to keep looking over my shoulder. These people are everywhere!"

For the first time since his arrival, he left his room and followed Norman down the hallway to the kitchen, taking care to keep his face hidden.

"Help yourself to some snacks and a drink. Let me know if you need anything else."

As Martin reached for the refrigerator door, he noticed a coaxial cable neatly secured to the wall near the ceiling. From what he could determine, it was probably connected to a camera concealed behind the parabolic mirror which was mounted on the other side of the wall in the common reading area. Using only his right hand, he managed to take a couple of individual-sized packets of peanut butter crackers, a banana, and a plastic bottle of juice from the refrigerator. He brought these items back to his room, while keeping his face concealed. A glance at the clock in the common reading area adjacent to the kitchen told him it was 7:30.

As he sat on the edge of his bed and began his first meal in Westwood Lodge, Quinn thought about how he was going to get a toothbrush and change of clothes. He considered how much he had taken even the simplest of things for granted. The few items of clothing he had acquired since leaving home had been left at the hotel. He made another trip back to the kitchen to dispose of the empty drink container and banana peel, before going to the bathroom opposite his room. Just as before, he kept his face covered while in the common area of the ward.

Suddenly he recalled that his friend Sean Feeney lived nearby and would probably be able to get him some clean underwear and toiletries at a local pharmacy. A notice in the common reading area had indicated that visiting time ended at 9:00pm. The only way to contact Feeney was by making a phone call from one of the two public pay phones at the end of the corridor, beyond the nurses' station. Not wanting Seahorse to be able to trace any calls from the hospital, Quinn thought it would be better to call Sean's father, Patrick Feeney. Patrick lived on Cape Cod and occasionally worked for Cove when the workload warranted. Quinn knew that he could be trusted to relay a message to his son.

Martin covered his face and made his way to the private call box. The 411 operator helped him with the phone number for the Feeney residence in Osterville, Massachusetts and using a pin-number, he was able to charge the call against his own home phone bill. When Patrick Feeney answered, Quinn briefly explained his predicament, while tempering the man's natural curiosity as to why he was calling from a psychiatric ward. Feeney, Sr. assured Quinn he would contact his son immediately and have him pick up the supplies.

"One more thing," Martin added before ending the call. "Don't use this phone that I just called you on to call Sean. Use your cell phone. There's a very good possibility that this call has been bugged and the phone numbers logged into a surveillance system. I don't want it traced easily."

When Sean got the call from his father, he responded immediately. Quinn had only been resting for a short while when his spirits were lifted by the sound of a familiar voice. His friend had rung the bell to access the ward via the door nearest Martin's room. As he got off the bed to meet his visitor, he could hear one of the staff members quizzing Feeney.

"I called him. He's here to see me," Martin interrupted.

"But you've hardly been out of that room since you got here," protested Warren.

"Well, I got the call and here I am. I have some toiletries, clean underwear, and socks for him."

"We need to check any packages before they're given to patients," Warren explained, reaching out and taking the two plastic pharmacy bags. "Why don't you come in for a few minutes before visiting time ends at 9:00?"

Sean smiled and thanked Warren as he followed Martin into his room.

"What the fuck's going on?" he asked when the two men were alone.

Sean was alarmed by everything that Martin shared with him, but did not have an opportunity to discuss any of it in detail before Warren returned with the toiletries and underwear.

"I'll come and see you again during the week."

"Thanks for the emergency supplies."

"No problem," Feeney acknowledged with a wave, before the door of the ward was closed and locked behind him.

Quinn returned to his room and lay back on his bed. His only other option was to sit on the wooden chair and read the packaging on his new underwear and socks. Until he was able to resolve the problem of surveillance cameras in the main ward, his social and recreational programs would be limited. As he contemplated his situation, he was quite pleased with his first full day in the mental hospital. "It's just like anything else in life," he thought to himself. "It's all really what you want to make of it." Satisfied and relieved, he wrapped himself in his bed clothes, oblivious to the fact that it was Margaret's birthday.

7:50AM - Sunday March 7, 1999

The next morning when Martin awoke, he felt even more refreshed than he had on Saturday. He had slept through the night without any interruptions. From the noise outside his room, he reckoned the other patients were gathering so they could be escorted to the dining room. Deciding that he would, in fact, eat breakfast with them, Martin quickly got dressed and joined the group outside the TV room. Once again he kept the lower half of his face covered by turning up his collar and holding it with his left hand. He did not feel the need to explain to the other patients that he was trying to conceal his identity more from the cameras, than from them. Quinn noticed, however, that they were puzzled by his behavior, which he tried to minimize by using a magazine to cover his face.

As he approached, a female counselor was counting the assembled patients.

"I'm sorry, but you can't come with us," she informed him. "We're not authorized to let any patient leave the ward unless we have their attending doctor's permission. You'll have to eat some fruit and snacks from the kitchen for the time being. Later this morning, we'll work on getting that paperwork in order."

Quinn did not give any indication that he had a problem with this news. He figured this was just a way for the staff to demonstrate who was in charge. Everyone else left via the set of double doors through which he had first entered the ward on Friday evening.

Once again, Quinn had to eat in his room in order to avoid the cameras in the main ward. The other patients were still at the dining room by the time he returned to the kitchen with a banana peel and other trash. He took this opportunity to browse through some of the materials in the reading area. Before returning to his room, he picked up a couple of magazines from a coffee table as well as a pencil. Martin was humbled by the delight he felt at being able to acquire these simple items.

A little while later, his reading was interrupted by a knock on the door. It was David Harrington.

"Hi, Martin, how are you feeling today? I'd like to follow up on our discussion from yesterday, if you don't mind."

"Not at all, but it's important you understand that you've yet to give me any reason to trust you."

"I'm sure that will come in time. I don't think you'll find any of my questions to be problematic. Yesterday, you indicated that you knew a lot about both this hospital and the Pembroke facility. However, there's no record of you having been a patient at either place. I also checked our employee records and that came up blank too. Did you have a family member or close friend who was a patient at either hospital in the past?"

"No, and I'm sorry that our conversation yesterday intrigued you so much to put you to all this bother. It was merely a question I thought up on the spur of the moment."

"But I checked and you're correct. The children's playground is exactly where you said it was. How did you know?"

"Don't worry about it, David. It's Sunday. Weekends are for relaxing. We can talk later during the week."

Quinn did his best to squint through the security grille on the window frame as he thought about Harrington's visit, "The staff may have control about who goes to the dining room, but I'll decide who I talk to in my own room, and when."

When he heard the patients assembling for lunch, Martin chose to remain in his room so as not to engage the staff regarding his eating arrangements. He did not want a repeat of that morning's communication when he was admonished like a young child. A few moments later, the woman who had prevented him from eating breakfast, peered around his door and invited him to join the other patients for lunch. He thanked her and picked up a magazine to shield his face. As he joined the other patients, they exited the ward with their escort. The dining room was not far along the corridor.

Quinn followed the normal routine of lining up at the beginning of a buffet service counter. The wall opposite the entrance door was constructed from floor to ceiling with windows. Unlike the windows in the ward, these did not have security grilles to obstruct the view of the hospital grounds. Vertical blinds on a track were neatly set off to the side. The cafeteria had the ambiance of a high school dining room. There were about fifteen circular tables, each accommodating six place settings. The vinyl tile flooring had a light gray and blue fleck. This same blue color was featured on the walls. A suspended 2x4 ceiling, twelve feet above the floor housed recessed fluorescent light fixtures with parabolic lenses.

Each patient, or staff member, was able to choose from three lunch specials being offered that day. Martin recognized his problem before he got to the stack of trays. It was going to be difficult to keep his face concealed behind the magazine while simultaneously negotiating the buffet counter to collect his food, plastic cutlery, and drink. He quickly surveyed the room, looking for cameras. Although he failed to detect any surveillance equipment, he was savvy enough not to let his guard down. He shuffled through this challenge to the best of his ability and then chose a seat facing the window wall since there were clearly no cameras on that elevation. After eating his lasagna and drinking a carton of milk, he covered his face before placing the tray with his dirty dishes on the assigned counter. He then returned to his seat and waited for the other patients to finish. This Sunday lunch was Quinn's first proper meal since eating dinner on Thursday evening at the hotel.

The clock on the wall of the dining room indicated that it was 12:55 when the two staff members got the patients assembled and ready to leave. After a quick head count, everyone was escorted back to the ward. From what Martin could ascertain from a notice posted outside the nurses' station, afternoon visiting time began at 2:00 and ended at 5:00. There was also an evening session between 7:00 and 9:00.

The afternoon passed slowly for Quinn who chose to remain in his room. He spent the time reading magazines; re-measuring various dimensions for his room survey; and engaging in an exercise program of sit-ups, push-ups, and walking. One issue that continued to preoccupy him was the need to cover his face whenever he would leave his room. Seeing the coaxial cable in the kitchen only heightened his suspicions regarding the presence of cameras. He did not know how long he was going to have to stay at Westwood Lodge, but something would have to be done about them. Concealing his identity was proving to be more difficult than Martin could ever have imagined.

He left his room at 5:00, to join the rest of the patients for dinner. Once again, he chose a seat facing the wall of windows. Although this enabled him to eat his meal while not having to hide his face, he was conscious of the difficulty this could present for communicating with fellow patients or staff.

Upon his return to the ward, Quinn took a couple of sections of the Sunday newspaper to read in the privacy of his own room. His second day in Westwood Lodge ended with him laying awake, consumed with thoughts of how he would deal with the cameras. He could not allow Grasso's people to use them to get information about his whereabouts or situation. Finally, he fell asleep without any resolution of this problem.

3:00AM - Monday March 8, 1999

Initially he thought it was a dream. By the time Martin realized it was not, the hysterical girl had already pushed open his door and was screaming, "I want to see his face! I want to see his face!" Fortunately, two members of staff arrived just in time to grab the intruder before she tackled Quinn. He kept his head down as he quickly put on his jeans, wrapped the dress shirt around his face just below his eyes and tied it behind his head with its sleeves.

After they had escorted her back to her room, Martin could overhear the warnings to his fellow patient. Any further problems were to be resolved by restraining her using straps and the slots in the bed frame. The only thing that prevented this from immediately being carried out, was the paperwork such a practice mandated. The girl also gave an assurance that she would remain in her room for the remainder of the night.

It was Norman who returned to make sure everything was okay.

"Don't let that bother you, Martin."

"And you wonder why I had no desire to leave my room."

"Try to get back to sleep. We'll keep a closer eye on things."

Norman closed the door, however, contrary to the assurances, Quinn was bothered. He got into bed, but this time, fully clothed. "Was this girl sent by Seahorse to identify me?" he wondered. "Why was she so intent on seeing my face?" There were no further interruptions and eventually he managed to fall asleep.

7:30AM - Monday March 8, 1999

L aying on his bed, he thought about the previous night's intruder. "If she's working for Seahorse, then I have more problems than just the cameras," he realized. "Plus, if they're able to infiltrate the hospital with bogus patients, I'm sure they could also have members of the staff working for them." If he could not control the surveillance information gathered by undercover agents or cameras, he could at least, corrupt it by faking insanity or mental illness. Quinn considered his options. He had neither medical training nor formal acting experience to draw on. Faking an illness requiring outbursts or twitches would be too difficult. With both cameras and professional staff observing him, it would require too much effort on his part. The solution needed to be simple. Suddenly he was inspired.

Martin sat up in the bed and removed his jeans. He then put them on backwards, but did not zip them up until he had also put his shirt on back to front and closed all but its top collar button. He proceeded to tuck his shirt neatly into his jeans and then zipped them up. His belt was with the belongings that he had given to Peter Dorian. After putting on his shoes, he walked around the room, extremely pleased with the results of his idea. If anyone associated with Seahorse Communications was spying on him, surely they would report that he was completely crazy and not worthy of any further concern. If they suspected Quinn had shared his theories about Seahorse's evil intentions with the doctors or staff, then harming him would only give credence to his story. Martin satisfied himself that his shirt was neatly tucked into his jeans before stepping out of his room.

Patients were already assembled for the breakfast trip to the dining room. Martin was relieved he no longer had to conceal his face which would make communicating with both staff and patients much easier. No one bothered to question him about his new fashion statement. When the remaining patients joined the group, they were all escorted out of the ward. Quinn left the buffet line with a full tray and sat at a table in the middle of the dining room. Norman joined him a few minutes later.

"I can't help noticing your clothes are on back to front, Martin. What's that all about?"

"I had an awesome idea this morning, Norman. I came in here last Friday, primarily to escape from some very sinister people. I'll constantly need to keep looking over my shoulder. But dressed like this; I can give my neck a rest and see behind me without having to turn my head!"

"That's a very good idea," Norman agreed, continuing to eat his blueberry muffin as if their conversation was no more extraordinary than a discussion about the weather.

Martin questioned him about the home decorating project, evident from the small traces of white latex paint at the top of his finger nails. He felt it was important to get to know everything he could about the facility, its staff, and his fellow patients. Now that he was close enough to Norman, he could read his ID badge.

"You're not a nurse then?" Quinn observed.

"No. I'm a counselor."

"So Warren, who was working with you on Saturday afternoon, is he a counselor too?"

"Yes, and so is Emily over there."

The two men chatted a little longer until they finished their meal. It was 8:50 by the clock on the wall when Norman stood up and announced that it was time to return to the ward.

Martin noticed that the ward was a lot busier than it had been at any other time during his stay. He had only experienced its operation in a weekend mode. Monday mornings were the busiest for the medical staff because of the intake during the weekend. Quinn wondered if there was a correlation between the daily volume of alcohol consumed by a community and the number of patients sent to its mental hospitals. Since most alcohol is consumed on Friday and Saturday nights, this guaranteed fresh new faces for the staff on a Monday morning. On this occasion, Martin's would be one of them.

Word of Quinn's new fashion trend had traveled fast. It was not long before he heard a knock on his door, heralding the arrival of a short, overweight gentleman who introduced himself as Dr. Bennet. His dark blue sports jacket did its best to contain his gut which oozed out over beige pants like ice cream on top of a waffle cone. A white dress shirt added to the effect. When Martin looked at the solid brown neck tie, all he could think of was a chocolate Flake bar, stuck into a large ice cream cone. Quinn repeated the explanation he had given to Norman, while the doctor listened attentively and made notes in his file.

"Would you like me to prescribe a sedative? It would help you feel less stressed and more relaxed."

"No thank you, Doctor. I appreciate you've only spent a few minutes with me and have no reason to believe that the people I was with last week pose a real threat, but when I signed into the hospital on Friday, I understood that I wouldn't be forced to take any medication. Since I've been here, I've enjoyed the best night's sleep I've had in months and I don't feel any stress whatsoever. In fact, I'd recommend it to you too and your colleagues. Surely the hospital gives employees a discount rate for weekend breaks?"

The doctor concluded his consult and as he left the room, he smiled at the thought of Martin's advice. Or was it the sight of him standing there with his clothes on back to front?

Half an hour later, he had another visit from Angela Curran, complete with her fishing tackle box. They chatted while more blood samples were taken, but without any reference to his attire. "Why rock the boat?" Quinn thought to himself. "With patients like me, she'll never be out of a job. More blood samples generate more invoices for my insurance company."

Before Angela was finished, Norman popped his head around the door.

"Excuse me, Martin. You're new to our program, but Monday through Friday; all the patients meet in the common reading area at 10:00 each morning. So we'll see you up there in fifteen minutes. Okay?"

Nurse Curran finished sticking labels on three vials of blood, placed them into her fishing tackle box and left. Martin used the time before the group meeting to do some push-ups and sit-ups. However, the latter exercise proved to be more difficult than in the past, due to the unfortunate position of the front zipper of his jeans.

When he joined the rest of the patients, they were already seated in a circle of chairs arranged for the meeting. A female staff member had claimed a position directly below the clock on the wall. Quinn's upbringing in Northern Ireland enabled him to recognize the strategic value of her location. She had an unobstructed view of anyone who entered this area. From her vantage point, no patient could approach from behind. With a clear view across the hallway to the nurses' station, she could easily summon immediate assistance if needed.

Quinn sat in one of the empty seats and introduced himself. She acknowledged his greeting and indicated they were waiting for one more patient. He sat back in his chair and studied the latest health professional associated with his treatment. He knew that like the other staff members, she would have considerable impact on his life during the coming days. It was important he pay attention to this woman. There was a bundle of patient files on her lap and one undoubtedly had his name on its cover. Quinn reckoned she was in her late forties or early fifties. A tall thin woman, her shoulder length red hair was held in place at the back of her neck with a brown barrette. Stylish black rimmed glasses were suspended like a necklace on a fine gold-colored chain. She wore a neat dark brown skirt with matching shoes and a tan tweed jacket over a mustard blouse.

The meeting started when the last seat was taken by a young woman. Martin counted eleven patients including himself.

"Good morning everyone. For those of you who are new to our program, my name is Cynthia Melrose and I'm a psychologist here at the hospital. We have these meetings every weekday morning at 10:00. Monday meetings begin by welcoming our new patients. Let's go around the circle one at a time, so everyone can introduce themselves."

Cynthia then expanded on the purpose of the daily ward meetings. They were a forum for the staff to work with the patients as a single unit, with the objective that everyone would benefit from the social interaction. Before requesting input from the new patients, the others were asked if they had any issues they wished to discuss. One girl had a problem because she was not permitted to go outside on Sunday evening for a smoke break and another gentleman wanted to know why he was not allowed to go to the dining room for breakfast. Apparently, each of them had violated a rule which resulted in suspension of their privileges. Staff kept order by rewarding good behavior. Difficult patients were initially punished by losing privileges. If this failed to correct the problem, the next recourse was removal from the ward.

Ms. Melrose then solicited input from the new patients.

The young girl, who had been the last to join the meeting, raised her hand.

"Yes, Mandy?"

"I'd like to know why his clothes are on back to front."

"Maybe Martin would like to answer that question himself," Cynthia responded.

"I don't know whether I'm coming or going!"

His response drew a laugh from everyone, to which he added, "And I don't want any of you talking behind my back, because I'll be able to see you."

"Well I don't know if that answered your question well enough Mandy, but perhaps Martin will discuss his dress code later with his doctors. Now before we break, I want the new arrivals to pick up a journal and pen at the office. Very often, we find that patients can accelerate their return to good health by privately recording their thoughts."

The meeting came to an end and the circle of chairs was tidied by the patients. Martin, Mandy, and another male patient followed Cynthia to the nurses' station, where each was given a notebook and pen. Quinn then returned to his room so he could rest.

After lunch, Martin received visits from a Dr. Kaskarelis as well as Mark Butler, a Boston University Medical School student. Both repeated the questions asked earlier by their colleague, Dr. Bennet. Shortly before dinner there was another visit from David Harrington who, like his colleagues, also expressed an interest in the new fashion statement.

During dinner, Quinn sat beside a patient who had also been given writing material by Cynthia Melrose that morning. This indicated that he, too, was a new addition to the ward. Martin was struck at how much information Andrew, a real estate broker from Walpole, divulged during the course of their dinner conversation. Seemingly, he had been admitted into the hospital after a failed suicide attempt.

Later that evening, Martin relaxed alone in the TV room. As he scanned the limited channel selection, the transmission appeared to stutter and jump. He suspected that some of the programming had been censored and attributed this to the need to shield patients from anything which could cause concern or anguish. News stories or fictional drama involving suicides or other stressful situations would be good candidates for such censorship. Martin joked to himself as he compared the weather forecast to the actual conditions outside. "Was this variance because the weathermen can't get it right, or has the staff substituted the real forecast with a nicer less depressing version?"

By 8:00 the ward was full with visitors, any one of whom, Quinn surmised, could have been an agent for Seahorse Communications. Conscious of the need to disseminate misinformation, he made a point of walking around the common reading area to give the cameras and visitors an opportunity to witness his apparent lunacy. He understood the social benefit of this behavior, since legitimate visitors could take solace in the belief that their loved one's condition did not appear to be as critical as his. Eventually he returned to his room, like a polar bear in the zoo, retreating into its private quarters, away from public view.

After all the visitors had left, Martin went to get a drink and some snacks. Norman intercepted his retreat from the kitchen and inquired as to how he was feeling.

"Awesome. Since I started wearing my clothes backwards, things have been great. No more wrenching my neck to see if anyone's trying to sneak up behind me."

"Well, I'm glad that we've got you out of your room. You'll soon realize you've no need to fear anyone in here."

As the two men talked at the entrance to the kitchen, they were approached by a patient. Like Martin, he was about six feet tall, but built a little heavier. Quinn remembered him from the group meeting earlier that morning. He did not contribute to any of the discussions and since he was not invited to get a journal, Martin deduced he was not a new patient. Rather than excuse himself, or wait for either man to step aside, he attempted to push his way into the kitchen.

"What's the big hurry?" Quinn challenged as he stiffened up to resist the patient's attempts to squeeze by. "There's plenty of drinks and snacks for everyone - there's no need to panic."

The new arrival obviously disbelieved Martin's audit of the juice and snack inventory because he continued his efforts to push through. Martin's limited experience of life in the hospital prepared him to expect such a response, so he had braced himself solidly against the entrance.

"Easy does it, Paul!" Norman instructed.

"Be careful, Norman, I'm sure Paul's a real tough guy. You've probably noticed that he's able to sleep at night with the light off."

Martin's caustic humor did not go down well with his fellow patient. He gave another shove at Quinn, but to no avail. Martin responded by squaring up to Paul, using the wall behind him for support as he pushed back. By now, Warren had left the nurses' station in response to the developing disturbance. Both counselors wedged themselves between the patients and prevented the situation from deteriorating further. The two adversaries continued to maintain eye contact as they were separated. Quinn managed to keep a tight grip on his juice carton and a small packet of peanut butter crackers as Norman herded him down the hallway towards his room. "Forget about it," the counselor kept repeating, in an effort to defuse the situation. It was obvious to Martin that he and Paul would not be playing checkers the next time they met.

"What were you saying about not having to worry about anyone here?" Quinn quizzed sarcastically.

Norman tried to respond and rationalize the situation, but both of them knew that recent events did not support his hypothesis.

Alone in his room, Quinn pondered the significance of this latest incident. "Did Seahorse Communications send Paul to check on me?" It reinforced his need to be more cognizant of the fact that neither staff nor patients could be trusted. Before getting undressed for bed, he spent half an hour doing push-ups, sit-ups, and some stretching exercises. Given his recent encounter, Martin understood the importance of keeping in shape. He had a crazy woman burst into his room on Sunday night and now this episode with Paul. He was beginning to question the wisdom of Dr. Dean's suggestion that he would benefit from a stay at Westwood Lodge!

7:00AM - Tuesday March 9, 1999

Martin was down to the last pair of clean underpants and tee-shirt that Sean Feeney had brought on Saturday evening. He set them aside to wear after he had taken a shower. Later, he would need to check out the laundry program. Although he had showered every day, he had not been trusted with a razor. This matter too, needed to be addressed.

As the patients left the ward for the dining room, he noticed that his sparring partner, Paul, had not joined the group. He ate breakfast with Andrew and discovered that they shared a common desire to see the Boston Bruins win the Stanley Cup again. Later, Warren supervised while Quinn shaved with a disposable plastic razor. When he had finished, the counselor reclaimed the blade and left him alone to shower.

* * * * * * *

When Martin joined the morning meeting, Cynthia Melrose was already seated along with some of the other patients. Paul, however, was not yet present. Quinn believed his fellow patient's bedroom was located between this common area and the double doors of the ward which led to the dining room. Accordingly, he chose a chair that provided a clear view of the direction from which he thought Paul would appear. Several others arrived before Martin spotted his nemesis walking towards him. Quinn lowered his head to avoid eye contact, and just as Paul approached the circle, Martin uttered the buzz phrase made famous by Michael Buffer, while announcing professional boxing matches in Las Vegas.

"LLLLLLLLLLLLLLLLLLLET'S GET READY TO RUM-BLLLLLLLLLLLLLLLE!"

Upon hearing the taunt, Paul erupted. He tossed a chair out of his way and charged across the room. Quinn jumped up to defend himself, while Cynthia shouted for assistance from other hospital personnel. Warren and another male counselor sprinted from the nurses' station, arriving just in time to intercede.

"You're extremely edgy when you don't get a proper breakfast," Martin observed.

"Shut the fuck up," Paul yelled.

Martin knew he was in no danger, now that he had help on each side.

"You do realize, Westwood Lodge is going to lose one of its star ratings after word of this behavior leaks out," Quinn joked to Warren and his two hundred and fifty pound colleague.

"I need you to sit down now, Paul, or you're going to be removed from this ward," Warren instructed sternly.

As Quinn surveyed the faces on the other patients, it looked as if they were disappointed that the staff had been able to intervene so quickly. It was now evident why the counselors wore athletic shoes. Cynthia did not appear to share the patients' disappointment. She had shuffled through her pile of files and was entering a note into one of them. Martin could not see whose file was being updated. Paul knew that being removed from the ward would most likely deprive him of any future opportunity to retaliate, so he complied with the counselor's command and took a seat opposite his rival. Warren's intimidating colleague sat next to Cynthia. The meeting continued without any further outbursts from Paul, or provocation from Quinn.

Regular meetings between a patient and his or her primary psychiatric doctor or psychologist, usually took place any time between 11:00 and 3:00. There was also a rotation schedule which ensured twenty-four hour access to these professionals in the event that a patient needed medical attention. Over the course of the next four hours, Martin received separate visits from his regular medical team. From their discussions he concluded that Dr. Kaskarelis and Dr. Bennet were psychiatric doctors, while David Harrington was a psychologist. Mark Butler was a medical student, satisfying a psychiatric medicine course requirement. The main development of the day's consultations was a suggestion by Dr. Kaskarelis that Martin permit him to invite Margaret to visit. Quinn had no objection to this, or to the doctor's recommendation that a colleague address the effects Martin's hospitalization could have on his family.

"Often, these events can be very stressful on the immediate family. Dr. Elizabeth Armstrong specializes in such issues and I think it would help if she spoke to both of you, to make sure all the Quinns are looked after."

"That sounds fine," Martin acknowledged.

3:00PM - Tuesday March 9, 1999

Before the end of his shift, Warren instructed Martin on the use of the laundry facilities, located adjacent to the TV room. The counselor stressed the need for consideration for other patients by not leaving clothes unattended in the machines, since they were available on a first-come, first-serve basis.

Walking back to his room, Martin met Jenna, one of the younger patients. She was with a woman who appeared to be her mother. Wearing a warm winter coat and carrying a small suitcase, Jenna shared with him the good news that she was going home.

"That's awesome," he replied when she reached out to give him a hug. "Look after yourself and stay safe."

"I will," she promised as they parted.

Quinn walked past his own room and into the one which had just been vacated by Jenna. It was better furnished than his, so he decided to help himself to some of the furniture. First he lifted one of the chairs and carried it to his room. Then he went back, leaving his door wide open, so he could push the chest of drawers from one room to the other. The whole operation took less than sixty seconds and was witnessed by no one. Again Quinn returned to Jenna's room where he rearranged the remaining furniture to minimize the visual effects of his work. Then he spent the next twenty minutes organizing his new furniture in various layouts, until he found one that he liked. With his toiletries and belongings neatly put away, Martin went to transfer his clothes from the washer to the dryer. "How lucky was that?" he mused. "Now I have somewhere to put my clean laundry." Content with his good fortune, he lay down on his bed for an afternoon nap.

7:00AM - Wednesday March 10, 1999

Wednesday morning followed the established routine of breakfast, ward group meeting, and private consults. Dr. Kaskarelis confirmed that Margaret would be coming in to visit at 2:00.

"I've arranged for both of you to meet with my colleague, Dr. Armstrong, tomorrow afternoon at 3:00," he continued. "Also, you should know that when I spoke with Margaret, she expressed how much she was looking forward to coming to visit you."

"Excellent! I'll clear my calendar for this afternoon and leave it entirely open for Margaret's visit and I'll put Dr. Armstrong into my schedule for tomorrow at 3:00."

The manner and tone of Quinn's response had the doctor almost believing he had just obtained approval for these plans from the hospital director. During consults with this patient, he constantly had to remind himself who was in charge.

After the doctor left, Martin reflected upon the upcoming visit with his wife. He had replied "Excellent!" to Andreus Kaskarelis' plans even though he recalled that the last day he had spent in her presence was very nearly his last one on earth. He had consented to being hospitalized in order to escape John Grasso and his cohorts. It had not been his intent to have the staff pry into the mental health of either himself or any of the Quinn family. As he left his room for lunch, Martin complimented himself on the new furniture layout. He was looking forward to hosting Margaret.

During lunch, Quinn sat with some patients who seemed keenly interested in the fact that he was born in Ireland.

"St. Patrick's Day is next week!" observed Jessica.

She was a good looking brunette who did not appear to be more than twenty years of age. Apparently, she was in Westwood Lodge because of substance abuse issues.

"Are you going to organize a party?" she asked.

Before Quinn could respond, the other patients around the table all voiced their support for her idea. How could he refuse?

* * * * * * *

It was a little after 2:00 and Quinn was in the TV room when he spotted Margaret walking past the window with Eileen O'Reilly. Eileen was a neighbor and good friend of the Quinn family. Her mother had emigrated from County Donegal in Ireland, where some of her relatives still lived. Eileen was very fond of the Quinns and treated them like they were her own family.

The two women stopped at the window of the nurses' station and were speaking with one of the staff by the time Quinn approached from behind.

"Can I help you ladies?" he interrupted.

Margaret and Eileen turned to see Martin standing, newspaper in hand, apparently oblivious to the fact that his clothes were on back to front. Neither of the two women could hide their shock at seeing him like this.

"Come on and sit down over here," he suggested.

"I want a hug first," demanded Margaret with a smile.

"Me too," added Eileen.

The three of them found a couple of empty seats around a coffee table in the common area.

"This was good of you to come along with Margaret today."

"We Irish folk have to stick together. How are you doing?" Eileen inquired.

"All the better for seeing you both."

"I brought you some things from home," Margaret began, "but they took them from me. Apparently everything gets inspected before it comes into the ward."

"Don't worry; they'll pass it along after they've checked through it."

He could sense that Margaret was distracted by his appearance.

"What do you think of my new fashion statement? Don't you think I fit in better, dressed like this?"

"I suppose you do," his wife acknowledged. "But is it very practical?"

"More than you could ever imagine, but enough about me. How's Brendan?"

"He's in Seattle."

"Seattle in Washington State? What's he doing there?"

"It was Shelley Tyre's idea. He's spending spring break with his classmate, Ryan Harrison. His dad's in Seattle and they're staying with him. It was short notice, but I managed to get him booked on the same flight as Ryan. Both boys were thrilled."

Martin thought how perfect it was that Brendan had been taken away for two weeks. He knew Shelley Tyre must have given serious consideration to his concerns after he had sent Chris Donovan to Thayer Academy on Friday morning. "That must have prompted her to contact Sarah Harrison to see if Brendan could accompany Ryan," he surmised privately. Quinn was touched by Shelley Tyre's thoughtfulness. He had to acknowledge that even if she believed Martin had no real reason for concern, she had decided it was prudent to protect her student. If, in fact, Brendan was not in any danger, then her plan merely resulted in a nice vacation for him. On the other hand, if the danger was real, then she had helped get him 3,000 miles away from Boston.

"Isn't she a very special person?" Martin responded.

"She really is," Margaret agreed. "Did you know she's leaving the school in June? Thayer won't be the same without her. From what I understand, she's taking a new post closer to her home."

"Her husband runs a SCUBA diving shop in Jamestown, Rhode Island and that's why we talked for so long when I was at the school last week," Martin explained. "She lives near the Jamestown Bridge where Seahorse wants to put the fiber-optic cable."

"That's incredible," Eileen remarked. "Do you mean she drives every day from Jamestown, Rhode Island to Braintree?"

"Yes," replied Martin. "That's at least a ninety minute commute in each direction."

"She's actually on a diving trip with her husband at the moment, in the British Virgin Islands," Margaret added.

"Hey! Do you guys want to see my room?"

"Why don't you two go down," Eileen suggested. "I'll stay here."

"Are you sure?"

"Yes, I'll be fine," she insisted.

"Well this is very cozy," Margaret remarked upon entering her husband's room.

"Thank you. I've tried to do my best with the furniture and a few items I've picked up."

"You've done a nice job, but how do you feel?"

"I feel fine, but the most important thing is that you and Brendan are safe. Now listen Margaret, it's very important you don't believe everything that you see and hear around you. Even in this hospital. Don't trust anyone, until they've proven to you they can be trusted."

"The people in here only want to help you, Martin."

"You don't know any of these people. Take your time and don't make any hasty decisions about the staff or patients."

Margaret decided it was better to avoid any further discussion on the matter. Besides, she would only be trying to reason with a man who was wearing his clothes back to front!

"We should be getting back to Eileen. Give me another hug before I go."

They found Eileen engrossed in a conversation with one of the patients regarding NASA's plans for future missions to Mars.

"Steve!" Quinn interrupted, "That's classified information you're divulging. You need to go back to your office and finish up that review. I thought you had a conference call scheduled at 4:30 with Mission Control. They're going to be looking for your evaluation on those trajectory calculations for the third phase of the launch sequence."

"You're right. It was nice meeting you, Eileen," Steve acknowledged as he excused himself.

"I trust we can rely on your discretion, Mrs. O'Reilly, not to disclose any sensitive information you become privy to, while here at Westwood Lodge?" Quinn joked.

"My lips are sealed," Eileen laughed.

"You seem to get on well with the other patients," Margaret noted.

"Some better than others. Let me show you an example of a patient who has some anger management issues."

Martin had spotted Paul coming out of the TV room, heading in the direction of the kitchen.

"Please observe the patient walking behind me," he instructed the two women while turning his back to Paul. "Note the classic Pavlovian Response to my command."

Martin then uttered the trigger phrase, "LLLLLLLLLLLLLLLLLLLLET'S GET READY TO RUMBLLLLLLLLLLLLLLE!"

His tone and volume were audible enough for Paul to hear, but not for the two members of staff standing by the nurses' station. With the aid of the parabolic mirror located in the upper corner of the common area, Martin was able to observe Paul's violent reaction. "You're such a fuckin' wise guy," he bellowed angrily as he scrambled towards Quinn, tossing chairs out of his way without regard to where they landed.

The two women were horrified as the patient charged towards their little group. They backed up as far as they could, fearing the two pursuing male counselors would not be able to catch the crazed man before he reached them. Martin smiled and remained motionless but kept his attention focused on events unfolding in the mirror above him. At the last second, Quinn took a quick step to the right just as his assailant went airborne.

The two counselors pinned Paul to the ground where he landed. Despite being outnumbered, the patient put up a valiant struggle. Finally, he succumbed. As they escorted him back to his room, he launched a tirade of threats in Martin's direction, littered with numerous expletives, which left everyone with a clear understanding of his future intentions.

"Someone ought to check his medication levels," Martin observed aloud.

"That's terrible!" Margaret muttered after Paul had been led away.

"I don't think so. He was the one who started to mess with me the other evening. Besides, I'm providing a valuable medical service by exposing these latent rage tendencies."

"I need to speak with the doctors," Margaret continued. "That guy really wants to hurt you."

"There's no need for that. His perception of himself as being a threat to me far exceeds reality. Now, you two have surely had enough for your first day here."

* * * * * * *

After dinner, Martin lay on his bed wondering how he had ever found the energy to work. Recently it seemed that he needed at least ten hours of sleep per day. The hectic pace of the last six weeks had certainly taken its toll. His mind and body were seizing every possible opportunity to rest and recover.

He awoke to the sound of Norman calling his name to inform him that he had a visitor. Quinn found Eddie Gallagher sitting in the common reading area.

"How are you feeling?"

Reflex had triggered the question; however, Gallagher had no intention of giving any credence to the assessment of a man who was wearing his clothes back to front. Quinn could tell from the expression that his business partner had not expected to see him dressed in such a fashion.

"Fine. How did things go in Ireland?"

"It was sad, but we all did what we had to do. Thanks for asking."

"Well, I guess you don't need me to tell you that things went a bit crazy here at the end of last week."

"I talked to Tom Sullivan and John Grasso. Both of them acknowledged that you were under a lot of stress. John wants to see you rested and back on the job."

Martin did not feel the need to share any details from Friday morning's events at the hotel. Rather, he decided to let Eddie reveal the information he had gleaned since returning from Ireland.

"Listen Martin, John Grasso wants Cove to continue with the bridge project. I've assured him we can still come through and get this job done. But to do it, I need you back healthy and involved."

Eddie paused briefly before continuing. "How do you feel about that? Are you up for it?"

Quinn considered Gallagher's proposition. He certainly felt rested enough to resume working on the project. Cove had the resources and the job had the potential to yield a very lucrative profit. His only reservation was, had John Grasso's people realized he had uncovered their plot to gain control over the telecommunications industry? He believed his best approach would be to continue with the pretense that he was mentally deranged and completely unaware of their true identity. Then he could work his way back into the program without anyone realizing he had discovered their agenda. Martin even considered the fact that there may not be any organized crime involvement with Seahorse Communications. In that case, there was every reason to continue with the fiber-optic bridge project.

"I've got no problem finishing the job, if that's what you feel is best, but I'm going to be in here for a little while longer."

"That won't be an issue. I'll bring you whatever you want from the office and you can tell me what needs to be done each day. Given Seahorse's schedule and its commitments to CellTell Atlantic, it's important that we get the job back on track. I'm not familiar with what you've done so far and the only way this job can be completed in time to get the $40,000 bonus is to have you continue to manage it."

"I've given Anderson Aluminum enough information to fabricate the bridge brackets, as well as order the extruded aluminum top sections from the foundry in Canada," Quinn explained. "However, they need a cutting list from Cove which indicates the lengths of the sections between the support brackets. Before we can give them this information, we'll need to carry out a detailed field survey of the entire bridge."

Eddie took notes as Martin continued with specific instructions and directions during their "job meeting." The irony of the situation did not escape Gallagher or Quinn. This construction project was now being managed by a man in a mental hospital who was walking around with his clothes on back to front.

"If this gets all screwed up," Martin laughed, "I'm going to stay in here and you can deal with the fallout."

"I want the phone number for your doctor so I can have him sign me up at short notice. I'll have him get me into this ward too."

"I know we can get this job back on track," Quinn confirmed. "I can call you from the ward without any problem; however, there's no guarantee I can receive a phone call and I may not be given your phone messages."

"Then I'll wait for you to call me. The next time I come in to see you, I'll bring you a current set of shop drawings plus anything else from the job files that I think you'll need."

"Sounds good, now would you like to meet Julius Caesar or perhaps Cleopatra? I believe they're in the TV room as we speak."

"Another time," Eddie joked back, "I really have to get going."

"You do realize that you can't visit me when Margaret is here. You're not at the top of her Favorite People List."

"I understand. Besides, it's not really convenient to visit during the day. Later rather than earlier works best for me. If I see your white Expedition in the visitors' parking lot, then I'll know to wait until she leaves."

9:20PM - Wednesday March 10, 1999

Martin was watching TV alone when a man he had never seen before entered the room and sat down. He was obviously a new patient since he did not have an ID badge, nor was he dressed as neatly as any of the hospital staff. He was not as tall as Martin, probably five foot - ten. Quinn could tell from the manner in which he sank into the chair that he had known happier times. Martin understood how tough it was finding oneself locked in a psychiatric hospital. The quality of the relationships with staff and other patients was key to easing the experience.

"Hi. Martin Quinn."

"Hi, I'm James."

"Did you just get in?"

"Yes, about twenty minutes ago."

"There really isn't any welcoming committee here in the ward. If you want some snacks or juice, there's a small kitchen just beyond that common reading area opposite the nurses' station."

"Thanks."

"Also, if you need extra bed linen or blankets, there's more in that cupboard behind me."

Quinn continued to watch television while he casually pitched the next question.

"How come you're in here?"

He felt that his own status as a patient entitled him to ask this intrusive question and strangely, it seemed appropriate.

"I killed a guy," James nonchalantly replied.

Even though the television program was far less interesting than anything the ward's newest patient had to offer, Martin opted to focus on the screen rather than continue their conversation. After James left the room, Quinn wondered, once again, why Dr. Dean ever thought a stay in Westwood Lodge would be therapeutic.

Martin decided to get a drink and a snack before going to bed. As he closed the refrigerator door and turned to leave, he realized that James had entered the kitchen and was now presenting somewhat of an obstacle to Quinn's exit. It was not an impossible task for two people to pass in the narrow kitchen; however, it did require an effort on the part of both.

As they squeezed by one another, Quinn gave James a friendly slap on the shoulder and asked, "How's it going, Killer?"

"It's all good," he replied with a smile.

Martin continued down the hallway to his own room. Another day in Westwood Lodge was coming to an end. Killer James was right, he thought to himself. "It's all good."

7:30AM - Thursday March 11, 1999

It had snowed during the night. Not much more than an inch or two, but enough to freshen up the landscape. After doing some exercises, Martin dressed and went to breakfast.

He chose an empty table at the window so he could look out at the picture perfect winter scene. The sight of this fine building showing signs of distress saddened Martin. Being involved in construction heightened his awareness of such things. In the distance he could see a fence that surrounded tennis courts which were no longer maintained. Unfortunately, the New England climate did not share Quinn's nostalgic appreciation for beautiful buildings and their grounds. It torched them mercilessly during summer months and abandoned them to the freezing elements of winter.

Martin's reflection on the scene was interrupted by Jessica and Hilary, two of his fellow patients. Hilary was in her mid twenties and probably two or three years older than Jessica.

"Hi Martin," the duet sang out. "Mind if we join you?"

"No, not at all ladies."

"What have you got planned for the St. Patrick's Day party?" Jessica asked.

"Well, I'm kinda lost for resources in here, Jess. To tell you the truth, I haven't really done anything."

"You'd better get to it," Hilary scolded. "We're going to be very disappointed if you don't organize something."

All three chatted away covering a wide range of topics which included their observations and opinions on the character of different staff members and patients.

"What's with that Paul guy?" Jessica asked. "Is he still in the ward?"

"Yes, as far as I know," Martin replied.

"The only times that I've seen him outside his room are whenever he's been charging at you," she continued.

"I don't believe I'll be inviting him to the St. Patrick's Day party," Quinn quipped wryly.

As usual, the morning's group meeting was chaired by Cynthia Melrose. Quinn was disappointed to see that Paul was on his best behavior. He was sure the other patients shared his feelings that life in the mental hospital was more interesting whenever the inmates acted up. He needed to contrive a way of triggering an outburst from Paul, but without anyone being aware of the provocation.

Shortly before lunch, Martin thought of a way to do it. He went to the two pay phones located just beyond the nurses' station and wrote down the number of the first phone which was mounted on the wall beside the message-board. He then proceeded further along the alcove and entered the private phone booth, closing the door behind him. It was standard procedure for patients to answer any calls that came in on the phone located beside the message-board. His plan was to place a call to that phone and ask to speak with Paul. Once his nemesis was on the line, Quinn intended to trigger a response by issuing the "LLLLLLLLLLLLLLLLLLET'S GET READY TO RUMBLLLLLLLLLLLLLLE!" challenge.

When Martin dialed the number, he was surprised that the phone rang in the nurses' station. From his vantage point in the booth, he was able to see Warren answer it. There must have been caller ID because the counselor knew immediately where the call was coming from.

"Who wants to speak with Paul?" he asked, looking directly at the booth while hastily signaling Cynthia Melrose to find out who was using the phone.

"Don King," replied Quinn with a smile, amused by the realization his plan had been scuttled.

Cynthia confronted him as he exited the booth.

"Who were you calling?" she demanded sternly.

"I think I got a wrong number. I didn't get the person I was trying to call."

By this time, patients had assembled outside the administration office so they could be escorted to the dining room for lunch. Cynthia knew it was pointless to pursue the matter, especially since Warren was standing at the office door and making no effort to hide the fact that he was laughing. Besides, she also found it difficult to converse seriously with someone whose clothes were on back to front.

At lunch, Martin sat with a new patient who had come into the ward the evening before. By the time the meal was over, Quinn understood as much as any of the doctors did about Dan. He was a twenty-eight year old computer programmer who worked for a bank in Boston. He was married and had one child, a two-year-old girl. His steadily increasing dependence on alcohol had eventually become an intolerable situation. With help from his company's Employee Assistance Program, a plan was put into action the previous afternoon, but with somewhat less than one hundred percent of Dan's own approval. He appreciated Martin's efforts to introduce him to life in the ward.

Margaret arrived at the hospital at 2:45 and was escorted to her husband's room by Dianne Russo. From what Martin could ascertain, Russo was one of the senior members of staff. He had never seen her cover a night shift and regularly witnessed her giving orders to other employees. He did not believe she was a very nice individual. She rarely smiled and her character seemed to be of a person who enjoyed having control over both patients and co-workers. Quinn could not help thinking of Nurse Ratched in the movie *One Flew Over The Cuckoo's Nest*. Diane Russo, however, was no movie star. She was at least forty pounds overweight for her five foot - four inch frame and had short gray hair. Although she was in her early forties, the thick gold-rimmed bi-focal glasses she wore made her look much older.

The Quinns were only alone for ten minutes before they were joined by Dr. Armstrong, a pleasant woman in her mid to late fifties. Despite the psychiatrist's unthreatening manner, Martin sensed that Margaret was feeling uncomfortable.

Dr. Armstrong was used to such responses and politely repeated the benefits of working with all members of the patient's family to ensure the best outcome for everyone. Her efforts to allay Margaret's anxieties were interrupted by a knock at the door. It was Dr. Kaskarelis.

"How is everyone?" he inquired.

The two doctors performed a well practiced professional duet, reinforcing the benefits of working with the whole family. Martin did not protest or argue because he believed Margaret would have her own reservations about such a program.

"Well, there's something else I want to run by you, Martin," Dr. Kaskarelis continued. "I work as a consultant with Monk Pharmaceuticals, assisting them with trial studies for drugs they are developing, as well as others which have already been released onto the market. Even after a medication has been cleared by the FDA for general use, its performance continues to be monitored by the pharmaceutical industry. With your permission, I'd like you to participate in a double-blind survey of Depakote. I believe your symptoms are consistent with bi-polar disorder. It's not an uncommon condition and is easily treated with the use of drugs such as this."

"I'm not too happy about getting involved with any drug program," Martin protested. "I thought I made that clear when I came into the hospital."

"That's why we're only discussing the issue and requesting your participation in this program. Perhaps I should explain it better."

Andreus Kaskarelis closed Quinn's medical file and returned his ball point pen to the inside pocket of his jacket.

"The double-blind survey is administered under strict controls by Monk Pharmaceuticals. Some of the participating patients receive the actual drug while others receive a placebo, which has no medication. Even the doctor isn't told if a patient is taking the real drug. That way, we can make a more balanced and objective observation during the trial. If you participate in this program and are given the placebo, then you won't be getting any medication."

Martin thought about it for a few moments.

"I think I'll go ahead and work with you on this," he conceded.

"That's great," Dr. Kaskarelis acknowledged as he reopened the file. "I have some forms here I need you to sign. It acknowledges that I have explained the testing program to your satisfaction and records your agreement to be a participant."

Quinn was impressed at the speed with which the doctor presented the pen and paper. Any life insurance salesman would have envied such moves. He did not mind getting involved in the trials because it was not his intention to take the drugs when they were administered. His objective was to give the impression that he was a cooperative patient.

"You see, Mrs. Quinn," Dr. Kaskarelis explained, "with double-blind tests on drugs that have already been cleared by the FDA, many people do not want to participate because of the possibility they'll receive a placebo during the study. This is certainly true for patients with cancer and similar diseases."

Margaret did not know how to respond to this assurance. "Is my husband a patient or an experiment?" she thought to herself.

"As with many drugs, Martin," Dr. Kaskarelis continued, "they should not be taken on an empty stomach. So you'll take it twice a day: once after breakfast; and again after dinner. All medications are dispensed at the nurse's station at 9:30am and 9:30pm."

Both doctors stood up in order to bring the meeting to a close.

"I'll check in and see you tomorrow," Dr. Kaskarelis suggested.

"I'll also include you in my patient consults over the next few days, Martin," his colleague added.

After the doctors left, Quinn attempted to reassure his wife that she had no reason to be worried about him being in Westwood Lodge.

"Have you heard from Brendan?"

"Yes. I spoke with him just before I left to come over here. He's really enjoying Seattle."

"That's good. Does he know his dad's in a mental hospital?"

"No. I told him Dr. Dean wanted you in the hospital because you were exhausted and needed rest. I didn't tell him where you were specifically."

"Well, if he's going to be in Seattle until the end of next week, then I need to set that as the goal for my release. I don't want him to come home from his vacation to find me here."

"Don't worry about anything like that. Just concentrate on getting plenty of rest and following whatever treatment the doctors prescribe."

After he and a staff member had escorted Margaret to the door of the ward, Martin returned to his room via the kitchen. He collected a few packets of peanut butter snacks and two lime juice cartons from the fridge and placed them in the bottom drawer of the bureau. He had decided to collect a stash of snacks and green drinks for their St. Patrick's Day party. If possible, he wanted to have a bottle of green lime juice for every patient in the ward. Given his circumstances, it was the best he could manage. Even though there would be no alcohol, Quinn anticipated this St. Patrick's Day party would be just as enjoyable as other years. If nothing else, it would be the first one he had spent in a mental hospital.

With the juice and snacks hidden, he lay on his bed to rest before dinner. He draped his right forearm over his closed eyes and thought about how tough this whole ordeal had to be for Margaret. Having her husband locked up in a psychiatric hospital had to be frightening. Furthermore, her own family was three thousand miles away in Ireland. Of course Martin's cousins, uncle, and aunt had reached out to offer support, but at a time like this, there really was no substitute for one's immediate family. What could he say to her in order to make her feel any better? No one was going to rely on assurances offered by a mental patient. His best course of action was to develop an exit strategy from the hospital. Setting the date of Brendan's return from Seattle as a goal for his release made good sense.

5:00PM - Thursday March 11, 1999

At dinner, Martin was sitting with Dan when they were joined by Jessica and Mandy. The four patients joked and laughed their way through the meal. This was a good thing for Dan since he had just spent a miserable afternoon meeting with several of his doctors. Apparently, his incarceration would extend, at a very minimum, until Wednesday of the following week. This news reinforced Quinn's decision to begin planning his own discharge from the hospital. That was never going to happen while he continued to wear his clothes back to front. He would have to give this issue some serious thought over the next few days. Many factors had to be considered including the need to gauge the threat from Seahorse Communications. He would assess this risk during discussions with Eddie Gallagher regarding the bridge project. After the weekend, if he thought things appeared to be safer on that scene, he would consider wearing his clothes correctly. In the meantime, he would maintain the charade.

Later in the TV room, Quinn encountered an extremely angry Killer James.

"What's up, Killer?"

"These fuckers are messing me around. I know my rights, you know! I want outta here before Friday night; otherwise I'll not get out until Monday. No one gets their papers signed off over the weekend. I'm getting the run around and I can't get a fuckin' answer."

Martin tried to pacify his fellow patient the best he could, however, he was more concerned about his own predicament. Brendan would be coming home from Seattle the following Friday. If Quinn wanted to be home before his son returned, then it was important he pay attention to matters like this. His discharge paperwork needed to be approved ahead of time to ensure that he did not become a victim of similar administrative traps. As long as his health insurance company continued to pay the bills, the hospital would have no incentive to release him. As he listened, he considered how lucky he was to have fostered friendships with both staff and patients. Had he not reached out to welcome James earlier in the week, Quinn very much doubted he would have been alerted to such a problem, until it was too late. While this was tumbling around in his mind, he happened to look into the ward, just in time to see his two cousins, Katie and Jane walk by.

"I'll catch up with you later, my cousins just got here."

"Those girls are your cousins?" James inquired with a smile as two attractive redheads disappeared past the window.

Martin responded in the affirmative as he made his way out the door. It was all very well engaging in idle chat with Killer James, but he did not need the conversation leading to requests for his cousins' phone numbers. He needed to quickly chaperone his visitors to the safety of his own room.

He caught up with the girls as they approached the window of the nurses' station.

"How are you?" they asked in sync, while taking turns giving him a hug.

"Awesome! It's great to see you two."

He cited the lack of privacy in the common reading area as a reason to hang out in his own room.

"Well, this is home for the moment!" he announced, opening his door.

"You probably don't want to hear this Martin, but I believe Grammy has a better room," joked Katie.

Grammy was her eighty-five year old grandmother who lived in a very comfortable assisted living community in the Chestnut Hill suburb of Boston.

"Well, you've certainly got the whole family talking now," Jane reported. "Uncle Dan and Aunty Lorna are all upset and concerned."

"There's no need to be," he assured them.

"I wouldn't be too sure of that," Jane countered, her eyes scanning Martin's clothes.

"Oh. Don't worry about the outfit. I'm dressed like this for a couple of reasons."

"Do explain," Katie insisted.

"Well, for one thing, you're only going to come off as aloof and pompous if you come into the hospital insisting that, 'you don't really belong in here.' Arguing that, 'everyone else is crazy, but you're not,' doesn't really endear you to either staff or patients. By dressing like this, I find everyone more accepting and friendly. It's just like when I came over from Ireland all those years ago. You girls made sure I got rid of my Irish clothes and started wearing what was more appropriate for living in America."

"The scary thing is," Jane responded, "it all sounds like a perfectly reasonable explanation. Does that mean I should be in here too?"

"In your case, I would exercise restraint. It wouldn't be wise to copy me. I imagine that wearing your bra backwards would be extremely uncomfortable!"

"Okay," Jane agreed, "I'll just remain a slave to convention and continue to dress the way that I do. Anyway, I brought you a Discman, so you can listen to some music. We stopped in at the house and Margaret gave us a few of your CDs."

"Great!" Martin replied as he accepted the items, secretly hoping they had not brought any Aerosmith CDs. "That was very thoughtful of you. I'm glad you gave me these items directly. Apparently, you're supposed to get the staff's permission before you give anything to the patients. It could take days before they'd pass something like this along."

His cousins had only been gone five minutes when Eddie Gallagher arrived with shop drawings and other information related to the Jamestown project. They spent the next twenty minutes going over the material.

"I have Bill Snow scheduled to go out tomorrow and survey the bridge like you asked. I should have his report for you by Monday at the latest."

Bill Snow was an independent professional land surveyor. Cove employed him when either a job's specifications required the services of a professional surveyor, or as in this case, when the task warranted engaging someone with his expertise.

"I spoke to Louis Fusco this afternoon at Anderson," Eddie continued. "He's making good progress with the brackets you ordered. He already has two hundred manufactured and sent to the anodizing plant. He expects to have the other six hundred fabricated by the end of next week. The anodizing will take another week after that. Then all eight hundred brackets will be ready for installation on the bridge."

"We can't allow this time schedule to drift out any later than what he's telling you. Make sure you speak with him regularly."

"I will," Gallagher promised, "but how much longer do you think that you'll be in here?"

"I intend to get out by next Friday at the latest."

"You can't get out any sooner?"

"I doubt it. The doctors here would be out of a job if the patients had any say about their own health. It's going to take some time. I don't even get a vote when they all get together to discuss my case. Next week I'm going to focus on an exit strategy."

When Gallagher left, Quinn stopped at the kitchen and took a couple of green juice cartons from the refrigerator, as well as some snacks. His plan to gather enough green juices for all the patients and staff members to celebrate St. Patrick's Day was coming together nicely. On Tuesday night, he intended to return all the green juices to the refrigerator so that they would be chilled and ready to distribute at Wednesday morning's group meeting. The juices were all vacuum sealed and did not require constant refrigeration. The peanut snacks were individually wrapped portions which also did not require refrigeration. Back in his room, he added them to the growing stash in the chest of drawers. He had just finished when there was a knock on the door. It was Angela Curran.

Martin knew immediately why she had come to see him. In her left hand she was carrying a paper cup half filled with water, as well as a smaller one containing a white almond shaped pill. He had not expected the course to start so soon.

"I have your Depakote medication that Dr. Kaskarelis prescribed. I wasn't sure if you realized you need to line up with the other patients at 9:30 each morning and evening at the nurses' station."

Obligingly, he placed the pill inside his mouth, downed the entire cup of water, and handed back the empty containers.

As soon as she left the room, he instantly retrieved the pill from under his tongue, wrapped it in a tissue, and placed it in his pocket so that he could dispose of it later.

It was only 9:30, so Martin lay on his bed and listened to some U2 on the Discman his cousins had brought him. "This isn't too bad," he thought to himself. He was beginning to accumulate a few luxuries, which added to his quality of life in Westwood Lodge. Margaret was safe and Brendan was enjoying a vacation in Seattle. Furthermore, it looked as if the bridge project would be continuing without any perceivable impact from Friday's episode in the hotel. In addition, Cove was also taking care of its obligations to other clients.

A little before 10:00, Quinn went into the men's restroom and flushed his Depakote tablet down the toilet in one of the stalls. After washing his hands, he used a paper towel to open the door of the restroom. Martin understood that mental illness was not contagious. Nevertheless, he was conscious of the propensity for diseases and illnesses to be transferred in an environment where people share common facilities.

As Quinn drifted off to sleep, he considered how he was going to orchestrate his exit from the hospital. He knew that he would have to begin wearing his clothes correctly, as well as win over his doctors' good graces. Ostensibly participating in the Depakote study, Martin hoped his apparent recovery would be attributed to the prescribed medication. He felt it would be prudent to wait a short time before showing signs of improvement. Consequently, he set Monday, March 15 as the day he would begin to dress properly. The subsequent week would be spent soliciting his release from Westwood Lodge.

6:30AM - Friday March 12, 1999

Quinn was amused by the fact that he was getting more rest than he ever did while staying in the best suite of the Boston Harbor Hotel. Before leaving his room for breakfast, he was able to spend a good hour reviewing the bridge material which Eddie had brought for him the previous evening. His mind was freshest in the morning and he wanted to get back into managing this project.

After breakfast, he lined up for his Depakote pill. Again he concealed it below his tongue so that it could be discarded later. Martin felt it was less suspicious if he was not seen to be hurrying to the restroom immediately after taking the medication. Instead he went to the TV room where he remained until the group meeting. His desire to get discharged within the week made him conscious of the need to be in compliance with all the ward's rules and regulations. Accordingly, he made sure that he was not late for Cynthia Melrose's meeting.

Once she began, Cynthia invited the patients to share any goals they had set for themselves during recent days or any they may have achieved. Hilary shared how, for the first time in two weeks, she had summoned the courage to call her mother at home. Prior to that, all her calls had been initiated by her parents. Then Jessica reported that she had cut down on her cigarette usage from six to three per day.

In each case, Cynthia complimented the women for both setting and achieving their goals.

"What about the guys?" she continued. "Have none of you anything to share with us this morning? Martin, you've been here for a week now.

Have you set any goals?"

"Cynthia, I've not really focused on myself during the past week. I regard myself as being just one person on a team that I like to call, 'Team Westwood.' When we meet here every morning, I look upon it like we're in the locker room with our coach. In my mind, Cynthia, you're the coach of Team Westwood. I'm not concerned if I don't get a goal. I'm happy with an assist, or simply being on the team when one of its members scores."

Cynthia did not know how to respond to Martin's pep talk to 'the team.' "Is he serious? Or is he just blowing smoke up my ass?" she thought to herself.

"That's very magnanimous of you, Martin, but as coach of this team, I want to see you scoring goals too. In fact, I want to see all of you scoring goals. I want everyone here to take some quiet time alone and set a goal that will improve your self esteem. On Monday, I want to know that each of you has identified at least one goal that you're going to work on."

Quinn was delighted with this order. Now he could return on Monday and announce to Cynthia that his goal was to secure his release from the hospital by Thursday evening. He would cite her inspirational coaching as the catalyst for this development.

When the meeting ended, once again, Martin returned to his room via the kitchen, so that he could retrieve more green juices and snacks. His free time before lunch was spent working on the bridge project. He wanted to go over all of his estimates for both material quantities and labor time, to make sure that he had planned the correct crew sizes and work schedules. After all, there was a $40,000 bonus at stake, provided the fiber-optic cable could be installed on or before April 15, but that was only one month away, and he was still locked up in a mental hospital. Furthermore, Cove did not yet have the stock available to even begin the job, nor was any of this material available at a local hardware store. It was all unique and highly specialized, requiring a lot of work and oversight in order to secure its timely acquisition. "Maybe that's why there's such a high bonus figure," Martin deduced with a smirk. "I guess if it was an easy project, anyone could have been contracted to do it." He continued to analyze the project's schedule to see where he could pick up time and overlap activities.

Before lunch, Quinn called Eddie Gallagher and got confirmation that Bill Snow had managed to get an early start on the bridge survey. From all accounts, progress was good and there was a possibility that this data would be available to be brought into the hospital on Sunday evening.

Martin decided to eat lunch with Killer James. He wanted to keep apprised of his efforts to get released. If James made any mistakes, then Martin wanted to be aware of them. His fellow patient was not in the best of moods.

"Don't worry, Monday isn't far away. Just stay out of trouble for the next few days," Quinn encouraged.

"It's not that simple. I have to watch out for some of the staff," James replied. "They like to stir it up and get a reaction from you, to put in your file."

"What do you mean?"

"They'll deliberately do something to annoy you, in order to spark a confrontation. Then the doctors have a reason to delay your release. You need to watch yourself too," James warned. "If there aren't any lunatics in the asylum, then all these people will be out of a job. It's in their interest to come up with reasons to keep us locked up."

Martin hung out in the common area and read the newspaper after lunch. Even though he had the paper in front of him, he was preoccupied with what his fellow patient had just told him. He would have to be extra vigilant. He also decided that he would not wait until Monday morning before wearing his clothes correctly, but would do so on Sunday instead.

Margaret interrupted her husband's newspaper reading shortly after 2:00.

"Hi. How are you?" Martin asked, as he stood up to hug her.

"Good," Margaret replied in a flat tone.

He sensed there was something not right about the way she had replied. "How could she be feeling anything but absolutely horrible?" he thought to himself. His intuition was correct. She had just spent the past twenty minutes alone in the car, wondering what was happening to her life. Her son was in Seattle, basically because her husband was in a psychiatric hospital, and she was three thousand miles away from the physical support of her own family. That day's mail included correspondence from the mortgage company which she could not bring herself to open. Furthermore, given her husband's condition, she could not discuss any of these issues with him.

The next two hours spent in the hospital went by in a blur. It was not until she was back home that she began to recall any aspects of the visit. Her life had become both stressful and frightening. The afternoon included Martin's consults with Dr. Bennet, Dr. Kaskarelis, and Dr. Armstrong. There were visits by two other staff members whose names she could not recall. Then there was her husband's new fashion sense, or lack thereof. While she was stressed and exhausted from everything that was going on, the whole hospital experience certainly appeared to be excellent therapy for him. He always appeared to be in the best of spirits. Nothing bothered him in the slightest. He greeted everybody in the hospital, both staff and patients alike, by their first name. He had even become acquainted with other patients' visitors. "Is all this an indication of his recovery, or is it a symptom of his mental illness?" she asked herself. The garage door closed and she turned off the engine. "What am I going to do?"

Back in the hospital, Martin was engaged in stimulating dinner conversation with Dan and Steve. The main topic of their discussion was the looming Y2K milestone, that was feared would adversely impact countless computer systems throughout the world. This was a subject Dan was more than qualified to discuss. Steve, on the other hand, had some extremely unique insights regarding the Y2K issue, which included some outrageous conspiracy theories. After dinner, Martin watched television with Jessica, Hilary, and Andrew. By 11:00, he had disposed of his Depakote tablet, added a couple of green juice bottles to his St. Patrick's Day supplies and was curled up in bed for the night.

Meanwhile, at the Quinn home, Margaret was finishing a long telephone conversation with Eileen O'Reilly.

"This can't be easy for you, Margaret. Why don't you come over here tomorrow and have dinner with us? It will help take your mind off things for a couple of hours and on Sunday, if you want, I'll go with you to visit Martin."

"Thank you Eileen, I know he'd love that. I really appreciate how good you've been to me during all this."

9:45AM - Saturday March 13, 1999

As Quinn read the newspaper, the Depakote pill which had been surreptitiously slipped into his pocket, was digging into his backside, a common affliction shared by everyone who wears their clothes back to front and needs to conceal medication. He had tried to do some laundry but the washer and dryer were being used by other patients. The pace of life in Westwood Lodge was nowhere close to the hectic program he had been used to before his incarceration. He was not upset that he could not do his laundry as planned. Instead he would simply relax and attend to it later. The morning dragged slowly since there was no group meeting on either Saturday or Sunday. His time with the newspaper was interrupted by Steve.

"Not too many people truly realize just how serious a problem this Y2K issue is," the scientist warned. "I've already made plans."

"You have? What sort of plans?"

"It's not safe to discuss them in here," he cautioned. "They listen and record everything we do and say. They have cameras and microphones hidden throughout the hospital."

Martin had been proud of the progress he had been making in his mind regarding such issues and now his fellow patient was unwittingly dragging him back over the edge.

"You're right," Martin agreed. "Let's not talk about it here. We can discuss it later."

He just wanted to stop Steve from saying anything else that might screw up his head any further. Martin was on a mission to get released from Westwood Lodge and did not want anything to detract from that. Apart from not letting Steve influence his thoughts, he did not need any staff members overhearing such a conversation. This coming week was going to be all about implementing his exit strategy.

At lunch, Quinn stalled in the service line to let Steve get well ahead of him. He then made sure not to leave the line with his tray of food until after Steve had committed to a table. While the rocket scientist shared more of his conspiracy theories with Dan, Martin sat on the other side of the dining room with Andrew and spent the lunch break discussing Boston's property market.

* * * * * * *

Again he avoided sitting with Steve at dinner and instead carried his tray over to Norman's table. Martin wanted the counselor to see how much he had improved since the previous Saturday when he had the two counselors ferrying cups of water from the kitchen. The effort was time well spent. The latex paint traces at the edge of his nails confirmed that Norman was still involved in some home improvement projects. Quinn took this opportunity to offer advice concerning repairs on a two-family residence in Dedham. Seemingly, the counselor had inherited the property from an aunt who passed away several years earlier. In order to pay the estate taxes, Norman took out an equity loan, intending to maintain the duplex as an income property. The legal paperwork had taken more than a year. In the meantime, the apartment where his aunt had lived remained empty. While he did his best to get it ready to rent, the tenant upstairs had problems with the second floor unit. The initial contact by the probate attorney seemed fortuitous at that time; however things had since deteriorated into a major headache.

"Don't let it get you down," Martin warned, "otherwise you'll find yourself locked up in here with the rest of us!"

"How ironic would that be?"

"These things can appear overwhelming, but if you step back, take a breath, and address the problems one at a time, you'll work through them okay. Just write out a list of the issues so you can prioritize the order in which you tackle them."

"You're right," the counselor acknowledged as he stood up from the table, lifting his empty tray. "I'll take your advice and get at least three estimates on any of the tasks that require a licensed tradesman."

"And don't forget their insurance. No one should be allowed to work on your property unless you have a current copy of their insurance certificate. Don't accept a copy from the contractor, but make sure you insist that their insurance agent sends it to you directly. That prevents them from giving you a forgery."

Norman rechecked the patients' head-count after dinner. As he unlocked the door into the ward, it amused him to think that he was being coached about his real estate property by a mental patient with his clothes on back to front. What made matters more ridiculous was the fact that the advice was sound.

* * * * * * *

Quinn was surprised to see Dianne Russo escorting visitors from the ward at 9:00. He was intrigued that she was working on a Saturday evening, since this was not her usual shift. Unbeknownst to Martin, his suspicions were correct. An influenza bug had left the ward short staffed, resulting in Russo having to cover two, twelve hour shifts that weekend. She would have to work until midnight and return again at noon on

Sunday, to work until midnight. By 8:00 on Monday morning, she needed to be back at the hospital for her regular shift.

Martin headed off to the kitchen and got himself a banana and two juices before going into the TV room. Andrew, Dan, and Jessica were watching a Boston Bruins hockey game. It was halfway through the third period and they were tied 2-2 with the New Jersey Devils. The game ended at exactly 9:30, with Boston losing after New Jersey had a five-on-three power play for the last ninety seconds of the game. As Quinn looked behind him, he could see through the windows that some of the other patients had lined up to receive their medication. He knew there was a strong possibility that Dianne Russo would oversee this activity and would be watching closely to make sure each patient swallowed his or her pills.

Before getting up from his seat, Martin quickly drank both drinks and ate the banana. He then went straight to the kitchen, ate another banana and drank two more juices before getting in line for his medication. Dianne Russo watched carefully as he swallowed the pill and washed it down with the small cup of water she had handed to him. Before turning to leave, he asked for a second drink so she could hear that his speech was clear and not impeded by any tablet concealed in his mouth. As Quinn approached his room, he casually turned right and went into the men's restroom. Fortunately, there was no one in either of the two toilet stalls. He entered the nearest one, closed the door, and vomited up at least one banana plus enough of the juice to flush out the Depakote medication. It was not hard to spot the white pill amongst the yellow banana and red juice. After two flushes, he washed his hands. Five minutes after thanking Dianne for the medication, he was outstretched on his bed, listening to his Discman.

At least half an hour passed before Martin's peace was interrupted.

"Where did you get that Discman and those CDs?" demanded Dianne Russo.

"My family brought them in for me. Is there a problem?"

"There certainly is. Anything like this should have been cleared through the ward's admin' office. There's nothing in your file indicating you have permission for these items. I'm going to take all this back to the office until your treatment team gives permission for you to have them."

Had this confrontation occurred earlier in the week, he would definitely have argued the issue with Ms. Russo. He immediately complied with the order because he was focused on securing his release and wanted to avoid a contentious incident.

After she left, he remained in his room to avoid any further communication with this woman. Quinn was not going to allow himself to be goaded into reacting to any provocation by the hospital's staff. He reached down and felt the slots in the side of the bed frame, reminding himself that these were not decorative. Having the beds designed to accommodate restraint straps was a feature which he did not want to try out first hand.

1:45PM - Sunday March 14, 1999

Martin was looking forward to seeing Margaret at 2:00 and was reading the sports section of the Sunday paper in the common area while he waited for visiting time to begin. His decision to wear his clothes correctly had produced no comment from either staff members or patients. Without a doubt, however, it had been noted in his file. The report on the previous evening's hockey game between the Bruins and Devils was as depressing to read as the last ninety seconds of the game had been to watch. To make matters worse, the paper had incorrectly identified one of the Boston players featured in an action photograph. Quinn knew not to share his finding with anyone else. He was on a mission to navigate the most expeditious exit from the hospital. Challenging the accuracy of the newspaper would not further this cause.

He was pleasantly surprised that Eileen O'Reilly accompanied Margaret to that afternoon's visiting session. Both women were delighted to see Martin and were thrilled with his choice of attire. Unfortunately however, Margaret's joy at being able to converse with her husband, who was showing obvious signs of improvement, was suddenly cut short. Dianne Russo stormed out of the nurses' station and demanded everyone's attention. She refused to continue until the other staff members had corralled all the patients and their visitors into the common reading area.

"There has been a serious breach of security and trust in this ward today," she bellowed. "A set of keys belonging to a staff member has gone missing. This ward is now in Lock Down Status until they are recovered."

"What does she mean by Lock Down Status?" Eileen asked Martin, in a hushed but indignant tone.

"Welcome to my world," he whispered. "Nobody is leaving until the keys are found."

"We can't be kept locked in here against our will," she protested.

"That's right," Margaret agreed, "we're not patients. They don't have any control over us."

Quinn was amused by the two women's fury at the thought of being confined to the ward. "They haven't even experienced sixty seconds of the captivity I've endured for the past week," he thought to himself.

"I know I can rely on the support and assistance of the visitors who are with us this afternoon," Russo continued. "With everyone's cooperation, we can resolve this matter quickly. At this time, I'm going to ask all visitors to leave the ward and regroup in the dining room. I'll have a member of staff accompany you there, where I need you to check inside your purses, bags, or pockets, in case the keys have been hidden without your knowledge. The patients will remain here until each of them has been searched. They will then be permitted to join you in the dining room for the remainder of the afternoon. Once the ward is cleared, the staff will conduct a thorough search of every room."

Margaret and Eileen continued to mutter protests under their breath as they lined up to leave. After the visitors had been escorted from the ward, Dianne Russo addressed the patients.

"If any of you has knowledge of the whereabouts of these missing keys, now is the time to step forward."

After thirty seconds of silence she ordered the male patients to line up at the door. Each of them was frisked before the whole group was brought to the dining room. This process was then repeated with the female patients. Since no keys were found, the staff commenced a search of the ward.

Martin was determined not to allow this episode to upset him. He remained focused on his goal to get discharged from the hospital by the end of the week. Whether or not any keys had actually been lost did not bother him in the least. If the staff had staged this episode in an effort to upset the patients, he was not going to react to their provocation. The only scenario that gave him cause for concern was if the keys were planted somewhere in his room.

Shortly before 5:00, Dianne Russo entered the cafeteria and announced that the keys had been found.

"I would suggest to our visitors that there is little point returning to the ward. Since visiting time for this afternoon is practically over, we would prefer that the patients remain here for their evening meal."

"It's good they found the keys," Margaret acknowledged.

"How do you know any keys were ever lost?" Martin replied in a low tone. "You only have their word for that."

* * * * * * *

As soon as Quinn stepped into his room after dinner, he knew things were not right. It had obviously been given a thorough search. The drawers of his dresser were not closed completely, which was not the way they had been left. When he opened them, he was horrified to see that someone had messed with the juice cartons, causing them to become swollen and bloated. The thin plastic lids on several of them had punctured allowing their contents to leak onto his clothes. These juices had survived for several days without any problem, until the time that Dianne Russo evacuated the ward. Quinn was absolutely sure that she, or one of her colleagues, was responsible for this damage. It appeared as if the cartons had been placed in a microwave oven and heated, before being tossed in amongst his clean clothes. Also, in another drawer, he found an extra-large pair of men's briefs which were in drastic need of laundering.

Martin was glad that Killer James had warned him about such behavior. He knew that he could not attribute this damage to every member of the staff. Unfortunately, he would never know who carried out this act of petty vandalism. He could not help thinking, however, that at least one of the employees was sicker and more disturbed than any of the patients.

Determined not to show any signs of anger or frustration, he immediately began to clean up the mess. First, he took several large black plastic bin liners from a cupboard in the kitchen. He placed them neatly in his pocket so no staff members would see that he was involved in a major cleaning program. It took almost two hours to tidy the mess and launder all his clothes. In light of what happened during the search, this also included the bed linens.

He had just sat down in the TV room when Martin noticed Eddie Gallagher walking along the corridor. Quinn hoped the large manila envelope in his right hand contained the bridge survey data, compiled by Bill Snow.

"Hey, what's going on?" Eddie greeted, consciously making no comment on his business partner's normal appearance.

"Things are going fine. Let's sit over here, so I can look at Bill's work."

Martin motioned to a vacant table in the common reading area where they were able to spread out the survey data. The volume of technical information compiled by the professional land surveyor was substantial and certainly looked out of place in the current venue.

"This all looks okay," Quinn confirmed, after careful review. "I should have a cutting list developed before noon-time tomorrow. I don't want to call Anderson from here, so I'll call you with the information and you can pass it along."

It was 9:00 when they finished discussing the Jamestown Bridge project, as well as other Cove jobs. Eddie Gallagher was the last visitor to leave the ward that evening. Norman locked the door behind him and walked back along the hallway with Martin.

"What's in the big envelope?"

"Just some calculations related to a project my company is working on."

"You know it's important that you get plenty of rest."

"I know, but this isn't stressful. In fact, it's the opposite. The days here would be too long if I didn't have something like this to work on. Besides, I'm the only one in my company who's up to speed on this project. Our client is relying on us to get this done."

"And you're feeling okay?"

"Absolutely. I'm actually looking forward to working with Dr. Kaskarelis and his team this week, so hopefully I can get released on Thursday or Friday at the latest."

"You shouldn't get your hopes up. The doctors have to consider your health before any timetable you might be developing."

"My son gets back from his spring break next Friday. He's in Seattle, and has no idea his dad is locked up in a mental hospital. I'd like to be out before he gets home."

By now, the two men were standing outside the nurses' station.

"Well, keep out of trouble. Just get plenty of rest and follow all the doctors' directions," Norman advised.

"I intend to."

After he had flushed that evening's Depakote tablet down the toilet, Quinn retired to bed. He wanted to wake up early and refreshed the following morning so he could develop the cutting list for Anderson. He was glad he had taken the trouble to wash the bed linens. He needed to be well rested and the freshly laundered sheets made it easier for him to relax.

8:00AM - Monday March 15, 1999

Quinn had already spent two hours formulating a cutting list by the time he joined the other patients for breakfast. He had checked his work twice before neatly folding the three pages of calculations and slipping them into the back pocket of his jeans. He certainly did not want his work to fall victim to another room search while he was at breakfast.

After he had been given his Depakote medication, Martin went straight to the private phone box where he removed the pill from under his tongue, and then called Eddie to relay the cutting list information.

"I'll fax this over to Anderson right away," Gallagher confirmed. "Call me later this afternoon just in case they have questions that I need your help with."

* * * * * * *

Cynthia Melrose was clearly happy to see that Quinn was sporting a more conservative and appropriate fashion style.

"All things considered, I had a very nice and relaxing weekend," he responded politely to her inquiry.

He knew the value of engaging the psychologist in such a normal and relaxed manner. It was important to have as many staff members as possible form a positive opinion regarding his behavior over the next few days. Cynthia made some notes on a legal pad while waiting for the remaining patients to arrive.

Midway through the meeting, she announced her desire to hear from patients who did not speak the previous week about their goals.

"I only have time to hear from a few of you this morning, but I do intend to call on each of you during the week. I think we'll begin with Martin. Have you set any goals that you would like to share with the group?"

"I certainly have," Quinn began, in an enthusiastic manner, leaning forward while resting his elbows on his knees and rubbing his hands together. "My goal is to get released from the hospital on Thursday afternoon because my thirteen year old son is returning home from spring break on Friday, and I would like to be able to meet him off the plane."

"That's quite a goal," Cynthia responded. "I hope it's not too ambitious."

"Well, the doctors told me that when a patient is in the hospital, it can be stressful for other family members. My son doesn't know I'm here. I know it would save him an awful lot of grief if I was at home when he got back from Seattle."

Cynthia continued to make notes in a file and invited others to speak. She finally ended the meeting after going over some general announcements. Martin was delighted that it had been her suggestion for goals to be set by the patients. Consequently, this positive change in his behavior could be attributed to her.

After the meeting, Martin went to shave and take a shower. His recent adherence to a normal dress code did not lessen the need for supervision while he shaved. After giving back the disposable razor to Warren, he was left alone.

Martin was impeccably dressed when he received a visit from Dr. Kaskarelis later that morning.

"Good morning, Mr. Quinn, how are we feeling today?"

"I feel great. I had a good weekend, got plenty of rest, and of course

I've been taking the Depakote tablets twice a day since last Thursday."

"Well, you do realize that you may, in fact, be taking the placebo," the doctor cautioned. "The pharmaceutical company doesn't even let me know whether a patient is taking the medication or not."

"Well, I don't really care who or what takes the credit. I feel very relaxed and not at all upset about anything."

"I see that you've stopped wearing your clothes back to front."

"Yes. I no longer need to keep looking over my shoulder. It would appear that I may have overreacted last week."

"Well, that's certainly good to hear."

"Before you go, Doctor, there's something I'd like to ask you."

"What's that?"

"I'd like to go home on Thursday afternoon."

"Well, that may be premature, Martin. The last thing we want is for you to be discharged too soon. But I'll bear it in mind."

Martin knew that any argument would be futile at this early stage. He was happy enough to have put his doctor on notice, and leave it at that.

11:40AM on Monday March 15, 1999

Xavier Santos was not used to speaking with law enforcement officers without his attorney. Usually he was the focus of their investigations, but on this occasion he was not. He did not have the benefit of George Grey's assistance during this interview with FBI Special Agent Colin Walker and knew that requesting his lawyer's presence would have given the impression that he was not one hundred percent behind their efforts to apprehend the kidnappers. He wanted to keep to himself any knowledge he had gained from his own inquiries, and consequently needed to be guarded in his response to Agent Walker's questions.

The impromptu meeting had taken place at Xavier's nightclub, The Cocoa Bean, on Lansdowne Street. The name was chosen by his father, which illustrated both his sense of humor as well as the source of funding used to launch and finance the business. When the meeting ended, Agent Walker had no idea about the progress Xavier had made uncovering the identity of the kidnappers. More importantly however, Santos was left with no idea about the progress the FBI had made.

12:10PM on Monday March 15, 1999

During lunch, Quinn sat with Jessica and Hilary, at which time he broke the sad news about the anticipated St. Patrick's Day party. He shared with them how the juice drinks had been tampered with during Sunday's lock-down.

"That's a bummer," Jessica responded.

"Tell me about it," Martin replied. "I had to launder all my clothes and that was after cleaning up the leaking juice cartons and snacks!"

"Maybe the Lucky Charms cereal leprechaun will secretly leave more green juice in the refrigerator on Tuesday night, when we're all asleep," Hilary offered as a way of consolation.

Considering the venue, he was unsure whether or not Hilary's remark was a joke.

After lunch, Quinn called Eddie again.

"We're all set with Anderson. I spoke with Louis after I sent the fax. He understood all your information. The only problem I had was avoiding questions regarding your whereabouts."

"What did you tell him?"

"I just said you were sick and left it at that. He wants you to give him a call. I couldn't think of anything else to say."

Quinn left the call box and made his way to the common area, where he picked up the newspaper. Now that he was wearing his clothes correctly and attempting to get released from the hospital, he wanted to stay out of his room and make more of an effort to be seen by the staff.

Just after 2:00, Dr. Armstrong walked by, on her way to the nurses' station. She was clearly pleased to see that his dress code was now in vogue with the rest of society.

"I spoke to your wife this morning and scheduled a meeting for the three of us at 3:00 this afternoon."

"That sounds good. You know that I'll be here."

"Excellent," she responded and continued on her way, adjusting a bundle of patient files under her arm as she walked.

* * * * * * *

The Quinns were chatting in the common reading area when Dr. Armstrong arrived and suggested that they use the empty TV room for their meeting. For twenty minutes, the doctor controlled the topics of their discussion before Martin expressed his desire to be released from the hospital on Thursday evening. Of all the health professionals with whom he had shared his goal, Elizabeth Armstrong appeared to be the most receptive.

"That's a healthy sign," she observed while standing up to conclude their meeting. "I'm sure Brendan would be delighted to see both of you together when he gets off the plane from Seattle. I'll speak with Dr. Kaskarelis and make sure that we keep this goal in mind."

Once the Quinns were alone, Margaret cautioned Martin about his plan to get discharged before the end of the week.

"The doctors aren't going to consider Brendan's travel itinerary when they make decisions about your treatment."

"Listen, Margaret, I came into this hospital voluntarily and I will be leaving at the end of this week."

It was clear that his mind was made up, so she avoided any further discussion. Since learning the details of the Jamestown Bridge project,

Margaret was privately troubled that Fred Ross could take advantage of Martin's hospitalization. She was conscious of the conflicting agendas of the doctors' treatment program and her husband's strong work ethic.

* * * * * * *

Before going to sleep that night, Martin reflected on his second day of dressing normally. The doctors had been put on notice of his desire to be discharged by the end of the week. The only thing missing was his Discman. He had no intention of asking for it to be returned, lest he give the staff the satisfaction of thinking that he cared. Furthermore, he wanted to limit his communications only to those encounters which would positively contribute to his early release.

8:05AM - Tuesday March 16, 1999

Quinn decided to sit with Steve the rocket scientist at breakfast. Even though he wanted to avoid incidents that would detract from his exit strategy, he felt sorry for his fellow patient. Martin understood that Steve was nearly sixty and had spent at least one month of each of the past seven years as a patient in Westwood Lodge. Apparently his visits began after he became the victim of corporate down-sizing. His employer was one of many companies which secured work from Raytheon, one of the country's largest defense contractors. When the Berlin Wall was taken down in November 1989, signaling the end of the Cold War, it triggered a domino effect. Unfortunately, one of those dominos was Steve's job.

It was sad to see him withdrawn into a life that appeared to be nothing other than ramblings about fantastic futuristic projects which no one had either the time or patience to comprehend. Nevertheless, this was how the scientist had spent thirty years of his working life. Martin felt genuine sympathy for the man and was saddened by his condition.

He tried to avoid discussing issues which Steve chose to talk about. Instead, he guided the conversation towards more normal topics which he thought might interest him. Quinn's favorite subject in high school and university had been mathematics. He hoped he could keep up with his fellow patient in that field, at least during a casual conversation at the breakfast table. Wrong!

"547, 557, 563, 569, 571, 577, 587, 593, 599, 601," Steve responded to Quinn's inquiry, as to how many prime numbers he knew. "That's the next ten prime numbers following the first one hundred."

Quinn knew that he was way out of his depth. He almost felt disappointed that the Cold War had ended. Surely someone like Steve did not have to be a casualty of peace.

Later that morning, Martin had another opportunity to confront Dr. Kaskarelis regarding his release from the hospital. The doctor had tried to finish his consult without making any reference to the issue. Quinn was not prepared to let that happen.

"It's still too early to commit to a time table. Let's just concentrate on your treatment and less on schedules and deadlines."

Since Andreus Kaskarelis had not been the one to raise the subject, Martin did not expect anything other than the response he received.

"Well, you know how important it is for me to be home in time for my son's return from Seattle. Besides, I need to call my friend, Peter Dorian, to come and pick me up. It wouldn't be fair to call at the last minute. I'd like to be able to give him at least one day's notice. Maybe we can firm things up tomorrow?"

* * * * * * *

Alone in his room, Quinn mulled over his latest consultation with Dr. Kaskarelis. It was obvious they were not on the same page regarding a discharge date. He closed his eyes and wondered how he was going to solve this problem. "One thing's certain," he repeated to himself. "When Brendan steps off the plane at Logan Airport, I'm going to be there to welcome him."

His thoughts were interrupted by a knock on the door. When he opened his eyes, he could see Dr. Elizabeth Armstrong silhouetted in the threshold.

"If you don't mind, Martin, I was hoping we could spend a little time together. Whereas my focus is the Quinn family as a unit and the relationships between each of its members, I also need to spend time with each of you individually."

"That's fine with me," he assured her; still confident she was his best advocate among his treatment team.

He responded in a cordial and cooperative manner to all her questions, while paying attention to the possible motive behind each one. Throughout the session, he stressed the strong bond between himself and Brendan.

"I appreciate your desire to get home before your son's return, but please understand that Dr. Kaskarelis is the physician in charge of your case. Although I'll have an opportunity to offer my opinion, the final decision is his."

She quickly realized from Quinn's expression that he did not want to hear qualifications regarding the weight her recommendations would carry in any discussions with Dr. Kaskarelis.

"I've observed a marked improvement in your condition," she added. "If you continue to progress like this, I'm sure everything will be fine."

Since it was only Tuesday, he reckoned that it was too early to be anything other than amenable and positive in his response.

"Thank you, Dr. Armstrong. I know that you'll do what's right for both me and my family."

"I will. Think positively, get as much rest as you can, and don't worry about any of this. We still have a couple of days before we need to make a decision."

At lunch, Quinn sat with Jessica, who was still upset that there would be no St. Patrick's Day party.

"It's a bit like having your tunnel discovered by the prison camp guards," he remarked in a dejected tone as she slumped down into her chair.

Who's that lady over there?" Martin continued, quickly changing the subject. "When did she come into the ward?"

"Last Friday, her name's Michelle. She stays in her room a lot."

* * * * * * *

Martin was shaved and showered by the time Margaret arrived at 2:00. He enjoyed hearing details of e-mails and telephone calls that she had received from Brendan. By all accounts, the Seattle trip was a big success. When the subject changed to his release from the hospital, Margaret did not share his optimism. She was, however, relieved to learn that Peter Dorian had promised to come and collect her husband. Since his Jeep was still in the hotel's parking garage, this would save her having to drive through the congested streets of Boston, an activity she did not relish.

"Besides, he still has all my belongings from when he brought me here."

"Perfect! Peter's a good friend," she agreed.

* * * * * * *

Quinn had not eaten more than two bites of his lasagna when he was interrupted. Dan shifted a chair with the edge of his foot so that he could step in closer and set down his tray. Martin deduced from his friend's cynical tone that he did not share his optimism regarding a release date at the end of the week.

"Have they started trying to weasel their way into your family?"

"Oh yes, but so far, my wife has resisted and my son's in Seattle on spring break."

"Well, they can be tenacious," Dan warned, cautiously looking around to make sure their conversation was not being overheard.

The only person who seemed to be showing any interest in their direction was Michelle.

"She seems pretty strange," Dan noted, motioning with his eyes for Martin to look towards her. "She always seems to be taking mental notes and observing everything that's going on."

"Aren't all the notes taken in here 'mental notes'?" Martin asked in jest.

Once everyone was back in the ward, Norman took the names of patients who wanted to go outside for a cigarette break. Quinn was never part of this group, but decided that he would join them on this occasion.

"I didn't realize you smoked," Norman remarked.

"I don't, but I haven't stepped outside in over ten days. I wouldn't mind getting some fresh air."

"Let me check with Dianne Russo first. Come back here at 6:15."

In his room, Martin contemplated the possible outcome of his request. He would use it as a barometer to measure how the staff gauged his condition. A negative response would, of course, be troubling. Being permitted to join the smokers would be encouraging; however, it was no guarantee of an early release. That being said, the Discman and music CDs had still not been returned.

"You're all set," Norman announced as Martin approached the nurses' station. "Any time you want to go out with the smokers, just meet here ten minutes after each meal."

"Do we have a new smoker?" Jessica asked, tapping a packet of cigarettes against her thigh.

"No, just the opposite, I need to get some fresh air."

The group also included Andrew, and the ward's shyest patient, Michelle. Once outside, Quinn immediately tried to orientate himself. It had been eight months since Cove had worked at Westwood Lodge.

A picnic table and benches were located to the right of the entrance door as they exited. At each end of the table was a metal cigarette butt receptacle to prevent this area from being trashed by the patients or staff members who took smoke breaks. Norman waited until they had each taken a cigarette from their own packet and then offered a light from a disposable plastic lighter. It was hospital policy not to permit the patients to carry matches or lighters.

Since neither Norman nor Martin smoked, they chatted together a few feet away from the others. Quinn kept the conversation topics away from any controversial issues, nor did he educate the counselor to the fact that he was familiar with the hospital's layout. Instead, he stressed how excited he was that his son would be coming home on Friday.

Quinn had a clear view of the smokers over Norman's shoulder. Every now and again, he got the impression that Michelle was looking in his direction. He was determined not to let his imagination get the better of him. "Perhaps she's looking at Norman," he thought to himself. He wanted to get out of Westwood Lodge and recognized the importance of not formulating ideas that people were watching him or were even remotely interested in anything about him. Martin was open minded to the fact that his evaluations of John Grasso and Seahorse Communications were completely wrong, and that exhaustion and lack of sleep had caused his paranoia to thoroughly distort his perception of reality.

Michelle appeared to be in her late thirties or early forties with shoulder length blonde hair, parted in the middle and pushed behind her ears. Martin had seen her wear glasses during lunch and considered the apparent glances in his direction may have been an effort to focus contact lenses. A loose fitting pink sweatshirt concealed the slimness of her five foot - ten inch physique. The hems of her denim jeans were frayed where they had been trapped under the heels of athletic shoes. As she nervously shuffled a packet of cigarettes from one hand to the other, Quinn noticed how stained her fingers were from nicotine. The expensive looking engagement and wedding rings were very loose on her finger. He concluded this was a symptom of a considerable weight loss. Martin had never seen her interact with any patients. Despite both Jessica and Andrew's efforts, she proved to be no more communicative outside the ward than she was inside. As the group responded to Norman's direction to head back, Quinn decided to introduce himself. As soon as she finished shaking his hand, she continued to walk, directing her stare at a spot on the ground approximately thirty inches in front of her feet.

6:30AM - Wednesday March 17, 1999

"Happy St. Patrick's Day, Martin," Quinn greeted himself, conscious that it was acceptable to engage one's self in conversation, while being treated as a patient in a psychiatric ward. "Happy St. Patrick's Day to yourself," he replied, using the same logic to justify a response.

"The early bird gets the washing machine," he remarked in a celebratory tone as he tossed in his dirty laundry. Since Margaret was not around to supervise, he was able to mix in "whites" with "colors." This was one of the perks of living in a mental hospital.

After starting the wash cycle, he went next door to watch TV and wait for the "breakfast parade" to assemble. Morning television featured the obligatory Irish dancers and traditional musicians in celebration of the holiday. He was soon joined by Jessica, who wanted to be the first to wish him a "Happy St. Patrick's Day!" Martin thanked her and acknowledged her disappointment that the ward's own little party had been scuttled during the search for the missing keys.

* * * * * * *

As the patients returned from the dining room, Quinn announced there were clothes in the dryer.

"Oh, they're mine," Michelle replied. "I put them in last night."

"Can you do me a favor and take them out? My wash cycle is over."

"No problem, I'll do it for you now."

Martin was surprised she was able to construct two consecutive sentences. He waited outside the door of the laundry room as Michelle retrieved her clothes. The room was barely large enough for one person, let alone two. Quinn stepped back to let her leave.

"Is that your brother who comes to visit you?"

Martin was puzzled by such a question coming at him without any warning.

"No, he's my business partner."

"I thought he might be your brother since he has an Irish accent too."

There were no more inquiries regarding his visitors, just an obligatory, "Thank you," as she left. "Michelle is quite observant," he pondered, transferring his laundry from the washer to the dryer. "And she appears to be quite interested in who's coming to visit me. Could she be an agent for Seahorse Communications?" Quinn scolded himself and consciously stopped pursuing such thoughts. "I'm never going to get out of here if I allow myself to formulate conspiracy theories like this."

Many of the staff wore at least one item of green clothing in honor of Ireland's national holiday. Cynthia Melrose made a point of wishing Martin a "Happy St. Patrick's Day," when he took his seat for the group meeting. He availed of this one on one exchange to remind her to lobby Dr. Kaskarelis on his behalf.

Quinn's only consult visit that morning was from Mark Butler, the BU medical student.

"Good morning, Mr. Quinn."

"Hi Mark, and Happy St. Patrick's Day!"

"And you too! How are you today?"

"Good," Quinn replied, gesturing for his visitor to take a seat. "I feel good."

"Any reactions to the Depakote?"

"I'm not having any, but I may be getting the placebo for all I know."

"That's true," Butler agreed while he took some notes.

"What are your plans for tonight?" Martin asked as Mark clicked his ball point pen. "I'm sure they include a visit to one or two Irish bars in Boston."

"I'll probably go over to The Kells bar in Allston. It's not too far from my apartment. No doubt it'll be packed to the rafters tonight!"

"Why don't you stop by after dinner and I'll come along too?" Quinn joked.

"I wish I could," laughed Butler, "that would be fun, but I'd have to kiss goodbye to my medical career."

"Well, have a pint of Guinness for me tonight!"

"I will," the young man promised as he shook Martin's hand before leaving.

It was Warren's duty to accompany the patients to the dining room for their lunch.

"Do you think they'll be serving corned beef and cabbage?" he asked Martin.

In America (and especially Boston) corned beef and cabbage is a traditional dish served practically everywhere on St. Patrick's Day. The custom is as established as turkey and cranberry sauce at Thanksgiving. Martin was nearly thirty when he immigrated to America. Not only had he never eaten this dish on St. Patrick's Day in Ireland, he had rarely eaten it on any other day of the year. It amused him that it had become such a big part of this Irish holiday. Americans found it hard to believe he had not eaten corned beef any more than ten times in his entire life. Nevertheless, all of Boston seemed to believe this dish was what Irish folk fed on every day, and twice on Sundays! Quinn surmised that long ago this meal was probably eaten daily during the voyage across the Atlantic Ocean. Prior to the invention of refrigeration in the late nineteenth century, salting the meat kept it from spoiling and cabbage was easily boiled along with it. So, whereas it was not as common amongst the Irish who remained in their homeland, it became synonymous with this nationality when they stepped off the boat in America.

Quinn chose not to disillusion Warren regarding his ethnic dietary beliefs.

"Well it's not the same dish unless it can be washed down with copious quantities of Guinness."

"Then I wouldn't get your hopes up if I were you," the counselor warned.

Martin was relieved that corned beef and cabbage was not on the menu. There were, however, some shamrock-shaped cookies with green frosting on display in the dessert section, but that was the extent of the kitchen's contribution to celebrating the holiday.

Quinn went outside after lunch with the smokers, but for some reason this trip did not happen until nearly 2:00. All of the regulars were present except for Michelle. When Warren brought everyone back into the ward, there were already visitors sitting in the common reading area. As the group dispersed outside the nurses' station, Dan spotted Michelle and Margaret chatting privately in the TV room.

"Hey. You'd better go and save your wife," he suggested. "There's something wrong with that picture."

Approaching the room, Martin could see through the wall of windows that Michelle had spotted him. He detected she was alarmed that he was only steps from the door. Their conversation appeared to end abruptly, and as he entered, Margaret looked around to greet him. She too looked startled.

"What are you two up to?"

"Just girl talk," Margaret replied.

"Well, I'll let you two have some privacy," Michelle suggested.

"How did you end up confined to the TV room with her?" he inquired once they were alone.

"Oh, it was nothing," Margaret fibbed. "I think she's lonely and wanted someone to talk to."

Unbeknownst to Martin, Michelle told Margaret she had witnessed him signing papers brought in by Eddie Gallagher. She was ignorant of the fact that the documents related to the Jamestown Bridge project. This news, however, caused needless concern for Margaret. Apparently Martin's initial instinct about Michelle was well founded.

When they left the TV room, Dr. Armstrong happened to be standing outside the nurses' station.

"Martin, would you mind if I had a quick word with Dr. Armstrong?" Margaret suddenly asked, in reaction to the information just received from Michelle.

"Not at all. Why don't you use my room? It will be more private."

"Is that okay with you, Dr. Armstrong?" Margaret checked.

"Certainly."

Martin picked up a newspaper and took a seat in the common reading area.

Five minutes later, Dan sat down beside him.

"I thought your wife was here today. That was a short visit."

"She's meeting with one of my doctors."

"That doesn't sound too good. When the doctors are meeting with the family in your absence, it usually means they're justifying why you need more treatment and observation."

"I don't need that. I'm trying to get out of here by tomorrow night!"

While they were talking, Dr. Kaskarelis approached.

"Good afternoon, Martin. Happy St. Patrick's Day! Why don't we go down to your room, so we can talk?"

"My wife's down there at the moment. She's meeting with Dr. Armstrong. I can't imagine they'll be much longer."

"Well in that case, why don't you stay here while I go down to speak with them."

Quinn felt uneasy as the doctor took off in the direction of his room.

"Looks like they're both going to have a little private meeting with your wife," Dan observed, "and you're not invited."

Just as Dr. Kaskarelis approached Quinn's door, the two women stepped into the hallway. Both Martin and Dan could see that this impromptu meeting was developing into a serious discussion.

"Well, it doesn't take a rocket scientist to work out what the topic of their conversation is," Dan offered.

"Could it be, 'What are we going to do with Martin?'" Quinn suggested.

"Correct, Sir!" Dan replied, like an animated game show host. "I'm going down there to listen to as much as I can. I'll make like I'm going to the bathroom opposite your room. They probably won't suspect anything. Besides, I don't have either of those two doctors."

"Awesome idea, but be careful," Quinn cautioned as his cohort nonchalantly headed down the hallway.

As predicted, no one took any notice of Dan, who prolonged his presence in the corridor by dropping a tissue he had been pretending to use. Continuing past Margaret and the doctors, he entered the men's restroom adjacent to where they were standing. It required practically no effort for him to listen to every word of their conversation. Five minutes later, Dan reappeared as Dr. Armstrong suggested she and Dr. Kaskarelis meet the following day.

Dan walked briskly past the group and returned to where Quinn was sitting. He sat in a chair immediately behind Martin, positioned back to back. The scene was worthy of any Cold War spy movie. Dan did not want the doctors to realize he had been in the corridor solely to eavesdrop on their conversation.

"You're screwed," he whispered. "The guy doctor doesn't want you to be released this week. Plus our friend Michelle has your wife upset because your business partner has been making you sign all sorts of papers."

"This is bullshit!" Martin replied under his breath.

"Hey! Don't shoot the messenger."

"What about Dr. Armstrong? What did she have to say?"

"Well, the woman doctor doesn't appear to have a problem with you being released tomorrow, but from what I understand, the guy doctor is in charge of your case."

"That's enough," Quinn whispered, his mouth hidden behind the newspaper. "We're about to have company. They're walking this way."

"Hi, Martin," Dr. Armstrong began. "I'd like to spend twenty minutes tomorrow afternoon with both you and Margaret, if that's okay. Why don't the three of us get together at 2:30?"

Martin recognized a complete lack of indication that the following day would be his last in Westwood Lodge, but did not want to begin a contentious conversation in such a public setting.

"2:30 tomorrow works for me. Is that okay for you Margaret?"

Dr. Armstrong left the group when Margaret confirmed their appointment for the following day.

"Martin, I'd like to spend a little time with you now that your room is freed up," Dr. Kaskarelis announced. "We shouldn't be very long, Mrs.

Quinn."

Ten minutes into their meeting, the doctor had not made any reference to Quinn's prior request that he be released from the hospital on Thursday.

"So you're happy with everything that's been going on while you're here?" the doctor repeated. "Has anyone been pressuring you to do anything you're not comfortable with?"

"No, I've never felt better. However, I do have a company with nearly twenty employees, most of whom have a family to support just like me. I've been in here for nearly two weeks, so I think it's time I got back to running my business to make sure everyone continues to have a job."

"Well, I'm more interested in getting you healthy and I think it would be a good idea if we continued this conversation tomorrow."

"That's fair enough," Quinn replied as the doctor stood up to leave, "but please understand a couple of things. First, I need to make arrangements to get picked up at the hospital when I check out. Second, if I begin to get the feeling that I won't be released in time to meet my son when he returns on Friday, then I'll be engaging the services of an attorney who specializes in resolving situations like this. We have a saying back home in Belfast, 'there's no need to bark yourself when you already have a dog.'"

Andreus Kaskarelis was obviously disturbed by Quinn's candor and reacted by retreating as quickly as he could.

"We'll talk tomorrow," he repeated and promptly exited.

Quinn wanted to avoid any friction between himself and Dr. Kaskarelis being witnessed by other members of staff. Consequently, he waited a full sixty seconds before going to meet Margaret in the common reading area.

"We need to talk," he announced in a low tone.

Once in the privacy of his room, he reiterated in no uncertain terms, his intention to be released from the hospital prior to Brendan's return.

"Listen Margaret, some of the staff members here are extremely nice and caring individuals, but that can't be said for them all. You witnessed the nonsense that went on here last Sunday when those keys supposedly went missing. This hospital is a business. They rely on generating invoices for patients' insurance companies and state agencies. I have a company to run, jobs to take care of for Cove's clients, and a mortgage to pay. I don't have time for this any longer. I'm intent on leaving here this week and if that doesn't happen, then I'm going to get a lawyer."

"They only want what's best for you."

Martin interrupted her.

"There's nothing to be gained by discussing this matter any further. You've had conversations with the staff here regarding my treatment, and I'm sure you'll have more discussions with them before I'm released. Whether or not I'm present during any future meetings, I expect you to lobby for my immediate release."

Margaret attempted to respond again citing concern for her husband's health and his need to follow the doctors' advice. Martin would hear none of it.

"I want to be able to call Peter Dorian and arrange for him to bring me into Boston, so that I can get my Jeep. That's it - plain and simple."

After that, it was difficult for Margaret to initiate other topics of conversation with any degree of sincerity. When it was time for her to leave, he stood up and gave her a hug and an affectionate kiss on the cheek. He recognized how tense and strained the situation was for both of them. He understood the hospital's need to consult with his wife; however, this made it difficult for him to trust her and he was conscious that this showed. Martin tried to appreciate things from her perspective. He tried to project the impression that all was well, and with a combined effort on both their parts, he would be released in time to meet Brendan off the plane.

The couple left his room and walked down to the nurses' station so they could get a staff member to let Margaret out of the ward.

"Tell Eileen Happy St. Patrick's Day," he instructed as Norman unlocked the door.

"I will," she replied, giving her husband a smile and a wave as she left.

"Well, how's Norman?"

"Good, thank you. Happy St. Patrick's Day, by the way," the counselor added, while checking to make sure the door of the ward was securely locked.

"How come you're not out celebrating?

"I wish! Warren asked me to cover part of his shift because he's going to a party. He can drown the shamrock for the both of us tonight."

"In Ireland, if you volunteer to work on St. Patrick's Day, it's considered a mortal sin. I believe the obligatory penance is two cases of Guinness plus one bottle of whiskey to be drunk on each of the following two Sundays."

"I'd better ask for Sunday off as well as Monday, and possibly Tuesday morning too."

The counselor returned to the nurses' station and Martin went back to his room. It was Wednesday evening, so he had forty-eight hours to get himself to Logan Airport. He had not received a positive commitment from Dr. Kaskarelis, nor did it appear that he had Margaret lobbying for his release. There was nothing more he could do at that moment. He would keep pushing the agenda on Thursday and set noon on Friday as the deadline for calling his attorney, Tom Sullivan.

During dinner, Dan was anxious to know if there had been further developments since his surveillance mission on Martin's behalf. They also traded frustrations regarding their common predicament.

"What a way to spend St. Patrick's Day - arguing with your doctor to get released from a psych ward," Quinn sighed.

Later, the two men joined Mandy and Jessica in the TV room to watch, *The Quiet Man*, starring John Wayne. Made in 1952, the movie chronicles Wayne's character's return to Ireland in search of his family homestead. The ensuing trials and tribulations include his attempts to court a character played by Maureen O'Hara. Mandy was horrified at the sight of John Wayne physically dragging the actress off a train and through the fields of Connemara.

"That scene would never be tolerated today!" Mandy exclaimed. "Especially the line where an old woman offers John Wayne a fine stick to beat the lovely lady with."

Martin and Dan laughed while explaining that in this movie, Wayne doled out abuse without gender bias.

"Just look at the beating he gave Victor McLaglen, who played the part of Maureen O'Hara's brother," Quinn offered in mock justification. "I'll be right back. I have to get my Happy Pill."

Upon his return, he reclined in his seat, discretely removed the pill from beneath his tongue, wrapped it in a tissue, and placed it in his pocket. After the movie was over, the four patients laughed and joked for more than an hour.

That night as he lay in his bed, Martin recalled various scenes from *The Quiet Man*. Shot in the village of Cong, in the Connemara region of County Galway, this beautiful choice of location was a contributing factor to the movie's success. Not far from where Quinn's father was born, the family regularly vacationed in the area when Martin was growing up. It wasn't long before he was dreaming of being right there, cheering on

John Wayne as he swung hay-maker punches at Victor McLaglen, while the pugilists stopped to down pints of Guinness in pubs along the route of the fight. What a way to end St. Patrick's Day!

6:10AM - Thursday March 18, 1999

After a good exercise session, Martin went across the hallway to the bathroom. Of all the restrictions in Westwood Lodge, the one that bothered him most was not being able to shave in the shower. At home this was one of his favorite times of the day. There, he had everything he needed arranged around the various shelves; just the way he liked it. In Westwood Lodge, however, there was barely enough shelf room to hold a single bar of soap. He liked to shave as well as brush and floss his teeth while the hot, steamy water massaged his back and neck. Not being allowed possession of a razor while unsupervised meant he had to shave later. It just did not seem right and it bothered Quinn. In fact, it bothered him a lot.

Not long after the morning's group meeting, Martin was visited by Mark Butler.

"Sit down. How was your St. Patrick's Day celebration?"

"It was fun, and I saw one of the other staff members. I'm not sure of his name, but I've definitely seen him working on this ward. I went to The Kells for a beer and on my way out, I noticed him in the corner of the bar with some friends. I doubt he even saw me."

"Did he have dark hair and was he a couple of inches smaller than me?"

"Yes."

"That was Warren. He's one of the counselors."

* * * * * * *

Quinn went outside after lunch with the smokers, who were escorted by Warren.

"Well, did you have a good time last night at The Kells?" Martin inquired of the counselor, after everyone had their cigarette lit.

"How do you know I was there?"

"Did you think I wasn't going to find out that you were off drinking in an Irish bar on St. Patrick's Day?"

Warren was baffled that Quinn knew he had been in The Kells, especially since he had not shared this fact with his coworkers.

"Seriously, Martin, how do you know I was in that particular bar last night? It can't have been a lucky guess."

"I'm in here, because my doctor believed I'd lost a handle on reality. Even though I'm locked up I still know what's going on, what's real and what's not."

"You certainly do," Warren agreed, realizing he was not going to be given any more information.

As they were going back into the ward, Martin spotted Dr. Kaskarelis heading towards them.

"Good afternoon, Mr. Quinn. Let's take a few minutes so we can go over some things," the doctor suggested, stopping outside Martin's door.

In the privacy of the room, he explained that there were aspects of Martin's condition which concerned him to the degree that he was not comfortable discharging him from the hospital.

"Can you please give me one example?"

"Well, I understand you intend to ask someone other than your wife to pick you up when you're discharged. I find this troubling."

"I'm forty years old, Dr. Kaskarelis and it concerns you who comes to collect me. That's ridiculous."

"I beg to differ. I had hoped your relationship with your wife was improving and perhaps you would not have a problem with her taking you home."

"You have it all wrong. When I came here two weeks ago, my friend Peter Dorian brought me. He has my wallet with all my credit cards, money, and driver's license, as well as my briefcase and other belongings. He offered to return and pick me up whenever I was ready. The guy's a police lieutenant and I trust him with my life. Also, I need to be driven into Boston to pick up my car. Margaret hates driving into the city – ask her yourself. It just doesn't make sense to have her pick me up."

"This is what I propose. Tomorrow I have a meeting scheduled with Dr. Armstrong and Dianne Russo. We're going to want to speak with both you and your wife. If we can all come to an understanding on some issues, then it may be possible for you to go home tomorrow."

The doctor gathered his papers and left the room. Quinn was undecided as to how the meeting had gone. On one hand, he was concerned that his release would not be any sooner than Friday afternoon, while on the other, it was the first time the doctor had broached the possibility of his discharge.

"This meeting is going to be crucial," Martin thought. "I'd better make sure that Margaret is prepared for it."

His thoughts drifted to his marriage. It was obvious the doctors were focused on the state of his relationship with Margaret. In fact, they seemed to have given it more thought than he had during the past weeks. Quinn appreciated that recent events must have caused his wife considerable stress. He was of the opinion, however, that concentrating on symptoms was not the best course of action. He believed that things would get better for Margaret after he was released from the hospital. Only then would there be a chance to complete the bridge project in time to secure the bonus. This would generate substantial revenue for Cove, which in turn would solve the Quinn family's financial issues. Martin had a blunt and candid approach to the problem. As stressful as things may appear, they would be much worse if their house was foreclosed. He could only apply himself to what he thought to be the best course of action: get out of Westwood Lodge and complete the Seahorse project.

* * * * * * *

Margaret was uncharacteristically late and it bothered him. He looked up from his newspaper and the clock on the wall of the common reading area told him it was 3:30. He smiled as he saw her entering the ward.

"How are you?"

"Good," Margaret fibbed. "I'm sorry I couldn't get here any earlier."

"Not a problem."

"I had an appointment with Dr. Dean and when I got back to the house, the phone wouldn't stop ringing. The last call was from Brendan. He's looking forward to coming home tomorrow."

"That's good because I'm looking forward to seeing him too."

Martin sensed that something was bothering his wife. Perhaps it was connected to her visit with Dr. Dean. Nevertheless, he was sure that in time, she would confide in him what was troubling her. The fact that her husband was in a psychiatric hospital had to be taking its toll. He elected not to put pressure on her by probing. Instead, he put a positive spin on the news that his request to be released would be discussed and hopefully approved the following day.

"I spoke with Kaskarelis before you arrived and he's meeting with other doctors and staff tomorrow to go over my case. He asked that you come in at 2:00 to meet with his team. Can you do that?"

"Yes, of course I can," replied Margaret, however, she did not appear to be as happy about this news as Martin had hoped.

"Is everything alright?"

"Oh yes, it is," she lied again. "Sorry, I'm just a little tired."

"And everything's okay with Brendan?"

"Absolutely. Brendan's great. I'm just tired. That's all."

Whatever was bothering her was not open for discussion. He decided to change the subject and focus on the following day's meeting with Dr. Kaskarelis and his team.

After Margaret left, Martin sat alone in the TV room while he waited for the escort to the dining room. He wanted out of "Camp Westwood!" The culmination of: the censored television programs; the regimented eating arrangements; the restrictions on shaving; attendance at mandatory morning meetings; the searches of his room and private property; plus the medication program, was becoming intolerable.

At dinner, Quinn sat with Andrew and Dan and solicited their help for the following day. Andrew was amused to hear about Dan's earlier intelligence gathering mission and was a willing volunteer for similar duties.

"We should get together after the group meeting," Quinn suggested. "If we hang out in the common area, I'll be able to point out the different doctors who are involved with my treatment. And one more thing, I don't need help from any other patients. I trust you two guys and that's it. I don't want a repeat of earlier this week when Michelle was snooping around and reporting all sorts of nonsense to my wife."

"Don't worry," Andrew repeated. "Tomorrow's going to go fine. Relax."

After dinner, Martin called Eddie Gallagher and got an update on the bridge project, as well as other issues. He also briefed his business partner on his plans to get discharged.

"If it doesn't go my way tomorrow, I want you to contact Tom Sullivan so he can file papers in court to get me out of here."

7:15AM - Friday March 19, 1999

By 7:15, Martin had already showered and was sitting in the common reading area, browsing through Thursday's newspaper. "My last day," he thought to himself. "I hope!"

At 7:55, Norman walked past him towards the nurses' station.

"Morning, Norman."

"Good morning, Martin. How are you today?"

"Awesome, but hungry. Hurry up and get sorted out in there so you can get us down to the dining room."

The remainder of the morning passed quickly and without any problems. Martin joined the smokers outside for their break; flawlessly performed his Depakote disappearing act; had a shave, under Norman's watchful eye; and participated in the morning's ward meeting. He expected that Andreus Kaskarelis would elicit some contribution from Cynthia Melrose and her colleagues regarding his behavior, so he made every effort to be as normal as possible. "How does one act normal in a mental hospital?" he joked to himself as he sat through Cynthia's meeting. "It's not like I can look around and get an idea how to behave!"

The day continued smoother than Quinn could ever have anticipated. Dr. Kaskarelis and his team took over the TV room at 11:30. The furniture was rearranged with a table placed near the window, along with four chairs positioned behind it. Andreus Kaskarelis had claimed one of the middle chairs and was accompanied by Dr. Bennet, Dr. Armstrong, and Angela Curran. A fifth chair set at the end of the table to Dr. Kaskarelis' left, was occupied by Mark Butler. All the doctors appeared to have several files in front of them. Martin reckoned that other cases were also being reviewed. A single chair was set in the middle of the room facing the group. This was obviously for any patient they needed to interview during their deliberations.

Margaret arrived at 2:00 and both she and Martin waited in the common area, where they could see Dr. Kaskarelis and his colleagues inside the TV room. It was 3:00 before both of them were invited to meet with the panel.

The interview could not have gone any better. By 3:45, he was thanking the doctors for agreeing to his immediate release, on condition that he participate in their out-patient program. Although it was not what the couple had planned, they complied with Dr. Kaskarelis' request that they leave together. Quinn was also given two prescriptions. One was for Depakote and the other was for a blood test to be administered at his physician's office, within a week of leaving the hospital. The prescription mandated that the medication be taken first thing in the morning and last thing at night. Since the doctors wanted to read the drug level in his system when it was at its lowest, he had to have his blood tested immediately prior to taking the medicine.

When the couple left the TV room, Martin reported the good news to Andrew and Dan.

"You two guys can fight over my dessert tonight. I'm outta here - thanks for all your help."

"Good job!" both men replied as they each gave Martin a celebratory pat on the back.

"Margaret, let's go and get my stuff."

4:05PM - Friday March 19, 1999

Martin placed all his belongings into two large paper shopping bags provided by the hospital. After leaving his room, he made a point of saying goodbye to his fellow patients, as well as those staff members who were on duty. He was glad it was Norman who escorted the couple to the door of the ward for the last time. It had been his efforts two weeks earlier that coaxed Martin from his room. The two men shook hands, and when he thanked the counselor, it was genuine and sincere.

He closed the driver's door and reached over to kiss Margaret.

"It feels good to be free," he confided. "It feels really good."

"I know – me too. Shall we get something to eat?"

"I'd like to go to Peter Dorian's house first, and get my belongings."

Twenty minutes later, Quinn was ringing his friend's doorbell. Peter's face broke into a broad smile when he opened the door.

"Hey, how are you?" he asked, shaking Martin's hand firmly.

"Awesome."

"Come in. Come in," Dorian instructed, gesturing to the car for Margaret to join them.

Peter's wife, Erin, was also delighted to see Martin and witness the relief on Margaret's face. The two couples chatted briefly before the Quinns explained that Brendan's flight was due that evening. Peter recovered the canvas executive briefcase from his basement where he had put it for safe keeping.

"I guarded this with my life," he assured Martin as he handed it over.

"Thank you. It's been two weeks since I even had a belt for my jeans."

"I really appreciate what you did for me," Martin continued.

"You're more than welcome," Peter assured him as he accompanied the couple to his front door.

Martin plugged his cell phone into the cigarette lighter socket and started the engine.

"Let's get something to eat at Legends before we go into the airport," he suggested.

The cell phone chirped and chimed as it booted up and then rang an alarm indicating there was voicemail.

"I can't believe that I've got voicemail," he joked. "I've only been away for two weeks!"

"Surely you're not going to check it while you're driving?"

"Certainly not, it can wait until tomorrow."

As Martin negotiated the afternoon traffic in Holbrook and Randolph, he spotted a pharmacy where he decided to fill his prescription. Margaret remained in the SUV while he went into the store. He had not taken any medication while he was in Westwood Lodge. Now that he had to have his blood tested within the next seven days, he needed to take it until the results were sent to Dr. Kaskarelis. Once his blood had been tested, it was his intention to stop taking the Depakote.

While he waited for the prescription to be filled, Martin gave Eddie Gallagher a call.

"I'm out!"

"Good job."

"Why don't we plan on meeting for coffee early on Monday morning?"

"Let's meet at the Dunkin Donuts on Franklin Street at 7:00. That's pretty much en route to Marina Bay for you and it works for me on my way to Milano."

"Okay. Have a good weekend, Eddie. I'll see you on Monday morning."

* * * * * * *

While the couple waited for their drink order in the restaurant, Margaret finally shared with him what had been bothering her for the past few days.

"There's something I need to tell you, Martin, before we meet Brendan. Something terrible has happened. Shelley Tyre is dead."

Martin was stunned. It could not be true. Shelley Tyre, the Principal of Thayer Academy Middle School? Shelley Tyre, the person who helped organize Brendan's trip to Seattle and had been so supportive of the Quinn family?

"What happened?" he asked in disbelief. Martin was truly shocked by the news. He now understood why Margaret had seemed so distant during her recent visits to the hospital.

"She died last Friday in a SCUBA diving accident. She was on a trip with her husband and another couple in the British Virgin Islands."

Suddenly Martin was struck by the thought that somehow Shelley's death may have been connected to his visit with her at the school. There was also her involvement with getting Brendan safely to Seattle. "Surely there couldn't be any connection," he thought to himself. "It had to have been a tragic accident." Then Quinn remembered Shelley's comment to him, that she understood what it was like to be in a troubled relationship. "Was this really an accident?"

"She was such a sweet and gentle person," Martin lamented. "This is just too sad."

The waitress placed their sodas on the table along with two menus, "I'll be right back to take your order."

"I knew she lived in Rhode Island," Martin continued, "but until you told me last week, I wasn't aware she intended to give up her position at Thayer. Brendan was fortunate to have attended the middle school while she was in charge."

"He was very fond of her and she was very fond of him. Neither Brendan nor Ryan knows anything about her death. Sarah and I agreed not to tell the boys until they got home."

"That was probably the best thing to do. We can tell him together."

When Martin had finished his food, he recovered the medication bottle from his jacket pocket, took one of the pills, and washed it down with the last inch of soda. Even though Margaret did not comment on his pill consumption, he knew she had to be impressed with his commitment to following Dr. Kaskarelis' orders.

The traffic on the way to Logan Airport was congested due to a Boston Celtics basketball game being played that night. It was a little after 7:00 by the time he found a parking space. Brendan was scheduled to arrive on an American Airlines flight from Chicago at 7:30. This was the second leg of a connecting flight from Seattle.

Sarah Harrison smiled fondly when she spotted the couple walking towards her. Margaret hugged Sarah and then stepped back to let Martin say hello. This was new territory for him. He was to behave as if he had not just been released from a psychiatric ward; even though he was well aware Sarah knew where he had been for the past two weeks. "This can't be any easier for her," he thought to himself. "Both of us will have to act as if we know nothing of my recent medical history." Martin enjoyed observing the charade. He realized it was a game he would have to play during the next few weeks.

"I think this is their flight," Margaret observed.

"You're right," Sarah agreed as she craned her neck to focus on the passengers further back on the concourse. "I think I see Ryan."

Sarah was correct. As more passengers peeled off to their right for the escalator down to the baggage claim area, it became easier to see through the crowd and all three adults recognized the young man's beaming smile.

As Ryan reached out to hug his mother, Martin and Margaret became concerned. Something, or rather someone, was missing. There was no Brendan!

Martin felt a sense of panic rise through his body, and did not want to say what he was thinking, "First, Shelley Tyre is dead - perhaps murdered - and now our son doesn't return from Seattle. What's going on?"

"Where's Brendan?" Ryan's mother asked.

"He's on the next plane."

"How did you two get separated?" both mothers asked in unison.

Martin knew there was no need to appear alarmed by firing questions at Ryan. He had Margaret with him and knew she would quiz him just as feverishly.

"When we were waiting for our flight in Chicago, the airline announced that it was over-booked. They asked for volunteers to go on a later flight. Brendan said that he would do it."

It seemed like a reasonable explanation. Nevertheless, Martin would not feel comfortable until his son was physically standing beside him.

"When is the next flight?" Margaret asked.

"Fifteen minutes after this one, and Brendan's going to get a $200 coupon for giving up his seat!"

All three adults laughed with relief at Ryan's latest offering.

"Shall we wait to make sure he arrives okay?" Sarah Harrison suggested.

"Not at all, there's no need," Margaret assured her. "You two should get on your way. I'm sure Ryan has lots of news. I just wish Brendan was here to thank you personally for allowing him to be included on the trip."

"It worked out best for everyone. I know Ryan really enjoyed Brendan's company too."

"Thank you, Sarah," Martin added as he gave her a hug.

"You're welcome, Martin. You look after yourself."

He slapped Ryan a high-five before the teenager and his mother disappeared on the escalator down to the baggage claim area.

He went along with Margaret's jovial remarks about their son's decision to rearrange his flight schedule in return for a $200 coupon, even though he would have preferred Brendan had stayed on the same flight as his friend. Fortunately, within twenty minutes, his fears were proven groundless when the young man marched down the concourse, smiling proudly.

"Good to see ya, buddy," Martin welcomed him with a high-five.

"Likewise."

"Give your Mom a hug," Margaret instructed.

"One at a time," the young man joked as he hugged his mother.

On the drive home, the Quinns allowed their son to share many of the details of his vacation, before telling him the tragic news about Shelley Tyre. Brendan was truly saddened. He was extremely fond of Shelley and remembered several instances when she had singled him out for some special assignment or task. Ironically, the most memorable was when she asked him to wear her SCUBA diving equipment, so she could demonstrate its operation to the class.

"She did that only a few weeks before spring break," Brendan recalled.

"I hope she didn't suffer."

"Well, she's at peace now," Margaret consoled him.

The remainder of the drive home was fairly quiet. Not only were all three Quinns tired and relieved to be back together as a family, but they were also reflecting on their own memories of Shelley.

* * * * * * *

Brendan was obviously delighted to have his father back home. Since he was still operating on a Seattle time clock, the young man wanted to hang out and chat. Even though Martin was tired, he wanted to spend some time with his son and allay any fears he may have had regarding the hospital stay. Margaret, however, was too tired. The events of the last few weeks finally caught up with her and she headed off to bed, leaving the Quinn men to watch some late night TV shows and talk about recent events. Brendan accepted that it had been his father's decision to take some time out and required no convincing that he had good reason to do so.

"An awful lot has gone down over the past two months. I needed to spend some time in a safe place where I wouldn't be disturbed. The opportunity presented itself for me to go into Westwood Lodge and I grabbed it. I was never in any danger of being locked up there against my will. I did construction work at that hospital last year, so I knew my way around. If I wanted out at any time, it wouldn't have been a problem."

Brendan smiled at the irony of his father having previously worked at Westwood Lodge.

"What about the fiber-optic project? What's going on with that?"

"It's going ahead as planned. I have a busy schedule for the next three weeks because we've got to be ready to receive the cable on the bridge by April 15."

"Are you guys going to be ready in time?"

"You bet! That's why I had to get out of the hospital, as well as meet you off the plane tonight."

"I'm glad to be home, Dad, and I'm glad you're home too."

7:00AM - Monday March 22, 1999

Quinn turned off Franklin Street in Quincy and parked his Jeep in the parking lot of the Dunkin Donuts, where he called Eddie on his cell phone.

"I'm just leaving the house. I'll see you in five minutes."

Martin leaned back in his seat and thought about his first weekend of freedom. Everything went smoothly and without any problems. He laughed to himself as he recalled what happened on Saturday when he had returned to the Boston Harbor Hotel to retrieve his Jeep from their parking garage. When he approached the main entrance of the hotel, he was greeted by the doorman.

"You're back, Mr. Quinn," he exclaimed with pleasure. "How are you?"

"Awesome!"

"It's good to have you back with us again, Sir," he offered with a smile as Martin disappeared through the ornate doors.

Five minutes and $300 later, he was driving his Jeep onto Atlantic Avenue and heading back to Stoughton.

As Eddie Gallagher drove into the parking lot, Martin got out of his Jeep. The two men spent the next twenty minutes going over issues related to Cove's projects. Martin brought his leather bound Day-Timer into the coffee shop to take notes during their meeting. The last time he recalled using it was when he was in Dr. Dean's office, two weeks earlier. He smiled to himself as he moved the plastic page-divider forward to the correct date in the schedule. He skipped past two weeks of pages, which would forever remain blank.

After the meeting, he continued to Cove's office. As he steered around the cars at the drive-up window to exit the parking lot, Martin called Chris Donovan.

"Welcome back, Boss."

"Thank you, Chris, and thank you for looking after Brendan two weeks ago."

"You're welcome, Martin. The main thing is that everyone's safe."

"Well, that may be the case, but it's only because of the good team I have around me. Why don't we have a quick beer after work today?"

"Sounds like a plan."

It was 8:00 when Quinn walked into his office for the first time in over three weeks.

"Welcome back!" greeted Sandra, smiling sincerely.

"Thank you. How are things?"

"Oh, I think they're going fine."

Martin was amused at how smoothly his initial return to the office and encounter with Sandra had gone. "What else can be said when your boss arrives back to work after spending two weeks in a mental hospital?" he thought to himself. "Am I to assure her that I'm sane again?" Quinn had no doubt that there must have been considerable talk among the employees as to what had caused his sudden disappearance. Now that he was back, there was an obvious ignorance of protocol on everyone's part, including his own, as to the best way to address his return.

The morning passed quickly. He had a brief conversation with John Grasso and arranged to meet him for lunch at the bridge in Jamestown. Martin felt that it was important to reach out and meet John face to face. He needed to regain Grasso's confidence, while appreciating they obviously did not share the same sense of humor.

He left Cove's office at 11:00 since he wanted to review the progress in the field prior to his meeting. His employees were pleased to see him back on the job and were confident they would meet the project schedule. Phone calls to Anderson Aluminum confirmed that the remainder of the anodized components would be available before the April 15 deadline. Thankfully, his company was on target to qualify for the $40,000 bonus.

When John Grasso arrived he was delighted to see both Martin and the progress in the field. After reviewing the work on the bridge, the two men went to lunch at the small restaurant and ice cream shop where they had previously eaten. As he followed Grasso's truck for the five minute drive, Quinn thought about what he was going to say regarding his two week absence. Obviously, since the project was still progressing, Grasso had confidence in Cove. Hopefully Martin would also re-establish John's trust in him. Nevertheless, he felt sure that in three weeks time, when the fiber-optic cable was in position across the bridge, all would be fine.

After they had given food orders to the waitress, Quinn took a drink of soda and began to speak.

"John, I want to thank you for working with Eddie Gallagher while I was in hospital."

"Not at all, Martin. You've looked out for my interests as well as my company's. I'm glad that our paths crossed. I enjoy working with Cove Construction and you. I want it to continue."

"Well, I appreciate that you pushed the project along while I was away. I got burnt out and run down. I really needed to take some time out, and now I'm all the better for doing so."

"You don't need to explain. With all that went down on this job since Fred Ross got involved, it's a miracle anything got accomplished. And here we are, three weeks away from having the fiber-optic cable across the bridge."

John Grasso appreciated Quinn's frankness about his hospitalization. Martin reckoned that this was the best way to handle the matter. How else could he have explained such a sudden disappearance? They discussed other issues related to the project and finished their lunches without any further reference to the hospital stay.

* * * * * * *

As agreed, Martin met with Chris Donovan after work for a beer.

"Chris, I assume that you heard the tragic news about Shelley Tyre?"

"I did. I couldn't believe my ears when I heard her name on the TV news. She was really nice to me at the school that day. It's just so sad what happened."

"That's what I meant when I spoke to you earlier. I'm so fortunate to have the people around me that I do. Shelley Tyre was extremely kind to me during the last week of school before spring break. She arranged for me to see Brendan and spent time with me herself, when I went to the campus to pick him up. What a loss."

* * * * * * *

Martin got home by 5:30 and had dinner with Brendan and Margaret. Although he had only been on the Depakote for four days, he noticed that his shoes were tighter fitting than before. Tying his laces had now become quite the task. Furthermore, his belt buckle had to be set back one notch on his trousers. He only intended to take the medication until Saturday morning; nevertheless, he was beginning to wonder if he could last until then. He had a mental picture of his body growing to the size of a balloon in Macy's Thanksgiving Day Parade. Since he had not taken any medication in the hospital, Quinn was cognizant of how important it was to keep taking the pills for at least one week, before having his blood drawn.

8:10AM - Saturday March 27, 1999

Martin handed Dr. Kaskarelis' prescription to the receptionist at the laboratory reception waiting room.

"Have you had anything to eat or drink this morning?" she asked.

"Nothing."

"And you haven't taken any medications since last night?"

"Correct."

"If you take a seat, the nurse will call you," she instructed, setting his paperwork in a wire basket on the desk beside her.

Martin took a seat away from the television set which was hanging from the ceiling. He had no interest in what the bubbly morning breakfast TV presenters and their guests had to offer. Instead, he sat in the corner and opened his Day-Timer so he could make some notes.

He thought about the past week and how quickly it had gone by. All things considered, he was happy, except for the weight gain caused by the Depakote. He had attended his appointments with Andreus Kaskarelis and psychologist, Paul Richardson. Both meetings had passed without any problems as far as he could tell. He met with Dr. Kaskarelis at Westwood Lodge while his appointment with Paul Richardson took place in Quincy, not too far from Cove's office. For the foreseeable future, it appeared that he would have weekly appointments with each of them. Martin had thanked everyone who helped him three weeks earlier in the hotel. Tom Sullivan was delighted to see him and warned of the health risks associated with the sort of work load Martin had undertaken. Helen Costa, too, was thrilled to hear that he was back at his office and the Jamestown job was progressing well. But the call which impressed Quinn the most was not initiated by him. On Wednesday morning, he was contacted at his office by George Grey, the attorney he had first met at the hotel's health club and who had later responded to his frantic request for help. Even though they had only met briefly, he spent most of that fateful Friday making sure Quinn got safely out of the hotel with Peter Dorian. Martin surmised that George and Tom Sullivan must have kept in contact which was how he knew to call Cove's office. This really impressed him, since he felt that most people would have avoided further contact once they realized he had subsequently been locked up in a psychiatric hospital. Nevertheless, George Grey seemed genuinely interested in his wellbeing and expressed a desire to go to lunch. Quinn explained that this would have to wait until after he had completed the Seahorse project. He added that once the fiber-optic cable was across the Narragansett Bay, he would be heading to Northern Ireland to see his family, but promised to contact George upon his return.

Quinn wondered how he had allowed himself to become so paranoid and disturbed back in the Boston Harbor Hotel, when he was clearly sur-rounded by such good people. Here he was, committed to faking blood tests and weekly meetings with a psychiatrist and a psychologist. Could all this, as well as the two weeks he spent in Westwood Lodge, have been brought about solely by Fred Ross' underhand behavior? Each of the events over the past two months developed a momentum of their own until finally Martin was in such a frame of mind, that all it took was a detonator to explode the whole mess. The detonator was a simple act of genuine kindness. He had completely misinterpreted John Grasso's inten-tions when he ushered the hotel staff from the Presidential Suite, since it was clear to John that things were getting just a little bit too crazy. The consequences of this compassionate intervention were staggering. "Sir

Isaac Newton was incorrect when he said that every action has an equal and opposite reaction," he thought to himself. "Sometimes an action can have an excessive and overwhelming reaction."

Quinn's analysis of his situation was interrupted by a nurse in a white coat calling his name. "What a job this medication is doing. After only one week of being on it," he thought to himself with a smile, "I'm not bothered when people in white coats come looking for me!"

Martin's kind and professional treatment by the nurse further under-scored just how far off base he must have been three weeks earlier, when his paranoia spiraled out of control. He really appreciated how fortunate he was to live in Massachusetts with access to first-class health care services.

Twenty minutes later, he was driving to Anderson Aluminum. Louis Fusco was delighted to see him in person. They had spoken by phone during the week and Martin had promised to stop by and visit. He explained that he had to take two weeks off due to exhaustion. His friend understood and shared his observation that it was an excellent move, since Martin looked great and appeared to be well rested.

"I think you've put on some weight."

"I've been laying around too much and not working. Once I'm back in the field for a couple of weeks, I'll work it off."

On his way back home, he was relieved to know he would no longer be taking the Depakote. "How fat do I look," he thought to himself, "if people are commenting?" Now he was beginning to feel even more self conscious about it. "God, my feet feel cramped in these shoes," he winced. "I hope this whole weight gain process is reversible, now that I've stopped taking the medication."

The remainder of the weekend included bringing Brendan to a hockey game on Sunday morning, as well as helping him with his homework assignments later that evening. The teachers seemed to have piled on the workload since the students returned from their spring break. The mood at Thayer Academy had been melancholy during that week. It was the first time the community had been back together since the news of Shelley Tyre's death. A memorial service was scheduled for Friday morning, which was to be attended by Shelley's husband and parents. The school was anxious to give the students and their families an opportunity to grieve together and share with Shelley's family the positive impact she had made on all their lives.

9:40AM - Friday April 2, 1999

Neither Martin nor Margaret was surprised at how difficult it was to find a parking space near the Thayer campus. It was no surprise that Shelley's memorial service was very well attended by past pupils, friends, and parents of both middle school and high school students.

A section of the auditorium, immediately in front of the stage, was cordoned off and reserved for the students and faculty. Despite arriving twenty minutes early, the Quinns struggled to find two seats together. The atmosphere was bathed in a hushed buzz of parents and friends still expressing their shock at Shelley's untimely death. People were swapping memories and recalling occasions when Shelley did something special for them or their own child.

At 10:00, Eric Swain, Thayer Academy's Headmaster entered the auditorium accompanied by several others. As they walked up the aisle, Quinn realized who these people were. Eric Swain escorted Shelley's husband and parents onto the stage and led them over to a row of seats arranged behind the podium. He then asked everyone to rise, since the faculty and student body of both the middle and high schools were about to enter. Martin had just finished reading from the program and realized that the senior class included students who entered the middle school at grade six, in September 1992. This was the first group of sixth graders to have been under Shelley's care. She had not lived long enough to see them graduate from high school. One of her former pupils took a position at the entrance to the auditorium. He was a talented bagpiper and played a moving arrangement as Shelley's colleagues and students slowly processed through the auditorium and into their reserved seats. Eric Swain remained at the podium until the music stopped, when he then asked that everyone be seated.

Martin's mind wandered throughout the service. He thought about how special it was that one of Shelley's pupils played the bagpipes. It really underscored the sadness and sense of tragedy the whole Thayer community was feeling. Nevertheless, Quinn could not help noticing that he felt sorrier for Shelley's parents than he did for her husband, David Swain. He struggled with these thoughts because he understood that they were not appropriate. Martin tried to suppress any notions he had about the possibility of her husband's involvement in her death during the dive. Shelley's words, just days before her death, that she understood what it was like to be in a troubled relationship, continued to haunt him. Quinn admonished himself for having these thoughts, but the fact that her husband's address was brief and unemotional also bothered him. He tried to attribute this to the shock and horror of the whole ordeal. Nevertheless, he fought hard to separate fact from fantasy in his mind, thinking that very often real life is more surreal than any movie or television drama. "How ironic is it that two men on stage to eulogize Shelley have the same last name?" he thought to himself. "Is it possible that one's a dear friend and colleague, while the other's her husband and killer?" Martin forced himself to stop thinking such things. It was thoughts like these that had caused him to be locked up in a psychiatric hospital for two weeks.

Shelley's parents were devastated. They obviously appreciated the beautiful service that Thayer Academy was hosting. Nevertheless, they bore witness to one of life's most harrowing experiences - the loss of a child. Even though Shelley was forty-six years of age, it did not make it any easier. Their love for her was no less that day, than it was on the day she was born.

The bagpipes accompanied the closing procession which was led by the Headmaster and Shelley's family, followed by faculty and students. Martin failed miserably to fight back tears, as he thought about Shelley's Bernese Mountain Dog, Tory. "How was he holding up, now that his best friend in the world was gone?"

* * * * * * *

The next two weeks passed by quickly and without incident. The fiber-optic bridge project continued to come together without any major problems. Martin was able to finalize the details of his trip to Ireland, which he planned to take the week after Cove had the raceway in place. He delayed booking his ticket until he was sure that everything with the job was proceeding on schedule. He had not been to Ireland for several years and was really looking forward to the visit. His family was anxious to see him, especially his mother. He appreciated how difficult it must have been to be so far away when she got the news that her son was in a psychiatric hospital. It would be good to put her mind at ease and let her see that he was okay.

8:20AM - Thursday April 15, 1999

CC Good morning," greeted John Grasso as Quinn stepped out of his Jeep.

"Good morning, John. It's D-Day!"

"It certainly is!"

The bridge was a hive of activity, especially on the mainland's North Kingstown side. The Jamestown Police Department and Rhode Island State Troopers had combined to provide four police detail vehicles to control the regular traffic on the bridge. The police had requested that Seahorse not bring any cable trucks onto the bridge until after 9:30, in order to minimize the impact on the morning commute.

CellTell Atlantic also had its equipment standing by to install their fiber-optic cable. They planned their installation to follow Seahorse's by forty-five minutes in order to avoid congestion. It had been agreed that Seahorse Communications should be able to claim that it was the first company to have a fiber-optic service across the bridge.

Quinn had four of his crew on site, ready to react to any problems that arose. This would later prove to be unnecessary. The combined price tag for the operation was running at over $10,000 per hour. If Cove was responsible for causing any delay, it would have been a horrendous blow to both its reputation and its bank account.

"It looks like you've earned your $40,000 bonus," John announced when Seahorse's utility trucks began their slow crawl across the bridge to install the fiber-optic cable.

"Thank you, John. None of us could have done this by ourselves. It was a real team effort."

"Here's my boss," Grasso observed.

Kevin Shaw was smiling from ear to ear as he walked towards them.

"Well done, men."

"Thank you Kevin," Quinn replied. "Thank you for having the confidence in our company and giving us the opportunity to complete this contract for Seahorse."

"You're welcome, Martin. John never had any doubt that you and your company were the right people to do this job for us. It couldn't have worked out better."

By 3:00, both Seahorse Communications and CellTell Atlantic had their fiber-optic cable in position. CellTell Atlantic had not planned to make any connections that day. Seahorse, however, had overhead line crews waiting at both ends of the bridge, to splice the cable and bring it into service immediately. This was a major achievement for the company and their Rhode Island office was anxious to notify its corporate head office in Georgia of its successful completion as soon as possible.

Martin said goodbye to John Grasso at 4:00, before heading back to Boston. "Relief" would not have been a strong enough term to describe Quinn's feelings as he drove back home. It was ten weeks since he had first rolled out a set of plans related to this project on Eddie Gallagher's kitchen table. "What a roller coaster ride it's been!" he thought to himself. "Absolutely crazy!"

3:25PM - Sunday May 2, 1999

Martin's brother, James, lived in a large farmhouse, set on a forty acre estate, located only fifteen minutes from Belfast, Northern Ireland. All Martin's family and many of his friends had gathered to celebrate his birthday. The weather was unusually warm for that time of year, which meant everyone could enjoy themselves both outside and inside the beautiful home. James was a very successful venture capitalist and his home was an ideal venue to host the many guests who were present.

Martin had visited his parents and other siblings at their various houses during the previous week, nevertheless, Sunday's gathering was a nice occasion for everyone to come together and reminisce about their childhood memories.

Less pleasant memories were evoked by the live television broadcast from Scotland of a Glasgow Celtic versus Glasgow Rangers soccer game. Historically, Celtic drew their support from Northern Ireland's Catholic-Nationalist community, while Rangers' supporters were affiliated with the Protestant-Unionist segment of the population. The last time Martin saw these teams play each other was in 1988, the year he immigrated to America. On that occasion, six players were arrested as a result of their behavior on the field. Eleven years on, James' two young sons were watching the televised game and they too were gripped by the obligatory violence which accompanied this rivalry. This year it reached a new high (or low), when one of Martin's nephews struck his brother over the head with his mother's dumb-bell. Fortunately, the four pound weight had a foam molded cover to make it more comfortable to hold during aerobic exercises. Nevertheless, it inflicted quite a bump on the back of the young boy's head, which thankfully was not too serious. This was nothing compared to the drama unfolding on the screen. By half-time, several players had either been cautioned or sent off the field. The referee had to have a wound on his head stitched after he was struck by an object thrown from the crowd, and a spectator tumbled twenty-five feet off a balcony onto supporters below in another section of the stadium. Martin did not watch the second half of the game, but events apparently continued along the same vain, culminating with the referee's home being attacked during violence that followed, forcing him to go into hiding with police protection.

9:30AM - Thursday May 6, 1999

M artin's vacation passed too quickly for his mother's liking. She made this clear to him on the car ride to Belfast International Airport. He had really enjoyed relaxing with his family and even got to see many of his old friends during the trip. He gave his mother a hug before heading through the security gates to board his flight to London where he would make his connection to Boston.

Later that afternoon, during the second leg of his trip, Martin realized, yet again, that very little of his life passed without some noteworthy event. A few hours into the flight, the captain announced that Air Force One, carrying President Clinton, was flying alongside on the starboard side. Martin was disappointed he did not have a camera so he could take a picture to show Brendan. Air Force One appeared so close, one could imagine being able to reach out and touch it. About an hour later, when Quinn was visiting the restroom adjacent to the rear galley area, he saw a map showing the flight details and scheduled route.

"Does that map have to get filed at the end of the trip?" he asked one of the flight attendants.

"No, not at all, would you like to take it as a souvenir?"

"Do you think the captain could mark it up to show where we were when we saw Air Force One? I know my son would love that."

Soon, Quinn was thanking the attendant for being so helpful. He rolled out the map to see it had been signed by the flight crew. Apparently, President Clinton had been flying back from Germany where he had been visiting troops and attending an international conference concerning the

Kosovo conflict.

Martin smiled as he rolled up the map. Peter Dorian had brought him to the airport when he left and would be meeting him again at Logan when he arrived. "What's he going to think when I tell him I flew back to America with Air Force One?" Quinn thought. "Will he drive me home or bring me straight back to Westwood Lodge?"

* * * * * * *

Even though Peter laughed when Martin gave him his news, it did concern him initially.

"Cut it out, Martin."

"I didn't say that I was actually on Air Force One," Quinn explained, rolling out the map to show his friend, "I said that I flew home with Air Force One."

"I'm glad you have the written proof!" Dorian laughed as they made their way to the car park. "Listen, I haven't eaten anything since lunchtime and if you don't mind, maybe we can stop somewhere for pizza and catch some of the Bruins' play-off game with the Sabres."

"Sounds like a plan. I'll call Margaret and Brendan to let them know I've landed and tell them what we're doing."

Forty minutes later, the two men were stepping out of Peter's Jeep in the parking lot of the Town Spa restaurant in Stoughton. Quinn opened the door to let Dorian go ahead into the lobby. The hostess did not notice Martin until she looked back up from retrieving two menus. Her face lit up as she recognized him. It was Cynthia Melrose from Westwood Lodge. Unbeknownst to Quinn, she also worked two evenings a week at the restaurant.

"How are you?" she asked while guiding the two men to an empty table.

He interrupted their conversation to introduce Peter and explain that Cynthia worked at Westwood Lodge.

"Awesome. I just got back from a vacation in Ireland."

"Well you look great," she observed. "It looks like the trip really did you good."

"I actually flew back today with Air Force One."

It did not take anything else to be said for Cynthia's expression to change from delight to serious concern.

"It's true," Peter interjected, "but it doesn't need any more explanation than that."

She quickly set down the menus and assured the men their waitress would be right with them.

"Only you would meet a psychologist from Westwood Lodge and start teasing her like that." Dorian laughed, once they were alone.

They ate their pizza and watched one period of the hockey game, before continuing on their way.

"You're a good friend, Peter," Martin acknowledged when the SUV turned into his driveway. "Thank you for looking out for me over the past few weeks."

"You're welcome, Martin, but I don't do this just for you. You have a good family and I want to make sure that Margaret's husband and Brendan's father is okay. I'm glad I'm in a position to be able to help both you and your family."

Peter came into the house to say hello, but did not want to stay long. He appreciated both Margaret and Brendan were excited to have Martin back home. Nevertheless, Quinn did not let his friend leave without presenting him with a souvenir sweatshirt with a Guinness logo embroidered on it.

3:05PM - Wednesday July 28, 1999

To date, no amount of improvement to the infrastructure of Charlestown, Massachusetts, had been able to thwart its dubious distinction as being a fertile breeding ground for bank robbers and safe-crackers. Located immediately north of Boston on the banks of the Charles River, many of its cozy neighborhood bar rooms provided a surreptitious social networking platform for their criminal patrons, similar to what Facebook and Craig's List legally furnish online. Any gang with an employment opening such as: getaway driver; or perhaps counterfeiter, could rely on finding the right man for the job in practically any of Charlestown's drinking establishments. Such job interviews lacked the formality of a written resume; however, references could be verified in real time during the hiring process with subtle hand and eye gestures to which the casual customer would be oblivious. Guns, explosives, and many other items, not commonly available through regular retail outlets, could also be purchased without the arduous bureaucracy and paperwork which the law mandates.

George Grey finished his Irish whiskey and stood up from the secluded table where he and two other men had chosen to sit. Even though the bar room was practically empty, the attorney was conscious of the need to keep his voice low during their conversation so that the televised baseball game would drown it out. He had spent the last half hour trying to allay the fears of his clients. Unfortunately, neither of his two students for this impromptu tutorial could ever have scored high enough on an LSAT examination to warrant attending such a lecture in any of the area's law schools. The main theme of that day's "side bar conference" was the importance of legal doctrines, such as the right to remain silent. Bestowed upon the masses in the Fifth Amendment of the Constitution of the United States of America, Attorney Grey attempted to convey how this simple and basic right can present an insurmountable obstacle to even the most ambitious of police detectives.

"Listen, Jack. As long as you two keep your mouths shut, the police have nothing. It's that simple," George explained, setting down his empty glass. "Just call me immediately if they pick you up or hassle you in any way."

11:00AM - Wednesday August 4, 1999

Days merged into weeks and weeks became months as Martin's life regained an air of normality. Cove continued to work on its construction projects for clients other than Seahorse Communications, with one exception. Since no more payments were received for its work on the funeral home in Canton, Cove had to file suit against Commercial Construction Enterprises and cease work on that job. (It would take over a year before Cove would prevail in court and recover over $150,000 from the bond company.) On other matters, Martin's patent attorney, Arthur Watson had sent documents for review related to the patent filing. He explained that Quinn should not expect any response from the patent office for anywhere between twelve to eighteen months. The appointment schedule with Dr. Kaskarelis and Paul Richardson was less stringent than it had been when he initially left Westwood Lodge. He only had to meet with Dr. Kaskarelis once a month, while his appointments with his therapist were once every two weeks. Quinn liked to think that this was because his health care professionals shared his opinion of his improved health. The cynic in him, however, believed that restrictions imposed by the health insurance company may have been an overriding factor.

It was at the end of a meeting with Andreus Kaskarelis when Martin was thrown a curve ball that he never saw coming.

"You're too happy for my liking," the doctor observed.

"Too happy!" Martin replied in disbelief. "What sort of problem is that?"

The doctor did not answer him, but scribbled away on his prescription pad. Quickly, Martin thought about his prior weeks in an effort to identify anything he may have overlooked in his behavior. He had carefully monitored his medication audits so he would trash the pills at the same rate as he should have been taking them. That way he always knew when to request a refill on his Depakote prescription.

"I want you to have your blood tested again," Dr. Kaskarelis announced, handing Martin a prescription for the clinic. "Make sure you have the blood drawn either first thing in the morning or last thing at night, but before you take your medication. I need to see the drug levels in your blood when they're at their lowest."

As he took the prescription, it was all that Quinn could do to remain calm and nonchalant as Andreus Kaskarelis set the date for their next appointment.

"If I need you to come in sooner after I review the blood test results, then I'll give you a call," the doctor added as a parting instruction to his patient.

In the privacy of his Jeep, Martin began to think about what he should do. "I'm not an Olympic athlete," he thought to himself. "A negative blood test result will not be a good thing."

Two days later, on Friday evening, Martin put his plan to pass the blood test into action. Immediately after his supper, he took four times the regular dosage of medication since he was sure he would not be leaving the house again that evening. He had decided he would get his blood tested early the following morning and intended to take a double dose an hour before this appointment.

On Saturday morning, Quinn sat in the clinic and waited for his name to be called. Apart from a little queasiness in his stomach and a minor swelling sensation in his feet, he felt fine. "I hope this test result satisfies Kaskarelis," he thought to himself. "God forbid any of his patients walk around being happy. What an affliction!"

4:10PM - Thursday August 5, 1999

F ew actions can cause more serious problems for a criminal defense attorney than when his client, or clients, communicates with the police without him being present. George Grey was irate when he received the tip. The battery of his cell phone dislodged itself as a result of the force with which it struck the floor of his car after the call had ended.

"What the fuck were those guys thinking?" he yelled while pounding the steering wheel of his 7 Series BMW.

This was a serious problem which Grey needed to resolve immediately. He knew there was only one thing that could never be recovered after it had been given away. That thing was information. How much had his two clients revealed to the police? How was he going to repair the damage they had done?

12:45PM - Friday August 13, 1999

Like many others, the legal profession relies upon the services of various specialists and experts. Paralegals prepare court filings and contract documents; sheriffs and constables serve summonses and subpoenas; psychologists assist during jury selection and monitor proceedings as a case continues through trial; a litany of forensic professionals such as hand writing experts, scientists, accountants and the like, all provide support when needed. There is, in fact, a specialist or expert for every contingency. The challenge for any attorney, who cares about winning a case, is to assemble a team with more depth and expertise than the opposing counsel's.

Grey could neither overstate nor underestimate the damage his two clients had caused by talking to police without his presence. When it came to correcting a problem like this, he was satisfied that there was no one better than the gentleman with whom he had just met. George looked out across Boston Harbor from his table at the No Name Restaurant, while his lunch guest visited the restroom. "Twenty-one thousand dollars and all because those two couldn't keep their mouths shut! So much for attorney-client confidentiality!" George felt he had no other option and this was certainly a case he did not want to end up in the "L" column. Lunch finished with the payment of a ten thousand dollar retainer. The balance would be due only when all services were rendered to Grey's complete satisfaction.

9:45AM - Tuesday August 17, 1999

It had been nearly two weeks since Martin had his blood tested and he had heard nothing from Dr. Kaskarelis regarding the results. Quinn began to feel confident he had achieved drug levels in his blood which proved to be in line with the doctor's expectations. It was while he was driving to a jobsite in Milford, Massachusetts, content he was on the right path to getting his life back to normal, that he suddenly focused on a news article on the radio.

"A Boston area attorney was arraigned today in Federal Court on attempted murder charges, after being caught in an FBI 'murder-for hire' sting. Attorney George Grey appeared before a federal judge to answer these charges in a preliminary hearing following his arrest yesterday."

Martin could hardly believe his ears. Just when he was beginning to believe he had no grounds to support his paranoia in March, he discovered the attorney from whom he had solicited help in the Boston Harbor Hotel, was a criminal! He stopped at the nearest convenience store and picked up two newspapers. Both the Boston Globe and Boston Herald covered the story; however, only the Herald had a picture of George being led away in handcuffs from the Framingham Tara Hotel. There was no mistaking Grey's intimidating six foot - four inch stature.

As the story unfolded in the media over the following weeks, Martin learned that the charges stemmed from George's involvement in a kidnapping scheme he had orchestrated with two of his clients. These individuals had difficulty paying for legal defense services he had rendered. The victim targeted for this crime was one of the attorney's other clients, Xavier

Santos. Grey was confident that Santos had sufficient amounts of cash readily available and demanded a ransom which he felt could be easily paid by his wife. From all accounts, the kidnapping went as planned and generated more than enough revenue to satisfy the delinquent legal debts. It was then that George's law enforcement contacts alerted him that he was a suspect in the crime. Since only three people had knowledge of the kidnapping, it did not take the attorney too long to realize that one of his associates/clients was talking to the authorities. He decided to murder both of them, but a confidant suggested that he engage the services of a professional to complete this task. Unbeknownst to George, the hit man with whom he entered into negotiations, was an undercover FBI agent. Apparently, he even tried to get this gentleman interested in another kidnapping scheme involving the son of a prominent Boston area jeweler. The undercover agent insisted they stay focused on the mission at hand and negotiated a fee of $20,000 to kill George's two partners-in-crime. An additional $1,000 was charged when Grey was unable to provide a gun for the hit. "I guess even murder contracts have small print," Quinn joked to himself when he read details in the newspaper. He could not help thinking what George may have had planned for him. "He must have thought that I was good for a several hundred thousand dollar ransom. How else could I have afforded to stay in the Presidential Suite of the Boston Harbor Hotel?" Quinn continued to postulate several possible criminal scenarios involving Grey. "No wonder he contacted me and suggested that we have lunch. If anything untoward had happened to me, George would in no way have been considered a suspect. Surely there would have been enough circumstantial evidence to implicate other parties by bringing up the episode at the Boston Harbor Hotel."

The plea deal George Grey would subsequently negotiate with the prosecutor's office was a credit to his contacts, and familiarity with the criminal justice system. Martin now had to add the FBI to the list of people to whom he was indebted, even though their services were rendered somewhat unwittingly. Rather than give him further cause for alarm, the whole incident had the opposite effect. Quinn believed there was no guarantee that George Grey would not have targeted him for a similar kidnapping scheme, had he not left the Boston Harbor Hotel in the manner in which he did, and allowed himself to be locked up in Westwood Lodge.

3:55PM - Thursday November 18, 1999

Martin sat in the waiting area outside Dr. Kaskarelis' Westwood Lodge office. He had decided this appointment would be his last, given that the previous few months had gone by without any further drama. Quinn believed that surviving encounters with individuals such as Attorney Grey, along with everything else that went down during the Seahorse project, should be acknowledged as something worthy of praise. Even though he had no evidence that George Grey would ever have considered harming him, Martin had to appreciate that there had been a serious potential for it to happen. Residing in the Presidential Suite and sharing information about the profitability of Cove's contract with Seahorse, must surely have set him up as a viable candidate for kidnapping. Whereas Quinn felt he had skillfully negotiated pitfalls associated with the bridge contract, escaping any wrongdoing at the hands of George Grey was solely the result of the FBI's labors. He had managed to get paid $450,000 for a job that cost his company less than $200,000 to complete. But here he was getting taken to task by his doctor because he was "too happy." Why wouldn't he be happy?

Cove continued to undertake projects for Seahorse which involved underground installation of fiber-optic cables, and also consulted with their engineers regarding plans for taking their utilities across other bridges. Martin also heard that Fred Ross had put his house up for sale and moved his family out of state. Seemingly, the negative aftermath of the Jamestown project was too much and he was no longer able to effectively conduct business in New England. Meanwhile, Arthur Watson continued to work on the patent application for the raceway.

Quinn's thoughts were interrupted by Andreus Kaskarelis inviting him into his office. Their meeting followed the established format right up until the doctor thumbed through his diary to find an open appointment for the following month.

"That won't be necessary. This is my last appointment."

"No it's not," the doctor countered.

"It certainly is," Martin responded, standing up to lift his jacket from the back of the chair. "I need to get on with my life and it no longer includes coming here every month. I helped pay for your Thanksgiving Dinner this year, but I'm not going to be helping you with Christmas as well. This is my last appointment."

"I'm not going to get into an argument about this now, Martin. It's important you continue to keep your appointments. I'll be sending you an e-mail. I want to see you before the Christmas holiday."

Quinn put on his coat and extended his hand. "Have a safe and enjoyable Thanksgiving Holiday, Dr. Kaskarelis."

"Thank you Martin, you too. You'll be hearing from me."

* * * * * * *

The following morning, Quinn received a call at his office from his therapist, Paul Richardson.

"What did you do to Dr. Kaskarelis last night? You have him all upset."

"I explained that yesterday was our last appointment."

"We'll have to talk about that when we meet next week. We have an appointment on Tuesday morning, don't we?"

"We do, but there'll be no point wasting our time talking about Dr. Kaskarelis."

"He's concerned about the medication you're on. It isn't good to stop the appointments suddenly like this."

"I took the medication for one week after I left Westwood Lodge in March, so I'd pass the blood test. I haven't taken it since. Except on one occasion when he sprung another test on me a few months back."

"When were you going to tell me that you are all done with my appointments?"

"I was going to keep seeing you until January. I like you and wanted to help get you through Christmas."

"I suppose I should take that as a compliment. Just make sure you keep our appointment on Tuesday, please."

"I will," Quinn promised and hung up the phone.

* * * * * * *

The next day was Saturday and Martin spent the morning running errands before taking care of some paperwork back at his office. It was mid afternoon when he left to go home, and on the way, he made a quick visit to The Foxy Lady strip club. A couple of the girls joined Quinn at his table to chat during a break between their sets on stage. This was not unusual - what would happen next certainly was.

He could not believe his eyes when Paul Richardson walked into the club. "What are the odds of this?" Quinn smirked to himself.

Martin asked one of the girls to go over and see what Paul wanted to drink. He smiled as Richardson rejected the scantily clad girl's advances. The club was dimly lit and too busy for his therapist to identify who had sent the dancer to his table.

"He's very shy," the emissary reported back. "He wouldn't tell me what he wanted to drink. You'd better go over."

The look on Paul's face when Martin appeared in front of him was priceless.

"How come you wouldn't let Amber know what you wanted to drink?"

Paul smiled and shook his head in disbelief. "So this is where you hang out?"

"Now and again, I don't live too far away and I like to support the local businesses. It helps keep the residential tax base low."

"You're full of it," he replied with a smile.

"Come on over and sit at my table."

"Thanks Martin, but I can't. I'm supposed to meet a patient here at 4:00."

"Now who's full of it?"

"No, really."

"How come we never have my appointments here? Why do we always have to meet at your office?"

Quinn interrupted Richardson's attempt to respond.

"You don't need to explain anything to me. You have to consider the confidentiality of the doctor – patient relationship. I'll just go back to my table and I'll see you on Tuesday."

"Who's he?" the dancer asked when Martin returned.

"You wouldn't believe me if I told you."

"Try me."

"He's my psychologist."

"You're right. I don't believe you."

Martin left the club after only one beer, leaving Paul Richardson still waiting for his patient to arrive. "Who would be late for their appointment at a strip club?" he thought to himself as he gave Paul a wave on the way out.

9:00AM - Tuesday November 23, 1999

Quinn was on time for his appointment with his psychologist, who began by explaining that he had been contacted by a woman who wanted help with her husband's addiction to frequenting strip clubs.

"Would you rather sit over here, Paul, and let me sit in your seat?" Martin joked. "We're not going to cure you of your illness until you first admit that you have a problem."

Richardson laughed because he too recognized just how contrived his story sounded. The two men chatted for an hour and agreed that, for the time being, Martin no longer had to make any more appointments. Nevertheless, Paul made it clear that Martin was welcome to schedule an appointment at any time. Quinn was pleased to know he had ended his out-patient program on such a good note. He liked Paul Richardson and enjoyed his appointments. It was, however, time to move on. He wanted to make a clean break and leave behind all the craziness that had invaded his life. Episodes such as meeting Paul Richardson in the Foxy Lady and Cynthia Melrose in the restaurant when he returned from Ireland, reinforced this decision. Quinn felt like Dorothy in the *Wizard of Oz*, when the characters of her dream subsequently appeared in the real world.

5:05PM - Friday February 24, 2006

Nearly seven years had passed since Martin's initial involvement in fiber-optic installations for Seahorse Communications. His patent application had been delayed by administrative and processing problems that arose from the anthrax scare, prevalent throughout the United States during 2001 and 2002. The initial incident was detected in September 2001, a week after the 9/11 terrorist attacks, when letters containing anthrax bacteria were mailed to numerous recipients, including two United States Senators. At least five people died as a result of their exposure to the deadly agent and, to date, no one has been convicted of the crime. Since primary targets of the attacks were United States government offices, all legitimate government activity was severely impacted. Martin's patent, however, was eventually issued in early 2003. Nevertheless, not all events from those memorable ten weeks in 1999 had found closure.

Quinn was listening to the car radio when the newscaster announced, "Today a Rhode Island jury returned a verdict finding former Jamestown, Rhode Island councilman, David Swain, responsible for the unlawful death of his wife, Shelley Arden Tyre, during a SCUBA diving trip to the British Virgin Islands in 1999." Martin's conversation with Shelley, days before she left for that fateful trip, came back to him in an instant.

Subsequent news reports of the trial, including an extensive feature article in People Magazine, reported on the court case. A jury in the Rhode Island Superior Court found that Swain, "by a preponderance of evidence ... had killed Shelley with malice aforethought." Tyre v Swain, 946 A.2d 1189, 1196 (R.I., 2008). Unfortunately, Swain managed to avert criminal charges being filed by either the British Virgin Islands or United States' authorities. The doctrine of double jeopardy, in the United States legal system, places an arduous burden on the prosecutor to ensure there is enough evidence to proceed beyond an indictment in order to secure a conviction. Since the crime occurred outside of the United States, this made it very difficult for any charges to be filed through an American court. Sadly, a country such as the British Virgin Islands, which relies heavily on tourism to support its economy, would rather have the death filed quietly as an unexplained SCUBA diving accident, than deal with the negative publicity which may accompany a murder trial.

Thanks to the perseverance of Shelley's parents, however, Swain's callous and vicious actions did not go undetected. They were fortunate to find a local attorney, J. Renn Olenn of Warwick, Rhode Island, who shared their daughter's passion for SCUBA diving. He also had considerable experience working on investigations related to diving accidents. He enlisted the help of several respected experts and was able to show the jury that, despite Shelley's frantic efforts to fight for her life, Swain, who was her "diving buddy," shut off her tank valve and ripped the diving mask from her face. He then held her down until she was dead. Olenn cited Shelley's failure to remove her weight belt to hasten her assent to the surface, as further evidence that she had other urgent matters to contend with at the time of her death. One of her fins was subsequently found imbedded vertically in the sandy ocean floor, which supported Olenn's argument that there had been a violent struggle.

Whereas much of Martin's time during the events of 1999 was spent questioning the wisdom of trusting the people around him, he understood that Shelley's tragic death arose from her trust of the very person she should have had least reason to fear – her husband and SCUBA diving partner. Upon hearing the news of the verdict, Martin contacted Attorney

Olenn's office and informed him of the nature of his conversation with Shelley, the week before she was killed.

"Shelley was a very, very special person, Mr. Olenn. I'm so glad you were able to prevail in this civil suit. You have my contact information, should any other developments require my testimony."

Quinn reflected upon the news he had just heard on the radio. It was clear that in 1999 there were certainly others who were more worthy of the attention and care that mental health professionals had bestowed on him. Surely any list would have David Swain at the top, closely followed by George Grey. Fred Ross would also make this list, in Martin's opinion. But how does anyone recognize symptoms in these sorts of deviants before it is too late for their victims? Does it all come down to instinct? What if Shelley Tyre had felt suspicious or uncomfortable about the trip to Tortola? What if she shared those feelings with a confidant or decided not to get on the plane at the last moment? Would that have been enough for her to end up in Westwood Lodge after an intervention by family and friends? Would her exhausting daily commute, between Jamestown, Rhode Island and Braintree, Massachusetts, have been cited by doctors as contributing to a state of paranoia? What if Martin Quinn's lack of sleep had caused him to focus on George Grey as being someone of whom he needed to be wary? Would anyone have believed him? It would seem that the only tool available to us for evaluating such feelings is instinct. Its effectiveness however, depends upon how sharp it is, and how often we use it.

10:35AM - Wednesday November 14, 2007

Two US Marshals entered the premises of Ocean State SCUBA and confirmed the identity of the man inside as its proprietor, David Swain. Within five minutes the store was locked, and Swain was sitting, handcuffed, in the rear of their unmarked Ford sedan.

He had been arrested on a federal warrant stemming from an extradition request filed by the British Virgin Island authorities, demanding he stand trial for the 1999 murder of Shelley Arden Tyre. The Tortola police had reopened their investigation, pursuant to the successful rulings secured by J. Renn Olenn with the civil suits tried in the United States courts.

In July 2008, Swain stood in the dock of the Eastern Caribbean Supreme Court while Senior Magistrate Judge Valerie Stevens ruled that he be remanded, without bail, in Her Majesty's Prison, Balsum Ghut, pending trial for murder.

5:51PM - Tuesday October 27, 2009

David Swain avoided eye contact with the jury foreman, as Supreme Court Justice, Indra Hariprashad-Charles instructed that the verdict be read aloud. There are occasions in life when no amount of time can adequately ready an individual for what he or she is about to experience. Swain had three thousand, eight hundred, and eighty-two days to prepare for this moment, yet he could not control the constricting feeling of panic which wrenched his gut tighter with every breath. He knew what was coming next, just as sure as he knew the sun would set in the west and rise the following morning in the east, and that he would be watching its shadows from within the confines of a prison cell in Balsum Ghut. Four hours earlier, the jury had been charged with the duty of determining his guilt or innocence. Three weeks of trial proceedings had come down to this final moment.

"How say you? Is the accused, David Swain, guilty or not guilty of murder?" the judge asked the foreman.

"We, the jury, find the accused guilty."

3:45PM - Thursday September 29, 2011

"You're kidding?" Richard Tyre uttered in disbelief and disgust.

It was a rhetorical question because he knew Attorney J. Renn Olenn would never have phoned to joke about such a matter.

The call ended. Richard sat motionless and gazed lovingly at his wife, who was sleeping peacefully in her favorite chair. He closed the blinds to shield Lisa's face from the strong afternoon sun and continued to agonize as to how he would break this dreadful news to her.

An appellant court had set aside the guilty verdict, apparently due to procedural aspects of the murder trial.

David Swain had been released.

THE END

Acknowledgements

I am indebted to everyone who assisted and supported me in writing this novel. Apologies in advance for repeated use of the phrase, "Thank you."

Thank you Mary for your endless encouragement with everything.

Thank you to my editing team led by Chris Walsh. "The student has become the teacher." – Source unknown.

Thank you to those relatives and close friends who painfully ploughed through early manuscripts providing invaluable constructive criticism.

Thank you William J. Burns, Esq., CPA for both your counsel and friendship. Until recently I thought, "Pro Bono," meant that you liked U2.

Thank you Dave Bailey for your artwork and those sales to people who, "judge a book by its cover."

Finally, thank you men and women of the armed forces for your sacrifice, which permits the rest of us to enjoy the lives that we do. Thank you for your service.

CPSIA information can be obtained at www.ICGtesting.com
Printed in the USA
LVOW08s0048160416

483832LV00001B/3/P